Murder in Brentwood

MURDER IN BRENTWOOD

DET. MARK FUHRMAN

REGNERY
PUBLISHING
A Division of Salem Media Group

Regnery® is a registered trademark of Salem Communications Holding Corporation

ISBN 978-1-62157-321-0

The Library of Congress cataloged the hardcover edition as follows:

Fuhrman, Mark.
    Murder in Brentwood / Mark Fuhrman.
    p. cm.
    Includes index.
    ISBN 0-89526-421-8
    1. Murder—Investigation—California—Brentwood. 2. Crime scene searches—California—Brentwood. 3. Evidence, Criminal—California—Brentwood. 4. Simpson, O.J., 1947- —Trials, litigation, etc.
    I. Title.
    HV8079.H6F84 1997
    364.15'23'092—dc21
    [B] 97-363
    CIP

Published in the United States by
Regnery Publishing
A Division of Salem Media Group
300 New Jersey Avenue NW
Washington, DC 20001
www.Regnery.com

Manufactured in the United States of America

10 9 8 7 6 5 4 3 2 1

Books are available in quantity for promotional or premium use. For information on discounts and terms, please visit our website: www.Regnery.com.

Distributed to the trade by
Perseus Distribution
250 West 57th Street
New York, NY 10107

THIS BOOK IS DEDICATED TO two people I never knew: two people who came into my life with their mortal passing; two people who I tried to serve with every ounce of my passion for my profession. The crimes committed on their bodies will never be punished, but I pray their souls are at peace.

CONTENTS

PART TWO: THE TRIAL

PUBLISHER'S PREFACE

THE O.J. SIMPSON CASE is a study in deceptions. Nobody involved—not Judge Ito, not the prosecutors, not the members of the jury, certainly not the defense counsel, and most definitely not O.J. Simpson—was much interested in the truth. Instead, they were all interested in their own well-being, their own cause, and how they looked to the millions who were watching.

In that process, it became apparent that somebody would have to be sacrificed, very publicly, so that the deceptions could continue. That person was, of course, Mark Fuhrman. And the way he would be sacrificed would be to exploit racial conflict.

Fuhrman played a pivotal role in this, the most noted murder case of the decade. Ironically, as the case unfolded, it was Detective Fuhrman who became the central focus rather than the defendant, who happened to be one of the most famous Americans ever tried for murder. And, therefore, Fuhrman has a riveting story to tell.

As a publisher concerned about justice, about the state of American culture and values, and in a world fascinated by the Simpson case, we thought that a book by Mark Fuhrman was obviously a good idea. We started discussing the possibility with Fuhrman even before he testified in the Simpson trial, and were close to concluding a deal. As controversy surrounding the case, and Fuhrman, intensified, Darryl Mounger, Fuhrman's lawyer, advised him to wait. Finally, we did sign a contract.

But within days after signing that contract, the now-infamous Fuhrman tapes were released.

We knew Mark well enough to believe his account that the tapes were made exclusively to provide material for a screenplay and that he was "in character" when he used offensive expressions and racial epithets. The sworn testimony of Laura Hart McKinny, his co-writer, confirmed his story.

In the face of a media and propaganda firestorm against Fuhrman, we decided that we could do him little good and perhaps even more harm, and suggested he take his book to one of the major New York publishers better able to weather such a storm. But with his lawyer's advice, Mark again put off the idea of a book until things calmed down. We were certain that another publisher would sign him up with a huge advance.

But we were wrong. Several publishers, including virtually all of the major New York houses, turned Fuhrman down. We don't know, of course, what the reasoning behind any of those decisions was. But we do know that Fuhrman is controversial and very politically incorrect, and that authors such as Fuhrman are not what most New York editors are looking for. As anybody who reads his book will quickly discover, however, Fuhrman can shed more light on this famous murder case than just about anybody else.

And so for us it became a matter of principle, as books for us so often are, and we decided to proceed. As we have worked with Fuhrman, and as we have edited his manuscript, we are convinced that we are publishing a very good and honest book.

Fuhrman's role in the Simpson case is laden with ironies. The murder case had nothing to do with race until Simpson's lawyers injected it, with all of the intensity they could muster, into the trial. Yet Detective Fuhrman, as his book makes very clear, may be the only one who can bring a degree of candor to the issue as it involves the Simpson case.

The case was also full of deliberate deceptions and untruths, but it was Detective Fuhrman who was labeled the perjurer. How ironic that he is now the one person directly involved in the case who has no reason to deceive! His book is what the trial should have been—the facts, as they happened, and the evidence, as it was found.

And finally, *it was* a murder case involving only one suspect who was on trial for killing two people. Yet the only person convicted of anything was Detective Fuhrman—the detective who did everything he was supposed to do at the crime scene, and whose conviction involved a circumstance that had nothing to do with the murders.

The Simpson case has come to symbolize much more than the brutal murder of two innocent people. Instead, it symbolizes how racial prejudice can be exploited for the benefit of the few at the expense of the many. And it symbolizes how our system of justice, the very backbone of our democracy, is easily exploited and damaged, again for the benefit of the few and at the expense of the many.

If Mark Fuhrman can play even a small role in correcting these wrongs, he will have succeeded as an author, and we will have succeeded as his publisher.

—Alfred S. Regnery,
Publisher

FOREWORD

THERE ARE MANY VICTIMS in the Simpson murder case other than Nicole Brown Simpson and Ronald Goldman. But once we get past their surviving loved ones, no one has been unjustifiably victimized by these murders more than Mark Fuhrman. Awakened from his sleep at 1:05 in the early morning hours of June 13, 1994, he went to the Bundy crime scene and for several hours thereafter participated in the investigation of the murders. Among his observations, he found a bloody right-hand glove on the grounds of O.J. Simpson's estate which was the mate of a left-hand glove found at the Bundy murder scene.

Though he did nothing wrong at all (and no one as been able to produce a speck of evidence to the contrary), his involvement in the investigation has almost destroyed his life. Even before his unfortunate error or lie on the witness stand (I speak in the disjunctive because it is not clear, at least to me, which it was) that he had not used the "N" word in the previous ten years, he was publicly accused by Simpson's defense team of being a virulent racist who had done one of the most despicable deeds that one human can do to another—frame O.J. Simpson for the murders.

After his error or lie on the witness stand, he was maligned and vilified perhaps more than any other person within recent memory, not even excluding O.J. Simpson. At least Simpson has a significant percentage of the population who still believe in his innocence and sing his praises. Not so with Fuhrman by the end of the trial. It seemed he had no friends. In Johnnie Cochran's final summation to the jury he referred to Fuhrman as a "genocidal racist, a perjurer, America's worst nightmare, the personification of evil," and even compared him to Adolf Hitler. Unbelievably, even the prosecutors joined in the vilification of Fuhrman, Marcia Clark actually telling the jury in her summation: "Do we wish that there were no such person on this planet? Yes." In fact, even his superiors at the LAPD denounced him severely. And not one of the "Talking Heads" on television, who have made a cottage industry out of commentating on the Simpson case, had one good word to say about Fuhrman.

In a telephone conversation with Mark Fuhrman on the morning of October 14, 1996, he told me, "Vince, I just returned from my first meeting with my P.O. (Probation Officer)." Can you imagine that? Mark Fuhrman, who devoted years of his life, as all police officers do, so that the rest of us can live in a safer and more civilized America, and at the very worst had committed the most insignificant kind of perjury, was now a felon. But O.J. Simpson, who murdered two human beings, brutally cutting them down in the springtime of their lives, was acquitted of the murder charges and out playing golf with a smile on his face.

When my book *Outrage: The Five Reasons Why O.J. Simpson Got Away With Murder* was first published in June of 1996, and I pointed out the terrible injustice of what had happened to Mark Fuhrman, his mother, Billie, called me crying and said, "You're the only one who stuck up for my son." It wasn't difficult for me to do. After all, as I've said, Fuhrman had done absolutely nothing wrong at all during his investigation of these murders, and even if we assumed he lied on the witness stand, it probably wasn't even perjury. Lay people are under the erroneous impression that lying under oath is automatically perjury. But it's not. Granted, it's the most important element of the *corpus delicti* of perjury. But there is a second element to perjury under Section 118 of the California Penal Code. The lie has to concern some "material matter," i.e., it must be relevant to an issue in the case. For instance, unless a witness's age or weight is somehow relevant to an issue in the case, their lying under oath about their age or weight is not perjury. Fuhrman's alleged lie about not using a racial slur within the previous ten years was not, in my judgment, perjury, since it had nothing to do with whether Simpson was guilty or not guilty of these murders.

A great many people have asserted that the sentence imposed upon Fuhrman by the judge on the perjury charge (three years' probation and a $200 fine) was far too lenient. I don't agree at all. There is nothing sacrosanct about a person receiving punishment for a crime exclusively by way of a sentence handed out by a court. It's just that a court sentence is the typical and usually best way of bringing about justice. Many times, however, the punishment has already been imposed upon the defendant by extra-legal means. Nowhere is that reality exemplified more clearly than with respect to Mark Fuhrman. In addition to his name being defamed and besmirched throughout the nation and his becoming an object of ridicule and even satire on comedy shows, Fuhrman was forced into an early retirement, and after his no contest plea to the perjury charge on October 22, 1996, he is now a convicted felon, no longer having, among other things, the right to vote or even own a firearm of any kind.

And like all things in life, there are degrees of perjury. For those purists who maintain that perjury is perjury, and it is all equally bad, I would assume that to be consistent, they would believe that all conspiracy is the same, be it a conspiracy to commit murder, or conspiracy to commit petty theft, disturb the peace, or maybe bird-watch.

Perhaps the most serious perjury would be a witness knowingly and falsely accusing an innocent person of a crime. Though not condoning it in any way, on a scale of one to ten, Fuhrman's perjury, if we assume it was perjury, was a one. He simply didn't want to admit—he was too embarrassed to admit—in front of a predominantly black jury that he had used the racial slur "nigger" within the past ten years. But since his use of the epithet had no relevance to any issue in the case, Judge Lance Ito should have never allowed the defense to even ask Fuhrman whether he had used it. It was an egregiously erroneous ruling by Ito that was in contravention of Section 352 of the California Evidence Code. Section 352 provides that if the relevance of offered evidence (in this case, Fuhrman's use of the "N" word) is "substantially outweighed" by the probability of prejudice to the opposing side, the evidence should be excluded. Here, the relevance of Fuhrman using the "N" word was extremely remote at best. I mean, it is a non sequitur and broad jump of Olympian proportions to conclude that just because someone used the "N" word, or is even a racist, that they're going to go around framing black people for murder. But the probability of prejudice to the opposing side (the prosecution) was more than the requisite substantial; it was monumental, and hence, should have been excluded.

Even if Ito did not want to follow the law in this case, common sense, which Ito exhibited precious little of during the trial, should have told him that it was improper to allow the defense to ask Fuhrman the subject question. Every day throughout the land, thousands of white police officers arrest or investigate black suspects. Does anyone really believe that when these thousands upon thousands of cases come to court it is perfectly proper to ask every one of these officers whether he has ever used the "N" word within the previous ten years, and if he denies it, and you can prove that he did, have a separate, satellite trial on that issue, which is precisely what essentially happened during the Simpson murder trial?

In my opinion, the entire Fuhrman matter was blown completely out of proportion. The Fuhrman affair reminds me of the theoretical situation of a traffic ticket being contested and ending up in the United States Supreme Court. Much ado about nothing. Can you imagine that the Simpson defense was so preposterously weak that the cornerstone for their defense was that Mark Fuhrman had used the "N" word at some time during the previous ten years? That says it all, doesn't it? They built their whole case around the theory that because Fuhrman had used the epithet, he was a racist, and therefore framed Simpson by, among other things, planting the killer's bloody glove at Simpson's Rockingham estate. But it should be noted that Mark Fuhrman could not have planted the glove at Simpson's estate in the early morning hours of June 13, 1994, even if he had wanted to. Fourteen LAPD officers had arrived at the Bundy murder scene before Mark Fuhrman arrived at 2:10 A.M., and all fourteen saw only one glove at the murder scene. Therefore, there was no second glove at Bundy for Mark Fuhrman to pick up and deposit at Simpson's Rockingham estate.

The entire thrust of the defense position in the criminal trial vis-à-vis Mark Fuhrman is that he had framed Simpson because Fuhrman is a racist. But if Fuhrman was such a racist that he was willing to frame black people, how come out of the hundreds upon hundreds of black people he arrested throughout the years, how come there wasn't a parade of black people taking the witness stand at the criminal trial to testify that Mark Fuhrman had framed them? If, hypothetically, you're a black man who has been framed by Mark Fuhrman for a burglary, and you spend five years at San Quentin, and when you get out you see that Mark Fuhrman is in the news, don't you automatically call Johnnie Cochran or another member of the defense team and say to them: "Hey, this guy framed me"? You would do this not just to get even with Fuhrman, which would be your primary motivation, but in doing so you would also be a hero to many in the black community, and could even sell your story. Yet not one single black person took the witness stand at the criminal trial to testify that Mark Fuhrman, at any time during his twenty years with the Los Angeles Police Department, had framed him or her. And the reason no such black person so testified is no such black person exists. It's blather, tommyrot, moonshine! But remarkably, the prosecutors in the Simpson case, among a great number of other powerful arguments that had to be made by them but weren't, never made this obvious argument.

If one is interested in ironies, what could be more ironic than this? To most blacks, Mark Fuhrman is the very embodiment of the virulently racist white cop whom they fear and detest with a passion. O.J. Simpson, on the other hand, has been and unfortunately still is a hero to millions of blacks, someone they supported during his trial with an unqualified fervor, celebrating his acquittal with almost rhapsodic joy. That's one reality. But here's the other. For several long and gritty years, Mark Fuhrman worked South Central, a heavily black area of Los Angeles with the highest violent crime rate in the city; an urban jungle whose mean, squalid, and untamable streets the average white person would not dare walk through at night...and many wouldn't even in daylight. What was Fuhrman's job? For a barely livable wage, going down there every day to protect law-abiding blacks from the black criminal element. In other words, on a day-to-day basis, Fuhrman, the racist black-hater, was risking his life to protect black people, not white folks, since the latter don't live in South Central. What was Simpson doing during the same period? Living and moving exclusively in the white social and corporate world. If any reader believes that Simpson, who would need a road map to get back to the hood, would daily (or at any time) risk his life to save any of the black people of South Central, I can only say that your naiveté is staggering. Simpson, in fact, couldn't even find time to do infinitely less than that for fellow blacks. As reported in the August 29, 1994, edition of *Newsweek*, "[Simpson] would promise to appear at community centers or youth programs in South Central, Los Angeles, then bow out at the last moment." Football legend Jim Brown, who for years has devoted his life to helping rehabilitate the black criminal element, told me that throughout the years, "there was no evidence of O.J. in the black community."

For those people who think that the reason I have come to Fuhrman's defense is that I am an apologist for racist cops and the criminal behavior some engage in against minorities because of it, they simply don't know me. In fact, show me another white public personality who within the past five years has spoken out publicly, and in depth, about how to substantially reduce the police brutality problem against blacks in America. In a long article in the February 1993 edition of *Playboy* magazine prompted by the Rodney King case and subsequent riot titled *"NO JUSTICE, NO PEACE,"* I pointed out, with irrefutable statistics, that district attorneys around the country rarely ever prosecute the police for engaging in brutality and excessive force against members of minority communities, primarily blacks. I denounced this practice and strongly urged district attorneys to commence criminal prosecutions against the very small percentage of offending officers who, by their conduct, stain the blue uniform of the rest of the force. I reasoned that these prosecutions would be the most efficacious way, by far, to substantially reduce this type of police misconduct. So my sympathies do not lie with racist police who brutalize black people.

Since I have come to know Mark Fuhrman only relatively recently, I can't speak with any assurance whether or not he ever entertained strongly racist feelings toward blacks. Certainly, the so-called Fuhrman tapes suggest he did. However, there is no evidence that his feelings toward blacks ever manifested themselves in any criminal behavior against them. Moreover, the Fuhrman tapes go all the way up to 1994, and the last time Fuhrman uses the "N" word on the tapes is 1988, six years earlier. Also, in 1994, when the Simpson murders occurred, Mark Fuhrman had black friends, he was getting up two to three mornings a week at five to play basketball with fellow black officers, and in a 1994 case I verified before the publication of my book *Outrage*, worked very hard to free a black man charged with the murder of a white man when he came upon evidence of the black man's innocence. (And it's the view of virtually everyone that Fuhrman, who finished number two in his class at the Police Academy, was a thoroughly professional officer throughout his career whose daily work was a model of efficiency.)

But none of this, really, is relevant. The only thing that is relevant is whether Mark Fuhrman framed O.J. Simpson. And the evidence is conclusive that he did not. Therefore, even if he were the biggest racist ever to come down the plank, the vilification, calumny, and unremitting revilement and ridicule of Mark Fuhrman that has befallen him is very wrong.

This foreword is not to be construed as an endorsement by me of everything Mark Fuhrman says in this fascinating and highly informative book. For instance, I don't agree with his particularly harsh assessment of the investigative job done in the Simpson case by lead detectives Tom Lange and Philip Vannatter. But he, not I, was there, and he is certainly entitled to his opinion. What I do agree 100 percent with Mark Fuhrman on is that he did absolutely nothing wrong during his participation in the investigation of this case. He has been victimized, outrageously so, by a combination of lies by Simpson's criminal defense team, abject incompetence by the prosecutors, and ignorance by many members of the media, a group who can always be counted upon to do a minimum of thinking.

A terrible, perhaps irrevocable injustice has been perpetrated against Mark Fuhrman, and all fair-minded people can only hope that this book is Mark Fuhrman's first step in a successful effort to rehabilitate his image with the American people.

—Vincent Bugliosi
January 1997

PROLOGUE

THE WORLD DOES NOT KNOW ME; it knows of me. My private thoughts and fears are still mine. The mistakes I made and the pain I inflicted on myself, the citizens of this country, and the people I love will forever haunt me. This is not a book of justification or excuse, but one of truth. It is not an easy task for me, for all of us hide portions of our life that we hope will never be judged by our neighbors, let alone the world.

An apology for the racial unrest I caused seems painfully inadequate. My immature, irresponsible ramblings with a screenwriter were never intended to be heard by anyone but the two of us. Although truthful, this simple explanation is no excuse for the disrespect that I showed millions of people. People I never met, saw, or heard of were affected by my cruel words. These words echo in my mind daily, and I am ashamed.

Many will say my words of apology stem from the mere fact that I was caught on tape. This is not the case. In my heart, I always knew it was wrong, even if I said them only to create a fictional story. My first failure was the lure of greed, and the second was my lack of compassion. There is nothing in life that comes free. I failed myself, my friends, and my family when I grabbed the chance to make money.

True, my career did expose me to the dark side of humanity. But I cannot blame all of my troubles on that. Along the way I made choices: some were good, others were tragically misplaced. But it was always my choice. I take full responsibility for my life and career.

There are no words for what I want to express. No thoughts can describe the remorse I feel for the people I have wounded. No story that can begin to excuse my insensitivity. I simply return to a much-used phrase, but in this case, it comes from the depths of humility: I am sorry.

Part One

THE INVESTIGATION

Chapter 1

NOLO CONTENDERE

It's a real tragedy that we have a mountain of evidence to convict O.J. Simpson, and he walks free. Meanwhile, Mark Fuhrman, with an almost total absence of evidence against him, is convicted.

—BILL HODGMAN, ASSISTANT DISTRICT ATTORNEY,
LOS ANGELES COUNTY

O N WEDNESDAY OCTOBER 2, 1996, I walked into the criminal courts building in downtown Los Angeles to face charges of perjury. In twenty years on the LAPD, I had spent a lot of time there, testifying, filing cases, and waiting in the cafeteria. I had participated in hundreds of trials, but had always been on the side of the prosecution. Now I was the accused.

As I rode the elevator up to the ninth floor, these familiar surroundings became less comfortable. Flanked by uniform and plainclothes sheriffs, my attorney and I walked down the hall and entered Department 109. For the first time in my life, I sat with the defense. While this court had not yet decided my fate, in the court of public opinion, many already considered me guilty. My career, my reputation, and my privacy had been taken away from me. But I still had my pride. I sat up straight and made eye contact with everyone who stared.

The audience was silent. Judge Ouderkirk entered the courtroom and began to read, "This case number BA 109275, *the People of the State of California vs. Mark Fuhrman.*" .

With the judge's words, I felt my professional life pass away. A hollow, lonely feeling overcame me, and I fought to keep my nerve.

The perjury complaint against me stated, in part: "While perjury is always a serious offense, it is rare that a witness who has given testimony is prosecuted for that perjury. When there is prosecution, the usual case involves a situation in which the witness has given false testimony about an event related to the crime or provided a false alibi."

Of course, I had done neither, which the complaint made clear:

"Here there is no evidence that defendant gave any false testimony about his investigative efforts."

The judge delivered a brief statement to make sure I understood that in my case it would be be very difficult to prove that my alleged purgery was "material," that it had any bearing on the guilt or innocence of the accused, in this case O.J. Simpson. Materiality is an absolute requirement for a conviction of perjury. And he stated that I had a right to a trial.

I told him I understood.

"In the investigation by the attorney general, they found nothing wrong with your criminal investigation on this case."

The deputy state attorney general, John Gordnier, said to the judge, "That is correct."

Then the judge addressed me.

"To the charges of perjury, how do you plea?"

"No contest." I said. The plea of no contest, or *nolo contendere,* is not an admission of guilt. While the technical equivalent of a guilty plea, it allows a defendant to maintain his innocence while accepting the plea.

Judge Ouderkirk read the sentence. "You are hereby sentenced to three years formal probation and a two-hundred-dollar fine. It has been agreed upon that you will serve your supervised probation in your state of residency. And the order of this court is that you will obey all laws. Do you understand this, Mr. Fuhrman?"

"Yes, your honor."

Sometimes in life you have to do things that go against all that you believe in, and this was one such time. Perjury is a felony, with a possible sentence of four years in prison. To some people, probation and a fine might appear to be a light sentence, but in my heart it was "life without the possibility of parole."

As a convicted felon, I can never again vote. I cannot hold public office. I cannot serve as a police officer. I cannot work for any city, county, state, or federal agency where I would have to be licensed. I cannot possess firearms.

Through the term of my probation, I must report monthly to my probation officer, and I am subject to unannounced visits. I must get approval to travel anywhere outside the five northern counties of Idaho. I can't own any weapons at all.

In the eyes of the law and the world, I'm a convicted perjurer, a felon. But that tells only a small part of the story.

In October 1995, Gil Garcetti, district attorney for the County of Los Angeles, said, "What Mark Fuhrman did was not perjury. It was not material to the case."

Garcetti is in charge of all felony criminal prosecutions in LA. But one month after he made that statement, facing a tough race for reelection and not wanting to anger voters either way, he announced he was passing off the decision to indict me to Dan Lungren, the state attorney general.

Lungren works with the same law books as Garcetti. Unfortunately for me, Lungren is also a politician, and he wants to be governor. And he was getting lots of public pressure to indict me from people like Tom Hayden, a former member of the Chicago Seven, Jane Fonda's ex-husband, and now a liberal California State senator.

After several months of anxious waiting, on July 5, 1996, my attorney, Darryl Mounger, said that Lungren was going to press perjury charges against me.

"Nobody knows this. Nobody should know this." Darryl told me.

"Then I guess we should stop talking on the cell phone," I responded.

Lungren's case was flimsy at best. If the state of California were going to prosecute everybody who'd apparently perjured themselves in the Simpson trial, they'd tie up the courts into the next century. But Lungren went after me, because I had already been used as a scapegoat for the trial of the century.

Over the next few months, Darryl had several meetings with the attorney general's office. Meanwhile, my friends and supporters kept telling me that I had nothing to worry about. Some of them were lawyers and cops who were familiar with the law. They knew that I hadn't committed perjury. Other friends were well-connected politically. They thought that Dan Lungren would come to the same conclusion that Gil Garcetti did—there was nothing to gain and a great deal to lose by indicting me. Of course, they were wrong. They didn't know what I knew, but I couldn't say anything. It was very frustrating to hear their words of encouragement and support, knowing full well that charges against me were pending.

My anger over the perjury charges has nothing to do with the shame and embarrassment I feel about what I said on the tapes. There is a difference between moral and legal responsibility. I should not have said what I said. But whatever I said, no matter how cruel or stupid, should have had no bearing on the Simpson case. My recorded conversations with Laura Hart McKinny were an attempt to create a fictional screenplay, but my words were used as if they were testimonial fact. There was no place for imagined dialogue in a trial concerning the murders of Nicole Brown Simpson and Ron Goldman. I should never have been asked the questions that led to my perjury conviction.

Even if everything my critics said about me was true, none of it would have been relevant to the trial. Likewise, even if the tapes had not been a work of fiction, they would not have been relevant to the case or material to Simpson's guilt.

What did race have to do with Simpson's guilt or innocence? Race was not an issue in the way Simpson's case was handled by the LAPD. Simpson made no complaints about his treatment, nor did he have any cause to complain. He was treated better than any suspect I had ever seen in my twenty years on the force. Simpson was above race. He didn't even live in a racial world. He was accepted and loved by everybody, regardless of race.

The defense team and the media injected race into the trial, to play on the public's sensitivities and to shift all attention away from the defendant's innocence or guilt and onto an issue that America has struggled with for centuries, and bitterly in Los Angeles over recent years.

Dan Lungren's office undertook an investigation whose sole purpose was indicting me, yet almost immediately Lungren offered me a plea deal that was as lenient as the law would allow. Why? While Lungren couldn't leave me alone, he also knew that prosecuting me wouldn't be easy. His people wanted to get me without going to trial because they knew they would never win. At best they could hope for a hung jury and retrials.

But I couldn't win either. I could not afford to mount any kind of defense. I'm retired and live with my wife and children on a small farm. For extra money, I work as an apprentice electrician in town. I already owed nearly $20,000 in lawyers' fees. An effective defense would have cost hundreds of thousands of dollars. A trial would have required me to be in Los Angeles for several months, unable to work. In Los Angeles, I would have had to provide for my own security, and pay for food, lodging, and transportation. Just the daily living expenses would have been far beyond my means.

The Los Angeles Police Protective League would not help me, even though my alleged crime was well within the scope of my duties as a detective. This group has financed the defense of accused murderers, rapists, child molesters, and drug addicts. All I had done was deny using a racial epithet. But I was too much of a risk to the public image of the League and the department. When I asked the League to help with $17,800 in legal fees, they refused. Over the years I had paid that much in dues. Gary Fullerton, director of the Protective League, tried hard to help me, but he was fighting an impossible battle.

Darryl Mounger wouldn't be able to represent me *pro bono*. The case would take months, maybe years. If I got a hung jury, Lungren could try again, but next time around I would have to start bankrupt.

And what would happen to the city of Los Angeles? I had been in uniform on the street during the Rodney King riots, when some fifty people died. My trial could easily have caused another riot. What if innocent people, my friends, former colleagues or partners were killed? This wasn't my sole consideration, but it weighed heavily on my decision. I also had to think of the LAPD. I didn't want to be responsible for any more negative attention or bad morale.

Then there were the legal questions. Who would be given the case? Would the presiding judge be able to ignore political and media pressures? In the Simpson trial, Judge Ito hadn't. What kind of jury would I get? If Simpson had been acquitted in repayment for all the wrongs done to blacks by the LAPD, then I could certainly become the victim of that same anger.

Most importantly, I had to think of my family. Could they go through two or three more years of this? The media would be hounding us again. The expense, hassles, and danger would be enormous. I had to hold my family together, keep our home, and provide for their future. I had to stay out of prison. I had to hope that I could begin to put this all behind us and have some kind of life.

After I weighed my options and the potential consequences, I decided to accept the attorney general's plea offer. The only person I told was my wife. She didn't understand.

"How can you plead guilty to something you didn't do?"

"Because this world is not made of sugar and spice and everything nice," I explained. "We have a Constitution, but humans enforce it."

Twenty years fighting crime on the streets had taught me a great many lessons, but it wasn't until the Simpson trial that I saw how wide the gap was between the law and how it is enforced, between our ideals and noble words, and the way the system actually works. Out on the street, at least you know what to expect, and you can be prepared. In the criminal justice system, all the law books and fine talk too often allow criminals to get away with breaking the law.

On the other hand, policemen never get the benefit of the doubt; in the public's mind, they are always guilty until proven innocent. For two years I have been listening to people who don't know me, and many who think they know me, blaming me for a criminal investigation and trial that went wrong. I never wanted to be rich, or famous, or anything but a good cop.

Ever since the beginning of the trial, I have tried my best to just do my job and keep quiet about it. I was willing to take the blame while everyone else took the fame. I didn't like the way things turned out, but I was willing to put it all behind me and start over. I received countless offers from publishers, news anchors, radio, television and print journalists, but I said nothing. Even during the height of the media frenzy, I kept my peace. And once the trial was over, when I was retired and under no professional obligation to keep quiet about the case, I still wouldn't talk. I moved out of California, wishing only that my family and I be left alone. I told people that if they pushed me too far, they wouldn't like what happened. Still, they kept pushing. Now, after the plea, I have no choice but to speak out.

So I decided to write a book and tell my story of this case.

I apologize for the pain I caused with my insensitive words. However, one thing I will not apologize for is my policework on the Simpson case. I did a good job; I did nothing wrong. Yet I was blamed when the case fell apart. Throughout my ordeal, many people wanted me to fight back. Now I am.

Chapter 2

MURDER IN BRENTWOOD

"The dog got more nervous and was pulling me harder.
It stopped in front of a gate on Bundy."
"What did you see there?"
"I saw a lady laying down full of blood."

—TESTIMONY OF SUKRU BOZTEPE,
NEIGHBOR OF NICOLE BROWN SIMPSON

T HE PHONE RANG AT 1:05 the morning of June 13, 1994. I woke up and went into the kitchen to answer it, knowing full well it probably wasn't a social call. I immediately recognized the voice of Ron Phillips, my good friend and boss in West LA Homicide.

"We've got a double homicide," he said. "One of the victims might be the wife of O.J. Simpson."

I wasn't on call to handle a homicide that weekend, but I knew that if Ron called me, he needed the extra help. We agreed to meet at the station, gather our gear, and get a car.

On the drive over, I went through a mental checklist, as I often do. What would I need at the scene? What particular problems does a double homicide

7

present? By anticipating certain challenges, I thought I would be better prepared to meet them. But there was no way to prepare for the case I was about to get involved in.

Ron and I met at the station shortly before 2:00 A.M. We got our briefcases, flashlights, and other gear, then drove to the crime scene at 875 South Bundy Drive, arriving at 2:10. Two black and white police vehicles were parked in the middle of the street. My friend Sergeant Marty Coon was standing nearby with Sergeant Dave Rossi, the West LA watch commander.

Officer Robert Riske had been the first on the scene. I knew Riske only casually from previous arrests, but my impression was that he was quiet, professional, and competent. His performance at this crime scene did not disappoint me. He did an outstanding job under the circumstances.

Riske told us how he had discovered the victims' bodies, where he had been, and what he had seen. Even without Riske's direction, it was easy to see the blood-stained sidewalk and large canine paw prints in red leading away from the residence.

Dark red blood had flowed down the large cobblestone walkway; it appeared to come from the front steps where the female victim lay in a crumpled position. Her head hung limply, with blood-stained hair hiding her face. The blood had coagulated and pooled in the grout between the bricks. The male victim lay face up by the walkway.

Following Riske's lead, we walked along the side of the walkway to avoid stepping in the blood or other possible evidence. Riske shined his flashlight to point out items of possible value. A dark-colored stocking cap and glove were beneath a small shrub. There was also a white envelope near the male victim's feet.

The first thing that struck me is that the victims did not match.

The first thing that struck me was that the victims did not match. The male was fully clothed, wearing a jacket and lace-up canvas boots, while the female was wearing a short, one-piece black summer dress and was barefoot. They had obviously not been walking together outside. The front door was wide open; Riske said he had found it that way when he

THE BUNDY CRIME SCENE

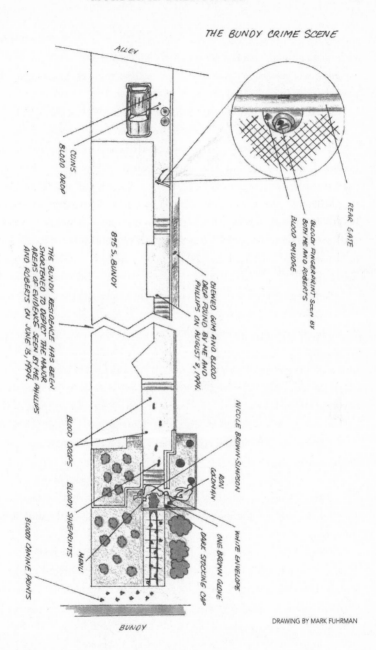

ALLEY

COINS

BLOOD DROP

875 S. BUNDY

REAR GATE

BLOODY FINGERPRINT SEEN BY
BOTH ME AND ROBERTS

BLOOD SMUDGE

CHEWED GUM AND BLOOD
DROP FOUND BY ME AND
PHILLIPS ON AUGUST 2, 1994.

THE BUNDY RESIDENCE HAS BEEN
SHORTENED TO DEPICT THE MAJOR
AREAS OF EVIDENCE SEEN BY ME, PHILLIPS
AND ROBERTS ON JUNE 13, 1994.

BLOOD DROPS

BLOODY SHOEPRINTS

MENU

NICOLE BROWN-SIMPSON

RON
GOLDMAN

WHITE ENVELOPE

ONE BROWN GLOVE

DARK STOCKING CAP

BLOODY CANINE PRINTS

BUNDY

DRAWING BY MARK FUHRMAN

arrived. I could hear music playing from inside the residence, and soft lights were shining from the house down onto the homicide scene.

Ron and I wanted to get closer to the female victim without damaging any possible evidence.

"Is there another way we can approach the victims?" Ron asked.

"We could come in from the back of the house," Riske responded.

As we backed out of the scene and walked around to the alley behind the house, I began making some preliminary deductions. The female victim was probably inside her residence just prior to her death, and had been there at least long enough to take off her shoes. She had returned, for whatever reason, to her front door and opened it. Conversely, the male victim was dressed for the outdoors. Either he had intended to enter the residence and never made it in, or he could have been leaving and the female victim was escorting him to the door.

At the rear of the residence, the garage was open, with a white Ferrari inside. A black Jeep Cherokee was parked outside on the driveway. Riske led us past the Ferrari and into the rear of the condo. As we walked up the stairway, Riske pointed out a Ben and Jerry's ice cream cup on the stairway rail. When he had first noticed it, the ice cream had not yet appeared to have melted. He explained that when he walked through the house initially he had not found anything unusual. Two children, a boy and a girl, had been sleeping in the upstairs bedroom, and he had arranged their transport to the West LA station.

As we walked through the house, I noted that there were lighted candles in the bathroom around the tub, and also in the living room. Romantic music was playing. The female victim had been home for several minutes prior to her death, at least enough time to light the candles and put music on the stereo. I also noticed a lithograph poster of O.J. Simpson on the wall in the front room.

Riske led Ron and me through the open front door, which showed no obvious signs of forced entry. From the front porch landing, Riske pointed to a bloody shoeprint heading west down the walkway. We could easily see the victims from the landing. We were within a couple of feet of the female victim and several feet away from the male victim, who was now in full view. The female victim's head was resting with her chin on her upper chest—or so it appeared, but her hair was obscuring her face. She was soaked with blood, which seemed to come from her neck or face area and drained down onto the walkway. Her right leg was wedged under the metal fence. On the ground nearby was a takeout menu.

Although the male victim was more visible now, his wounds were not so obvious, and I could not tell how much he had bled or from where. Riske led us around the front porch and down the walkway along the north side of the condo, pointing out a trail of blood drops just to the left of the bloody shoeprints. As the shoeprints faded out, we came to a heavy metal gate that was about two-thirds of the way open. Riske pointed to smears of blood on the upper rail of the gate. I noticed two blood drops on the bottom inside of the gate. We continued out to the rear driveway.

In the driveway, just north of the Cherokee, Riske showed us two coins on the pavement, intermingled with drops of blood. The blood trail stopped at the beginning of the alley. There, the person either had stopped bleeding or had entered a vehicle.

Riske walked around to the front of the residence while Ron and I went back inside the house. Ron had previously told me that I was the lead detective on the case, and I began making my preliminary notes. The initial indications were that the female victim was O.J. Simpson's ex-wife, but that could not be verified yet, and I was not about to jump to conclusions. The male victim was as yet unidentified, and my impression was that he did not fit with the female victim.

At this point in the investigation, my instincts leaned toward an attempted residential robbery. The cause of death seemed to be some type of traumatic force, maybe a blunt object or a firearm. The scene indicated that the female victim had opened the door, either answering it or possibly investigating a noise outside.

The male victim's presence was not as easily explained. He could have left the residence and been confronted by an assailant who then killed him, either intentionally or in the course of a struggle. The female might have heard the struggle and opened the door to investigate. Then she too was killed, and the suspect fled down the walkway.

I also considered the possibility that the male victim was a suspect. Perhaps he had been killed accidentally by another suspect during the murder of the female victim.

On any investigation, you can't jump to conclusions and then try to make the evidence fit your theory of what happened. Instead, you must let the evidence speak for itself. And you have to listen to it. Every aspect of the case must constantly be questioned. You must try to put yourself in the suspect's mind and walk through the crime in different ways. What did he see? Was the suspect mad or methodical? Was he sloppy or neat? Was the crime planned or spontaneous? Was this the work of a professional or an amateur?

I sat down on the living room couch and continued writing my preliminary notes. At that point my partner Brad Roberts arrived, walking into the house from the garage. I gave him a general briefing before walking him through the scene. He commented on the apparent lack of struggle inside the house, and I agreed. We moved onto the front porch, and I pointed to the shoeprints and blood drops. We both examined the drops more closely than I had before and noted that the bleeder appeared to have been moving west, corroborating the direction of the shoeprints. I also pointed out the other visible pieces of evidence—the cap, glove, and white envelope.

At this stage we couldn't get any closer to the victims, so I took Brad down the north walkway, showing him the bloody shoeprints and blood drops. When we walked toward the alley, we noticed two additional blood smears on the gate that were not observed in the initial walk-through. We were carefully scanning the gate with our flashlights when we were both shocked by the sight of a bloody fingerprint on the brass deadbolt knob.

In our years on the force, Brad and I had seen thousands of fingerprints. This print was no doubt at least several "points" in quality. The more identifiable points of comparison, the better the chance of identifying the suspect. This print was identifiable, comparable, and high in quality. I wrote these observations down in my notes.

As we walked onto the rear driveway, I pointed out the coins and the blood drops on the ground or nearby. Together, we came up with one possible explanation. The suspect had come down the walkway, bleeding as he walked, then reached for his car keys, turning the pocket inside out and sending loose change spilling onto the ground. This would suggest that the suspect was male, as females generally do not carry change in their pants pockets, and that the suspect was very excited, not calm and professional.

The suspect had dropped or lost a left glove in a struggle by the walkway at the front of the house. So, his left hand had been bare and apparently bleeding. As he approached his vehicle, the suspect reached into his pocket with his ungloved left hand, and the change fell from the pocket as it was turned inside out.

Brad walked around to join Ron Phillips in front of the house while I went back into the house to complete my notes. When I was about two-thirds done writing down my observations, Ron walked in from the garage.

"I just talked to Bureau Chief Frankel," Ron said, standing over me. "He's assigning the case to Robbery/Homicide."

I looked at Ron.

"Okay, just let me finish my notes, and I'll be right out."

Being relieved of a case such as this one brings on a combination of emotions. Initially, any good detective, particularly a homicide detective, wants to keep a "Whodunit." But if the female victim was really Nicole Brown Simpson, there would be extreme pressure to solve the case, and a lot of people would be putting their fingers in the pie. From the beginning I knew that Ron, Brad, and I could not handle the case purely from a logistical point of view. The case would absorb the attention of the detectives assigned to it every waking minute. Brad and I could not take such a case. We were responsible for all the murders committed in West Los Angeles, and those investigations could not come to a halt because of a single case. Conversely, Robbery/Homicide does have the luxury of assigning detectives to only one case, as would be necessary in this case. Having the case reassigned to Robbery/Homicide was inevitable.

My notes completed, I walked through the garage to the rear alley and around to the front, where I joined Ron, who was standing in the street talking with Lieutenant Frank Spangler, commanding officer of West LA detectives. I gave my notes to Ron, who put them in his notebook. Then we stood in the street and waited for the Robbery/Homicide detectives to arrive. I felt that I had done a good job in the short period that I had been on the scene, and was confident that my notes would assist the detectives taking over the investigation.

By now it was about 3:00 A.M. Brad and I were talking about being relieved from the scene and eating breakfast before beginning our normal shifts. Ron was standing nearby, and we asked him, half-jokingly, to take us to breakfast at Coco's restaurant, one of our favorite early morning eating spots. Maybe he

MARK FUHRMAN'S NOTES
THE SCENE AT BUNDY

NOTES BY DET.
FUHRMAN
#14464

— AT SCENE 0210 HRS — 875 S. BUNDY

— SGT. ROSSI, AM WATCH ASST W/C
COMMANDER BRIEFED DETS ON
SCENE

1) OFCR RISKE REC'D R/C " POSS 459
SUSPS THERE NOW 874 S. BUNDY."
RESIDENT OF 874 HEARD SOMETHING
ACROSS STREET.

2) TWO PEOPLE WALKING DOGS FOUND
BODIES.

3) RISKE FOUND FRONT DOOR TO
TO 875 S. BUNDY WIDE OPEN. TWO
BODIES INSIDE THE WALKWAY GATE,
ONE FEMALE WHITE, ONE MALE
WHITE BOTH EXPIRED — UNKNOWN
CAUSE OF DEATH — POSS GSW.

4) RESID. APPEARS UNTOUCHED — NO
RANSACKING. STEREO PLAYING, LIGHTS
LOW, CANDLES LIT IN LIVING ROOM
AND UPSTAIRS BATHROOM.

06129 ·

5) HANDWRITTEN NOTE ON UPSTAIRS
   COFFEE TABLE, "CARA   575-5713
   CAL PIZZA KITCHEN." PIZZA MENU
   BY FEMALE VICTIM'S LEFT LEG.

6) CUP OF ICE CREAM AT BOTTOM OF
   STAIRS (REAR OF RESID) LEADING INTO
   GARAGE. NOT YET MELTED WHEN OFCR
   RISKE ENTERED RESIDENCE.

7) CHILDREN (2) SLEEPING IN UPSTAIRS
   BEDROOM — AWOKEN BY OFCRS.

8) PAGER LYING ON GROUND NEXT TO
   MALE VICTIM.

9) BLOODY FOOTPRINTS LEADING FROM
   VICTIMS W/B TO ALLEY.

10) CANVAS OF NEIGHBORHOOD BY
    PATROL DIDN'T YIELD MANY RESPONSES,
    RESIDENTS WOULDN'T OPEN DOOR.

11) "AKITA" DOG FOUND RUNNING LOOSE
    BELONGS TO VICTIM (FEMALE).
                    → WHT FERRARI/BLK CHEROKEE
12) NEITHER VEH IN GARAGE/REAR
    PARKING WERE WARM TO TOUCH

00200

13) AT REAR GATE ON N/S OF RESID - TWO
BLOOD SPOTS AT BOTTOM INSIDE OF GATE.
THIS AREA MIGHT HAVE BEEN WHERE
THE DOG WAS KEPT. SUSP RAN
THROUGH THIS AREA. SUBP POSSIBLY
BITEN BY DOG?

14) REAR GATE, POSS BLOOD SMUDGE
ON UPPER RAIL OF GATE.

15) REAR GATE, INSIDE DEAD BOLT
(TURN KNOB TYPE) POSS BLOOD SMUDGE
AND VISIBLE FINGER PRINT.

16) BLOODY PAW PRINTS OF LARGE DOG
LEADING FROM RESID, S/B ON SIDEWALK
APPROX. 60 FT S. OF RESID.

17) SKI MASK, ONE GLOVE BY FEET
OF MALE VICTIM.

would, the look on his face seemed to say. We were tired, hungry, and knew we had a long day ahead of us. Looking back, that was the only conspiracy we engaged in at the crime scene—trying to get the boss to buy us breakfast.

While we were waiting for the detectives, Ron sent Brad to interview the couple who had found the Akita, believed to be Nicole Brown Simpson's pet, wandering near the scene. Although the case had already been reassigned, Ron wanted those witnesses interviewed before they went to sleep or had to go to work.

Meanwhile, Lieutenant Spangler, who had been trying to get a clearer view of the male victim through the wrought-iron fence on the north property line, said he thought he saw a gunshot wound. I walked over, looked through the fence, and shined my light on the victim. It was then that I recognized the wound as a laceration, not a gunshot. Walking back to Spangler, I informed him what I thought.

"How can you be so sure?"

"Because I'm the detective, and you're the lieutenant."

We both laughed.

"I guess you've got a point there," Spangler said.

At about 4:05 A.M., Detective Philip Vannatter from Robbery/Homicide arrived, and Ron and I were introduced to him for the first time. Ron briefed Vannatter on the situation, gave him my notes, and led him on a walk-through of the crime scene. Shortly after Vannatter completed his initial walkthrough, Detective Tom Lange arrived. Once again, Ron and I were introduced to a detective we had never met before. Ron briefed Lange and led him on a walk-through.

Lange, Vannatter, and Ron Phillips all stood in front of the house discussing the scene until Ron walked away and started talking on his cellular phone. After a few moments he turned his head away from the phone and asked me if I knew the way to Simpson's estate on Rockingham Avenue. I told him I had been there in 1985 or 1986 on a family-dispute call, and thought I could find it again. Ron went back to his phone call.

Even though I had been to the Rockingham estate before, I didn't know if I could locate it immediately. I also didn't know if I could give precise directions to someone else. I knew that Riske worked the area, and he gave me the exact address and brief directions, which jogged my memory.

I returned to the front of the Bundy residence and saw Lange walking toward an unmarked police vehicle.

"Ron, Mark, let's go," he said.

Lange and Vannatter were going to follow Ron and me to Simpson's Rockingham estate. While Ron drove, I gave him directions and asked why we were going to the Simpson house. Ron told me that Keith Bushey, the West Bureau commander, had asked that an "in person" death notification be given to O.J. Simpson.

The lead detectives would talk to Simpson. Then we would reunite him with his children, and assist with any notifications of the other family members. Although I didn't convey my thoughts to Ron, I knew our chances of breakfast at Coco's were gone.

Chapter 3

THE ROCKINGHAM ESTATE

*"O.J., you did get a call telling you your wife got killed,
didn't you? . . . Where your wife was killed there was
a blood trail. And that blood trail led here." At this point
Simpson stopped asking questions. He broke into a sweat
and began hyperventilating. He just kept muttering:
"Oh man, oh man, oh man."*

—NOTES OF DETECTIVE BRAD ROBERTS

E ARRIVED AT SIMPSON'S Rockingham estate about 5:05 A.M. The neighborhood was quiet. The large mansions, manicured lawns, and meticulously maintained properties were the homes of millionaires, not working people. I noticed two vehicles parked nearby, a dirty and cluttered Nissan 300ZX car just east of the Ashford Street gate and a white Ford Bronco parked on Rockingham. The Nissan did not seem to fit the neighborhood, so I ran a check on the license plate, which came back clean, with a Hollywood address. Phillips parked along the curb on the north side of the residence. Lange and Vannatter parked behind us. Lange, Vannatter, and Phillips all approached the large iron gate and rang the doorbell for several minutes. No one answered.

EVIDENCE FOUND BY DETECTIVES FUHRMAN AND ROBERTS AT
360 N. ROCKINGHAM AVENUE ON JUNE 13TH, 1994.

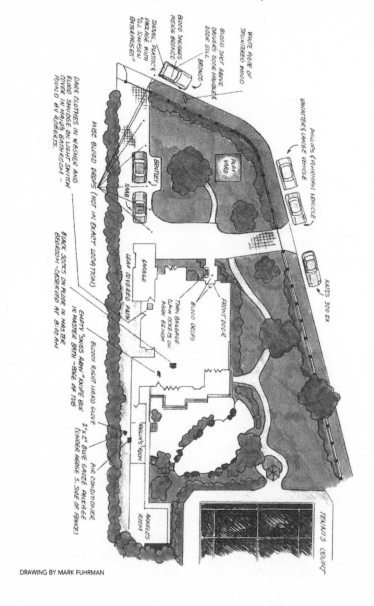

DRAWING BY MARK FUHRMAN

There certainly seemed to be enough people at the gate, so I walked to the corner of Ashford and Rockingham to look at the front of the house. Two rooms had lights on. The Bronco was parked haphazardly, at an odd angle.

I walked over to check out the Bronco and noticed a piece of splintered wood lying on the parkway next to the right front corner of the car. The wood appeared to be a piece of a white picket fence, approximately one foot long. Closer inspection with my flashlight showed a very weathered exterior paint that looked very much like old, oil-based lead paint. The wood was freshly splintered; the interior wood was naturally colored and not yet oxidized. There was a small, rusty nail hole where the wood had broken. I figured the rust meant it had been held in place by a non-galvanized nail. That indicated an old fence. The piece of wood alone might not have appeared suspicious, but the parkway was as well groomed as a golf course, with not a picket fence in sight.

I approached the Bronco's driver's side and placed the back of my hand on the vehicle's hood, which was cold. Scanning the exterior, I noticed a very small, reddish-brown spot above the driver's side door handle. The vehicle was very clean, so the stain stood out despite its small size. Using my flashlight, I viewed the spot closer. It appeared to be blood.

Was this Bronco connected to the crime scene we had just left? I searched for other evidence of blood on the door. Down on my hands and knees, I discovered three or four small stains on the doorsill which also appeared to be blood. My first impression was that they could be small brush marks from the soles of the driver's shoes. Shoes with blood on them.

I continued to examine the vehicle. The side windows in the cargo area were tinted, so I had to cup my hands around my flashlight in order to concentrate the light inside. In the rear cargo area, there was a brown, wrapped package with "O.J. Simpson Enterprises—Attention: Cathy" written on the front. There was also a shovel and a folded piece of heavy gauge plastic. The shovel, an old, used, dirty gardening model, seemed out of place in the Bronco, which didn't look like a work truck.

I looked toward the house and saw that Lange, Vannatter, and Ron were still standing near the gate. Ron was talking on his cellular phone. I walked closer and called them over, saying "I think I saw something on the Bronco." I didn't want to shout, both because of the early morning hour and the possibility that this could be important evidence.

Lange and Vannatter came over immediately. As I walked with them toward the Bronco, I explained the awkward position of the car, the splintered piece of wood on the parkway, and then showed them the spot on the door. I told them that I thought it was blood. Phillips joined the discussion, and I remember him saying "If Mark says it's blood, it probably is."

Vannatter asked if I had run a DMV check on the Bronco. I hadn't, so I went ahead and ran one. The Bronco belonged to Hertz Rent A Car.

To me, these pieces of possible evidence had serious implications. We had just come from a gruesome, bloody double homicide. Blood on a hastily parked vehicle that could be rented to O.J. Simpson might mean that we had another crime scene at Rockingham. Our initial reason for going to Rockingham—to tell O.J. Simpson of his ex-wife's death—was slowly evolving into the suspicion that something was amiss. Whether Simpson was a victim, a possible suspect, or not even involved, the Bronco seemed to be connected in some way.

Lange and Phillips went back to the front gate and tried the doorbell again. Vannatter and I stayed near the Bronco and discussed the newly discovered evidence. We both agreed that the spot looked like blood and the vehicle was probably O.J.'s. I said there could be more victims in the house, possibly injured or unconscious. We might be looking at a murder/suicide or a kidnapping, but we were definitely facing an emergency situation. Vannatter agreed, offering similar concerns.

"I don't care whose house this is, there could be people injured or dying in there right now," I told him, raising my voice. "We have to do something!"

Vannatter agreed.

Phillips got on the phone to the West LA station's watch commander, Sergeant Rossi. From what I overheard of their conversation, Rossi was trying to get the phone number inside Simpson's estate from Westec, a private security firm.

Within minutes, a Westec patrol car arrived. Phillips asked the security guard for Simpson's phone number, which the officer could not give us without his supervisor's approval, so Ron asked him to get his supervisor.

Several minutes later, I saw another Westec patrol car driving slowly along Rockingham. I walked toward the car as the driver stopped and got out near the white Bronco. I introduced myself as a detective, although my badge was in plain sight, and told him we needed to reach someone inside the house. The sergeant informed me that a live-in maid should be there all the time, which I relayed to the other detectives.

If ever there was probable cause to enter private property, we now had it. We had just come from the scene of a brutal double homicide, where one of the victims was apparently the ex-wife of O.J. Simpson. The Bronco, which Simpson probably used, had what we believed to be blood on the door. The vehicle was parked haphazardly, and there was a shovel and some plastic in the rear cargo area. A maid was supposed to be at the estate, and lights were on upstairs and down, yet no one was answering the door.

We had to make a decision and quick. After a brief discussion, Vannatter decided we should go in. As the junior officer, and the youngest among us, I volunteered to climb over the wall. Vannatter told me to go ahead. I jumped the wall and released the hydraulic arm on the gate, admitting the other detectives to the Simpson residence.

We walked to the front door and rang the bell several times, but no one answered. After a few moments, someone (I believe it was Phillips) decided we should go around to the rear of the estate. A stone path was visible to the north of the house, which appeared to lead to the backyard. We all walked in that direction, with me in the rear. A large black dog appeared, but let us walk by him.

As we turned into the pool area, I could see three bungalows on the south side of the property. Ron approached the first bungalow's glass French door and looked inside. He turned back toward us and said, "There's someone on the bed."

When Ron knocked on the door, a white male about thirty years old answered. Ron asked him if Simpson was in the house. One of the other detectives, I'm not sure which one, said that there was an emergency. The man, later identified as Kato Kaelin, a permanent houseguest, told us that Simpson's older daughter Arnelle was in the next bungalow, and pointed toward her room. While Ron, Vannatter, and Lange went toward that bungalow, I stayed with Kato Kaelin.

Even for someone who had just woken up, he appeared more than a little disheveled, with glassy and bloodshot eyes. When I asked if he had been drinking, Kaelin replied that he didn't drink. Because of his demeanor and appearance, I was suspicious of narcotics use and asked him to let me examine his eyes, and he complied. I checked for vertical or horizontal nystagmus, which requires having the subject face you and follow your finger, or an object such as a pencil, with his eyes while keeping his head still. Certain drugs, alcohol, or a combination of the two will make the eye bounce as it reaches the limits of its movement. Kaelin showed no symptoms of nystagmus. As I sensed then and realized later, Kaelin was a little goofy, a little unorthodox, and actually pretty funny. He was just being himself.

I asked Kaelin for permission to look around inside and to make sure no one else was in the bungalow. Again, he made no objections. While I looked around the room, I asked him his name, where he was last night, and other routine questions. There was a pile of clothes and pair of boots next to the bed. With his permission I inspected the boots, checking for blood and the design of the sole. There was no blood, and the sole didn't resemble the shoeprints at the Bundy scene.

I kept asking Kaelin questions in no particular logical order. I asked what he did the previous night, and then followed with, "Who owns the white Bronco out front?" While he was telling me that O.J. drove the car, I quickly followed with "Anything unusual happen last night?"

His answer stopped me cold, although he didn't seem to realize its importance.

Kaelin told me at about 10:45 P.M., he heard and felt a couple of loud thumps on the wall above his bed. He thought there had been an earthquake, because the thumps had caused the picture above his bed and to the right of the air conditioner to shake. He went on to describe a limo parked outside the Ashford gate around the same time.

I asked Kaelin to follow me out of his bungalow. By that time a door to the main house had been opened. I walked inside with Kaelin and asked him to sit at the bar and wait for someone to come talk to him. Unfamiliar with the house, I walked toward the sound of voices, which led me to the kitchen where Phillips, Lange, and Vannatter were standing. Phillips was talking on the phone. Vannatter was closest to me, so I asked "Phil, would you talk to this guy at the bar?"

Vannatter appeared to acknowledge my question, so I continued outside, hoping to see if there was any access to the south side of the bungalows where Kaelin had described the thumping on his wall. Walking toward the garage, I noticed a chain-link fence running along the edge of the property. Along this fence was a narrow cement sidewalk with an open gate that led down the south side of the house. The sidewalk was dark and shadowed by overhanging trees and shrubs.

As I stared down the path, I suspected that a person walking down it had caused the thumps on Kaelin's wall. The possibility that someone could have been injured, near death, or already dead was still on my mind. That the thumps could have been made by a suspect was possible, but still remote to me at that point.

I looked down the dark path and noticed a gate about three feet tall that was half open. Looking up, I began to orient myself to the buildings, and determined where the garage began and ended. I continued down the leaf-covered path and gave this part of the house a cursory look, but nothing appeared disturbed.

Returning my attention to the path, I looked up to a very high wall that continued to the end of the buildings. This appeared to be the bungalows, as I remembered they had a steep, single-pitch roof. I looked further along the path and noticed a dark object. At first I thought it was dog droppings, but as I walked closer, the object began to resemble an old gardening glove, either lost or discarded. As I knelt by the glove, I saw that it wasn't old or a gardening glove. It was a right-hand, dark brown leather glove with something slightly wet-looking on it. One of the fingers seemed stuck to the palm, and I concluded that the substance on the glove must have been somewhat sticky, perhaps dried or drying blood. There were no fallen leaves from the overhanging trees, no dirt—virtually nothing on top of the glove, which indicated it hadn't been there long.

The glove looked very much like the one at the Bundy residence. I immediately looked around. Directly above the glove was an air conditioning unit that protruded from the wall about two feet and was braced underneath with 2 x 4 studs. Could someone have bumped into the air conditioner and dropped the glove? My heart started pounding. Was I on the trail of a victim, or possibly a suspect?

Adrenaline shot through my system. I was in a dangerous position, halfway down a path that a murder suspect had possibly used. Should I turn back or go forward? If I turned around, my back would be exposed to anyone who might still be hiding further down the path. Going forward seemed like a better idea. As I started to walk slowly forward, surely I held my gun, though I don't remember pulling it out or even thinking about it. After twenty years, some things become reflex.

Within my first few steps past the air conditioner, my face hit cobwebs. Since I was slightly crouched, lower than most people would stand, I concluded that whoever had dropped the glove did not continue walking down this path. The rest of the leaf-cover was undisturbed; no one had crawled or dragged along the path either.

I continued walking and looking for other evidence, ending at the southeast corner of the property in what appeared to be a gardener's potting area. I spent a few minutes making sure that no one had collapsed, that there were no obvious pieces of evidence in the area, and then returned to the glove.

Kneeling next to the glove, I noticed a small, light blue paper package immediately on the other side of the cyclone fence. The package was roughly two inches square and appeared to be the wrapping for a gauze bandage. I scrutinized the immediate area, looking for evidence of blood, footprints, or disturbed ground, but saw nothing.

I returned to the front of the house and told Phillips what I had found, and led him to the glove. I related all my observations and conclusions, as it was important first to get his impressions. Phillips agreed that the glove looked very much like the one at the Bundy scene, and that it did not match the surrounding condition of the path.

Ron went to get Lange and Vannatter, and I took them in turn down the path, explaining things as I went. Vannatter was very interested in the discovery, although Lange was reserved. The three of them returned to the house while I stayed outside, in part to keep an eye on the glove, but also to let the adrenaline rush wear off.

After a short time, Phillips came back outside and told me that O.J. Simpson was in Chicago on business. He had left the previous night about 11:00 P.M. As we looked at each other, I could tell we were thinking the same thing: the dog was discovered wandering the streets at 10:30 to 10:45. Kaelin heard the bumps about 10:45. The possibility that O.J. Simpson could have been responsible for the bloody murder scene on Bundy seemed both bizarre and remote, but it loomed large in our minds nonetheless.

Several minutes later Phillips came back to tell me that Vannatter wanted us to go back to Bundy and look at the glove to see if it matched the one I had discovered behind Kaelin's bungalow. I didn't think this was a good idea, since by going from one crime scene to the other I could transmit trace evidence with my hands and clothes. Detectives call this cross-contaminating a scene, and avoid it whenever possible. But Vannatter was an experienced detective, and he was in charge of the investigation.

Phillips and I drove to Bundy together, arriving between 7:00 and 7:15 A.M. There was already an LAPD photographer at the scene, and Ron told me to have him photograph the glove before I inspected it. The photographer's name was Rokahr, and I had worked with him before. Together, we walked around to the back of the condo and inside, since this was still the least contaminating way to approach the victims. I stepped over the female victim, careful to place my foot on a portion of the step that was not splashed with blood. Another long step and I was standing in the flower bed, just a few feet from the male victim. I knelt close to the glove and cap. On Rokahr's direction I pointed toward the glove, and he shot the picture.

After the first photo was taken, I inspected the glove. Moving it with a pen, I easily saw it was a left-hand, large, dark brown leather glove with beige/gray knit fabric lining. It appeared to be the mate of the right-hand glove I had found behind the bungalow at Rockingham, although this glove's leather had a duller appearance. I left the scene as carefully as I had entered it, and walked back around to the front of the property. I drove back to Rockingham with Rokahr following me.

Upon my return to the estate, I parked just south of the Rockingham gate and was joined by my partner Brad. I left Brad at the gate by the Bronco and walked through the Ashford gate with Rokahr, looking for Vannatter. I found him and told him that the glove at the Bundy scene was for a left hand and looked like a match for the glove I found behind Kaelin's bungalow. Vannatter instructed me to have Rokahr photograph the glove behind the bungalow, at the same time saying that now we were going to have to handle the Rockingham estate like a crime scene.

I went with Rokahr to photograph the glove. The only instructions I gave Rokahr were that I wanted the photos to depict the ambient light as we now saw it. He took several shots, and then we returned to the front of the estate.

Brad had not been to the estate before. I explained my initial observations about the Bronco, showing him the blood spot above the door handle; the small brush lines on the doorsill; and the shovel, plastic, and the package addressed to O.J. Simpson Enterprises. While briefing Brad, I noticed Vannatter walking toward the Bronco from the corner of Ashford and Rockingham. I introduced Brad to Vannatter and then continued my briefing, explaining the difficulty I had seeing through the tinted windows in the dark. On his own, Brad walked over to the passenger side of the vehicle and looked inside, cupping his hands around his eyes to see through the glass. After a short time he looked back at me.

"There's blood all over the inside!" Brad said. He described reddish-brown stains on the steering wheel, console, seats, and door panels. I looked for myself; there were blood smudges all over the Bronco's interior.

Vannatter was still standing close to the Bronco, and I called him over to the passenger side to look. Brad and I described the stains Brad had found inside the Bronco as Vannatter looked inside. Surprised and excited, Vannatter went back to the Ashford gate while Brad and I stayed close to the Bronco watching Rokahr photograph the blood spot on the door. As Brad and I walked back toward the Rockingham gate, he made another timely observation. Brad saw drops of blood on the street by the driver's side of the Bronco leading toward the Rockingham gate. The gate was not locked, but it was closed. Brad and I walked through the gate, observing more drops of blood on the driveway. To my knowledge, this was the first time anyone had gone through that gate from the street that morning.

Brad and I walked up the driveway past the Saab and the black Bentley to the front of the house. Looking toward the open front door, Brad saw a large drop of blood on the cement walkway outside the door. He brought this to my attention, then together we noticed three drops of blood just inside the door on the light-stained oak floor.

I believe Vannatter was talking to someone inside the house, but within seconds he came outside where Brad and I had seen the blood drops. When Brad showed them to him, without hesitation Vannatter said, "That's it. This is now a crime scene. Let's get everybody out of the house."

Vannatter asked Brad and me to help evacuate the premises of all non-police personnel. Arnelle Simpson had gone to the West LA station and picked up O.J.'s two small children. She had also called O.J.'s good friend, Al Cowlings, who was now with her and the kids watching television in the next room. At our direction, Arnell, Cowlings, Kaelin, and the kids left the house through the patio door and the Ashford gate. Brad and I had them use the patio exit to keep foot traffic away from the blood evidence we had just found near the front door.

Vannatter also asked us to check the house to make sure no one else remained. Brad and I had already walked through most of the bottom floor, so we went upstairs to check the other rooms. When we walked into the master bedroom, which we assumed was O.J.'s room, we noticed that the room was neat except for a pair of black socks on the floor at the foot of the bed. The socks were lying there as if someone had taken them off and thrown them on the floor. This seemed odd, not just to a detective, but to anyone who might have observed the immaculate condition of the rest of the room and the entire house. After we completed securing the house, I found Vannatter in the kitchen and told him about the socks.

Brad and I went back outside, where we saw Kaelin milling around near the Ashford gate, looking confused. We were both concerned that he could be "in the wind" if someone didn't get him to the West LA station. Although Kaelin seemed to be a witness, we were not exactly sure of his status at this point in the investigation. One thing was certain; we needed to hang on to him. I went back into the kitchen and suggested to Vannatter that someone take Kaelin to the station before we lose him. Vannatter listened, but made no comment. So, I made a decision and asked Brad to have a patrol officer transport Kaelin to the station for a witness interview. Then I told Vannatter that it had been taken care of.

Vannatter said he was going to the station himself to write a search warrant and asked Brad to write a description of the property for the warrant. Placing his hand on my shoulder, and with confidence in his voice, Vannatter said, "You're in charge of this crime scene."

One of the first things I did was instruct an officer to complete an impound report for the Bronco and have it transported to LAPD headquarters at Parker Center. I made sure to have the officer indicate on the report to hold the vehicle in the print garage and have special notification for the serology, fingerprints, and trace evidence sections of the Scientific Investigations Division (SID). I told the officers to fill out the necessary reports, but delay the actual impound until the criminalist had taken a sample of the blood spots. Just as the officer was completing the impound, Vannatter came over and asked what I was doing. I explained that I was protecting the possible evidence on the Bronco by impounding it and placing it under cover instead of leaving it exposed to the elements and possible contamination. Vannatter canceled the impound and told me to leave the vehicle on the street with the guard officers. I didn't understand his decision, which increased the risk of sensitive evidence being compromised. The only justification I could even entertain was that Vannatter didn't believe he had enough probable cause to impound the vehicle. Anyway, it wasn't my case, so I did what I was told. Vannatter left to write the search warrant.

While Brad and I waited for the warrant to be written and signed by a judge, I went to the house that shared the south property line with Simpson's. I knocked on the door, and a female answered. I could not see her face behind the mesh security panel, but she greeted me and I identified myself. I told her that there might have been some trouble next door and asked if she would mind if I walked along their fence and into the rear yard. The woman gladly gave me permission, adding that if I needed to come back, her permission was not necessary. The woman spoke perfect English. Much later, we learned that she was Rosa Lopez, who had such trouble with her English during the trial. After speaking to Rosa, I spent several minutes looking around the backyard but found nothing unusual.

When I returned to the Simpson property, an SID criminalist van was parked in front of the Bronco and a criminalist named Dennis Fung, whom I had never met or worked with before, was busy unloading equipment from the van. I showed him the blood spot on the door and the streaks on the sill. Although he tested the spot, which did prove to be blood, he apparently never tested the streaks. And strangely enough, Rokahr never photographed them.

While Fung was testing the blood spot on the Bronco's door, Brad was just inside the Rockingham gate placing small plastic numbers along the driveway leading toward the house. He had found a blood trail that made a path from the Rockingham gate to the front of the house, and now was marking the spots to keep people from walking on the possible evidence and to document their position for photos. Together, we looked for additional blood spots and found several more.

At one point Brad looked back toward the gate and saw Fung picking up Brad's numbers and replacing them with his own. But Fung was only putting numbers on every fourth or fifth drop.

"Why don't you recover every drop of blood? It looks like you're missing a lot of drops," Brad asked the criminalist.

Fung replied that taking samples of every fourth or fifth drop would be good enough. Brad and I looked at each other in disbelief. Without saying a word, we both knew that had we been in charge of the case, every drop of blood would have been recovered.

As Brad and I talked by the front door, I noticed a couple of small pieces of paper lying on a park bench near the front door. Brad and I looked closer at the paper scraps and recognized them as airline baggage tags. Anywhere else, these discarded tags would not have merited a second look, but, as we had seen inside, the rest of the estate was immaculate. We both made a mental note of the tags.

At that point Vannatter called to tell me to have Fung test the glove behind the bungalow for blood. Fung used a swab to obtain a sample from the surface of the glove and tested the sample by the front of the garage. The substance was indeed blood. I called Vannatter at the West LA station to convey the results of Fung's test. Vannatter instructed me to take Fung to the glove and recover it. I led Fung down the south walkway to recover the glove and the small blue wrapper I had noticed earlier. With me holding a brown paper bag, Fung carefully placed the glove into the bag and closed it.

We went back inside the house. The phone kept ringing, and I answered it, thinking the calls might be police-related. Most of the calls were from friends of Simpson who wanted to know what had happened. One of the calls was from Bruce Jenner's wife, Kris. Another was from Ron Shipp, an ex-cop who was close to Simpson.

"I'm a good friend of O.J.; my name is Ron Shipp."

"Ron, this is Fuhrman."

His tone warmed to that of a friend. I had known Ron for nine years.

"Mark, what happened? Is everyone okay? O.J. didn't hurt Nicole, did he?" I couldn't tell him anything.

"Ron, it's not my case."

"Mark, you can trust me, you know that."

"If it were my case, things would be different. But I can't, it's not my case. Sorry, buddy."

I had not been to the front of the house for a while; when I went outside, I was shocked to see dozens of media trucks and crews scurrying around carrying minicams and cameras. All of a sudden, I felt like a panda bear on loan from China. That feeling would last quite a while.

It must have been between 10:30 and 11:00 A.M. when Vannatter called to say that the warrant was signed. By this time, there were at least three or four additional Robbery/Homicide detectives at Rockingham. Although it was no longer our case, at Robbery/Homicide's request, Brad and I assisted with the search.

Earlier, we had seen the torn baggage tags near the bench, and I had noticed a discarded airline ticket envelope in a waste-basket in the downstairs bathroom. We alerted the detectives to these discoveries. I watched one of the other detectives attempt to open a door in the hall, which was locked. Finding a set of keys in the house, I unlocked the door and entered Simpson's office and den.

From this room, I could see the premises and the Rockingham gate through a large window. Sometime afternoon, I was looking around the room when I noticed a disturbance outside by the gate. O.J. Simpson had arrived and entered the gate. A black uniformed officer was chasing after him. The officer, Don Thompson, handcuffed Simpson and led him toward the house.

From the den I heard Brad's voice.

"O.J.'s here. He's coming up the driveway."

I saw him go out and approach Simpson and Officer Thompson to intercept them before they reached the house. Brad took control of Simpson. They stood together beneath a tree by the children's playhouse. The following conversation was later related to me by Brad.

"What's this all about?" Simpson asked.

"What's all what about?" Brad responded.

"This. All the police all over my house."

"O.J., you did get a call telling you your wife got killed, didn't you?"

"Yeah. Yeah. I know that. But what's this all about?"

"I'm not the detective handling this case. So, I'm not at liberty to talk with you. I'll tell you this. Where your wife was killed there was a blood trail. And that blood trail led here."

"A blood trail?"

"Yeah, a blood trail."

At this point Simpson stopped asking questions. He broke into a sweat and began hyperventilating. He just kept muttering:

"Oh man, oh man, oh man."

Moments later, Vannatter approached Simpson and engaged him in conversation. Simpson asked to have the handcuffs taken off, saying it was really embarrassing with all the media cameras on him. Vannatter took the cuffs off. It has been previously reported elsewhere that Howard Weitzman, Simpson's attorney, asked to have the cuffs removed, but the truth of the matter is that Simpson himself asked.

Vannatter approached Brad and asked if we could take Simpson down to Parker Center. Then he asked if just Brad could assist him with the transport. Brad went back inside to give me his car keys. By the time he came out, Vannatter was driving off with Simpson and Weitzman.

As Vannatter and Simpson were driving away from the estate, Brad related to me the conversation he had had with Simpson. We both realized the importance, not only of the statement, but the involuntary bodily reaction that Brad had observed. I suggested Brad put this to paper immediately, which he did. His written statement was then given to Vannatter and Lange. Brad's statement could have been very helpful when they interrogated Simpson, but they did not use it.

Then we all returned to searching the residence and premises. Brad alerted Robbery/Homicide to freshly washed clothes in the washing machine. Brad described the clothes as black sweats, then and now. Also, in the half bath next to the maid's quarters, Brad found blood smears on the light switch and various other locations. Up in the master bathroom, at the edge of the tub, we found an open knife box with the Swiss Army logo. It was empty, but meant to package one of the larger knives. I also pointed this out to the detectives.

The interior of the house was now being searched quite thoroughly, so I walked downstairs and turned into the living room area. As I entered the room, I could not help but notice the Plexiglas-encased Heisman trophy. Looking around the room, I saw other awards and photos of a successful and popular athlete who very well might be involved in the murder of his ex-wife. It was sad to be investigating a double murder in this room of accomplishment and memories.

Searching the room, I looked toward the television and VCR, for no other reason than curiosity. Seeing an empty video box, I turned on the VCR and pushed eject. The videotape that I pulled from the machine was the movie

Ghost. Although it had no evidentiary value, the tape's being left in the VCR indicated that Simpson had probably just watched this story about love, jealousy, and murder.

If my twenty years as a cop taught me anything, it's that people get away with murder every day.

I left the living room and proceeded to search the more unpopular areas of the warrant, like the crawl space under the house, and the roof and the bushes behind the estate, but found nothing of interest. Brad and I had agreed that the shovel in the back of the Bronco was a gardening shovel, but neither one of us could find other gardening tools anywhere. The garage housed Simpson's Ferrari, a workout machine, and lots of golf equipment, but no tools used to maintain the grounds.

Around noontime, Marcia Clark from the district attorney's office arrived. She was another person I had never met before. Clark asked to be shown what I had seen, what I did, and where I had found any evidence. So I walked her through the crime scene and explained my discoveries and observations. She was soon joined by Bill Hodgman, a high-ranking district attorney, and they both wanted to speak to me. We all went outside and sat at a table on the patio.

Clark asked me if I could describe everything that had taken place at Bundy and Rockingham that concerned me. Before I could start talking, a news helicopter began hovering overhead just a few hundred feet above us. It was impossible for us to hear, so we moved inside to the living room.

As I described everything that I observed, noted, and found, she sat smiling and nodding. Hodgman listened and took notes. When I had completed my story, they stated they were very satisfied. They asked no questions.

I spent the rest of the day on the scene while the photographers and criminalists completed their time-consuming jobs. I finally left at 6:00 P.M.

It had been a long day, and I knew this was just the beginning. But I thought the killer would be found and justice served. I should have known better. If my twenty years as a cop taught me anything, it's that people get away with murder every day.

Chapter 4

COSTLY ERRORS

---

*To distill this case down to its irreducible minimum, if
your blood is found at the murder scene, as Simpson's was
conclusively proved to be by DNA tests, that's really the end
of the ball game. There is nothing more to say.*

—VINCENT BUGLIOSI

I HAD ALWAYS THOUGHT that the Robbery/Homicide Division (RHD) was the cream of the crop when it came to murder investigations. But mistakes made in the first fourteen hours of the investigation, mostly by lead detectives Vannatter and Lange, would compromise the case and change my life forever.

The murders at 875 Bundy should have been investigated just like any other murder, by the book. But they weren't. One of the first avoidable mistakes was my returning to the Bundy crime scene after having been at Rockingham. When I found the bloody glove behind Kato's room at Rockingham, Vannatter felt we had to compare the color, hand, and material of that glove to the one at Bundy immediately. Had this information been necessary to establish that the Rockingham

35

estate was a crime scene, or to gain a search warrant, I could understand the need
to send me to the other scene. But neither case applied. If you find two gloves at
two separate scenes that are linked by a blood trail and look similar, you have
enough probable cause. And even if you do feel the need to establish the match,
you don't send a detective from one crime scene to the other and risk cross-
contaminating the scenes. Had the case remained mine, I would not have sent a
detective back to Bundy.

But this was Vannatter's case and he was calling the shots, so I went to the
Bundy scene to inspect the glove. In doing so, I possibly took anything on my shoes
or body with me that I came in contact with from Rockingham.

Probable cause for a warrant could have been easily established without close
comparison of the two gloves. We had already found blood on the Bronco, blood
drops in the foyer, and a bloody glove behind Kato's room. The Rockingham estate
was clearly a crime scene. Would it have ceased to be a crime scene if it turned out
the two gloves were not perfect matches? Just the evidentiary discoveries as they
occurred and the obvious connection of the two crime scenes would have resulted
in a signed search warrant, if the warrant had been written accurately and
completely.

Unfortunately, it wasn't. Vannatter's June 13 warrant was only two and a quarter
pages long, double spaced. There is no way that all the details of the probable cause
and evidence we compiled at Rockingham could be described in a document of
that length. And they weren't. This brief and faulty warrant would become a focal
point of the defense's claim there had been suspicious police conduct at the scene.
(Search warrant reprinted in full in Appendix B.)

In the warrant, Vannatter did not establish a strong initial connection between
the Rockingham estate and the Bundy scene, but merely noted the fact that one
of the victims and Simpson had two children together, and that detectives had
gone to Rockingham to make a notification. Upon arriving at Rockingham,
Vannatter stated that "detectives were unable to arouse anyone at the residence."

Vannatter went on to describe the Bronco and the blood found on the door
handle. But he did not mention the fact that the Bronco was parked at an odd
angle, or that there was blood observed inside the car; a package addressed to O.J.
Simpson, a gardening shovel, and a piece of heavy gauge folded plastic in the rear
cargo area; or that a piece of wood that did not fit the neighborhood was found

near the car. These items were not easily explainable, and taken together indicated that the Bronco might have some connection to both Simpson and the Bundy crime scene.

The search warrant also failed to describe a Nissan 300Z that was parked on Ashford, which DMV records showed was registered in Hollywood. Although the Nissan later proved to be Kaelin's, it was at that early stage important to establishing probable cause: who did the vehicle belonged to, and why it was parked outside the estate?

Vannatter described waking and interviewing Arnelle Simpson, at which time he learned that Simpson was the primary driver of the Bronco, and that Simpson had gone to Chicago. The warrant mistakenly describes his trip as "unexpected," an error that was made much of during both the preliminary hearing and the criminal trial. I don't know why Vannatter said the trip was "unexpected." To my knowledge, no one characterized it as such.

These errors were minor compared to the truly tragic loss of evidence that could have put the case away that morning.

Why didn't Vannatter even mention Kato Kaelin in the warrant? Not only was he interviewed before Arnelle, but he described suspicious thumps on his wall that he thought so unusual he went outside to investigate.

Although Vanatter did note the discovery of the glove behind Kaelin's bungalow, his description was vague and incomplete. The search warrant described the glove as being found "during the securing of the residence," almost implying that someone tripped over it, rather than its being discovered during a search following Kaelin's statement. And by the time Vannatter wrote the warrant, he knew that the gloves matched, but even though he sent me back to establish exactly that detail, he never put it in; he simply described it as a brown leather glove.

Throughout the warrant Vannatter missed important details. He did not describe the blood seen inside the Bronco or the three drops of blood in the foyer. He did not include the theory that the suspect probably left the Bundy scene in a vehicle parked where the blood drops stopped and that blood drops started again from the Bronco and led into the residence.

Because so many easily described pieces of evidence and easily explained observations and conclusions were omitted from the first search warrant, Vannatter appeared to be groping for probable cause, when it was staring him right in the face.

A second search warrant was executed on June 28, after Simpson had already been arrested and the preliminary hearing was well under way. It gives a concise and detailed description of all of the probable cause leading up to the June 13 search warrant. There were few similarities between the two documents, except for the first three paragraphs of both warrants, which are almost identical, with the exception that Ron Goldman is identified as the male victim in the second one.

The first warrant was obviously written in haste, while the second might well have taken days. Even beyond that, however, the style, verbiage, and syntax of these two warrants have little in common. Vannatter signed both, but the documents are so different they could have been written by two different people. If Vannatter didn't write the second search warrant, who did?

When Vannatter established the Rockingham estate as a crime scene and asked Brad and me to evacuate the home of family and friends, we checked all the rooms for people. As we walked into Simpson's bedroom, we immediately noticed a pair of socks on the floor. After completing our search, I told Vannatter about the socks. This was about 8:00 A.M.

There was nothing obviously sinister about the socks, except that they were the only pieces of clothing on the floor in an otherwise neat bedroom. Later these two socks became crucial evidence, when it was discovered that they contained blood evidence from Nicole and Simpson. Brad and I could have established the socks being on the floor in the master bedroom long before the search warrant was signed or Simpson gave a blood sample to Vannatter and Lange. Instead, because the socks did not show up on a videotape shot to memorialize the condition and possessions of the Rockingham house, the defense was able to question whether the socks had been in the bedroom, creating doubt in the juror's minds. Later, it was proven that the videophotographer had shot the room after Fung had already removed the socks. But doubt had already been planted.

Another crucial source of evidence mishandled was Simpson's Bronco. From the moment I saw what appeared to be blood stains on the door, it was apparent that this vehicle contained important evidence. It should have been treated with extreme care, following standard procedures.

As I related in the previous chapter, when Vannatter put me in charge of the Rockingham scene, one of my first actions was to order the Bronco impounded. But Vannatter cancelled the impound and simply had two officers guard the vehicle. Because of Vannatter's decision, the Bronco sat outside for several hours with countless people around it.

The decision to leave the Bronco on a public street bothered me then and still does. Did Vannatter think he didn't have probable cause to impound the Bronco prior to having the search warrant? That seems very odd, considering the fact that Vannatter eventually testified that he looked inside and saw blood in the Bronco. Just how much probable cause did he think he needed to impound a vehicle which he thought was connected to a crime?

When the Bronco was finally impounded, it was taken not to Parker Center, but to a contract impound lot. There, the worst that could happen did. A tow lot employee went inside the Bronco and took a receipt from the glovebox for a souvenir. The defense now could rightly argue that the evidence inside the Bronco was compromised, but it was still a stretch to call it contaminated. However, it once again looked as if we were careless or had mishandled evidence. And once again, the defense had reason to cast suspicion on the actions of the LAPD officers and their support staff.

One of the most important responsibilities of detectives at a murder scene is the handling of the bodies. They shouldn't be moved until all evidence around them is collected or secured, and any forensic tests at the crime scene should be delayed until it is certain they will not interfere with the proper collection of evidence. While the defense argued that Vannatter and Lange should have given the medical examiner earlier access to the bodies, in this case they did the right thing. But that's not to say the detectives were flawless in their handling of the bodies.

When I read the autopsy reports during the trial, I was surprised to learn that Lange and Vannatter didn't have Nicole checked for semen. They reasoned that since her panties weren't torn, the possibility of rape was almost nonexistent. That may be true, but consensual sex was still possible.

Simpson reportedly had consensual sex with Nicole many times during their separation and divorce. Ron Goldman was also rumored to have been sexually involved with Nicole. Wouldn't it have been useful to know if Nicole had sexual intercourse just prior to her murder?

I cannot imagine not trying to acquire every piece of forensic evidence possibly available at a murder scene. It would be far better to have it, or try to obtain it, than to be criticized by the defense for not even attempting to retrieve it. The detectives simply had to request the sample be taken, and we would have been covered.

Another mistake was Tom Lange's decision to cover Nicole's corpse with a cotton blanket from her house. Simpson had no doubt slept over at the house occasionally. So, even though it was later argued that the blanket had been laundered the day before the murder, it was still a mistake to allow even the possibility of hair and fiber contamination.

Then there is the issue of Simpson's blood sample. After Vannatter got a blood sample from Simpson on the afternoon of June 13, he carried it to the Rockingham scene instead of booking it as evidence. He claimed that he wanted to give the sample to Dennis Fung, so the criminalist could put it in with the other evidence. But Vannatter could just as easily have put the blood vial in an evidence envelope and stowed it in an evidence locker. When Fung returned to the station, Vannatter could have given him the blood. There was no reason for Vannatter to carry the blood back to the crime scenes, and doing so only opened him to criticism. His actions showed a lack of presence of mind, and frankly I agree with the defense for questioning them. Vannatter should have realized that in such a high-profile case his every movement would be dissected in court. If both he and Lange had simply stayed at their respective crime scenes, many of the problems eventually exploited by the defense would have been avoided.

Every crime scene is different, and the process of evidence collection changes with the conditions of each particular scene. The Bundy residence was the most challenging type of crime scene: outside, and without much room for us to move around the bodies. In any outdoor crime scene, you have to worry about wind, rain, and other factors that could degrade or destroy evidence. The entire block should have been sealed off until we had gathered every piece of evidence that we could possibly find, but we did not.

Still, these errors were minor compared to a truly tragic error by which the prosecution lost a single piece of evidence that could have put the case away that morning.

Hindsight is always 20/20, and it would not be fair to say that the Bundy crime scene would have been better served by Phillips, Roberts, and myself. But this much is certain: Had we remained in charge of the case, Brad and I would never have gone to Rockingham. Instead, we would have stayed at Bundy and investigated the scene completely and without pause.

Remember, at the Bundy scene, Brad and I had found a bloody latent fingerprint on the north walkway gate. We both saw the print as we shined our flashlights on the other blood evidence on the gate. The print was formed in blood on the brass-plated doorknob turnstile. We both commented that it appeared to be several points in quality and very clear.

Once my preliminary walk-through of the Bundy crime scene was complete, I carefully wrote my observations, including the print on the gate, in clear, neat notes. I had a meticulous system for taking notes at crime scenes. During the first walkthrough, I noted every obvious point of evidentiary value and gave each of those items a number. As the investigation proceeded, I would make more extensive notes concerning each numbered item and use the originally assigned number to connect these notes forever to my initial observation. This system is immensely important for prioritizing evidence collection.

When the case was reassigned, I gave my notes to Ron Phillips and told him there was a fingerprint on the gate. Then Brad and I walked out to the street and waited for the RHD detectives to arrive. We felt we had done a good job and the case was just about over.

When I was turning over the Bundy crime scene to Robbery/Homicide, it never occurred to me to lead two veteran homicide detectives by the hand and show them the bloody fingerprint. It would have been an insult for me to emphasize a single piece of evidence to senior detectives. The fingerprint was clearly described right there in my notes, and I had no reason to think they wouldn't read my notes before walking through the scene, since doing so is standard procedure. The importance of the fingerprint was obvious. Brad and I agreed completely that whoever walked down that path left bloody shoeprints, blood drops to the left side of his body, and a bloody fingerprint on the gate. The suspect just about signed his name in blood before he escaped.

Whose blood was it? At least some of it belonged to the suspect, because there was enough blood to suggest that the suspect was bleeding. A blood smudge beneath the fingerprint indicated that the suspect transferred blood, most probably from his hand or finger, onto the gate. And as he swung his hand up to open the gate, he cast droplets of blood there as well. But if we were lucky, the blood stain would include blood from the victims. By linking the victims' blood to the suspect's blood and identifying the suspect, the fingerprint could have closed the case.

Later, after Simpson was arrested, it would have been virtually impossible for him to claim that the print was left there at some prior date. The print was in blood. Simpson told Lange and Vannatter that he cut himself the night of June 12, 1994. But he also claimed he had not been at Nicole's Bundy townhome for a week. Eleven hours after Brad and I observed the print, Simpson made these statements and locked himself to that story forever.

Standing on the street discussing the case while waiting for the RHD detectives to arrive, Brad and I felt absolutely confident that with a bloody fingerprint this case was all but solved. Sure, there might be questions or challenges. Whoever left the print might have pressed a finger into blood already there, leaving a latent print behind. But that would mean this person had been at the murder scene at some point after the murders and before the first officer arrived at approximately 12:15 A.M.

A defense attorney might argue that the print had been made by one of the first uniformed officers at the scene accidentally touching the gate. But the blood would have been drying for at least an hour and a half.

My observation of a bloody fingerprint and its recording in my contemporaneous notes also showed something else, the significance of which I had no way of knowing at that time. I had no idea whose print it was. This makes the defense's later claim that I planted a bloody glove at Simpson's Rockingham estate completely absurd. Why would I plant a glove to implicate Simpson if I already knew we had a fingerprint at the crime scene, but I didn't know whose fingerprint it was?

Other than an eyewitness report or a confession, you can't get a more powerful single piece of evidence than a fresh bloody fingerprint at a crime scene. Had the bloody fingerprint been properly handled and analyzed, it alone could have put the case away. But there was only superficial mention of the fingerprint at the trial. What happened to this crucial piece of evidence? Somehow, the fingerprint was lost, and so, eventually, was the case.

While Dennis Fung was at Rockingham testing the blood on the Bronco door, latent print specialists from SID were at Bundy, eager for something to do. Instead of having the latent print specialists wait until Fung returned to secure all the blood evidence, Lange had them dust the exterior and interior of Bundy for prints. Left to themselves, latent print specialists would not be concentrating on the blood evidence. In fact, they would avoid anything with the obvious indication of blood, knowing full well that their fingerprint dust would most probably contaminate that evidence. But with a fingerprint on the rear gate, the SID personnel should have been directed to photograph and inspect it.

If Lange merely told latent print specialists to print the area but did not actually supervise what they were doing, his police-work was sloppy. This might seem like a petty charge, but after all, fingerprint people are not detectives. They do not have experience with how a crime might progress, what a suspect might touch, how a crime scene might develop, or what might have taken place.

During Lange's criminal trial testimony, he stated that he showed Fung the gate and ordered him to take blood samples from it. Lange further testified that he never checked the evidence report to make sure that this was done, and only became aware on July 3 that it hadn't been done. At that time he observed the same blood he had asked Fung to recover.

Later in court the defense attorneys disclosed that a photograph with Fung pointing to blood on the rear gate was not taken until July 3, when he returned to get the blood he had missed. If the blood was still on the gate two weeks after the murder, the fingerprint might also have still been intact. But someone who was not specifically looking for the fingerprint probably would not have found it. At some point, the fingerprint was destroyed.

The coins found in the rear alley might also have put a bleeding O.J. Simpson at the murder scene on the night of June 12. I have been unable to find out whether those coins were ever fingerprinted, but during Lange's testimony, his orders as to which items should be dusted for prints did not specifically include the coins.

Sometimes, important evidence can look mundane or even insignificant. Around the first of August, Ron Phillips got a call from Captain Gartland of Robbery/Homicide. Gartland explained that because it was late on a Friday afternoon, he had no one to go investigate the discovery of yet another piece of blood evidence at the Bundy scene. Nicole's friend Ron Fischman had been over at the townhome doing some chores when he saw another blood drop which hadn't been noticed before. Gartland asked us to see if the blood was indeed there, and to recover it if possible. Of course, we agreed and went over to Bundy. There it was, a drop of blood on the step of the north walkway, leading toward the alley gate. Ron got on the cell phone and called a criminalist and a photographer to recover the blood drop.

While we were waiting, I looked around. The planter to the side of the walkway was covered with leaves, yet I saw a flash of color among the fallen foliage. I began poking through the leaves with a pen and saw a very large piece of bubble gum with visible teeth impressions of adult molars.

"Look what I found," I said.

"Oh, no," Ron groaned. "Don't do this any more. Why do you have to keep finding stuff?"

So it wasn't exactly a bloody glove, but this piece of gum could tell us something. "What do you expect RHD to do with it?" he asked.

"They can get a search warrant or court order, take dental impressions of O.J. Simpson, and see if they match this gum. Check it for DNA."

The piece of gum was covered with leaves, which meant it had been there a while, anywhere between the last time the gardener visited and the night of the murders, after which the gardener had obviously not returned. If the gardener came toward the end of the week, that would close the time frame even more tightly.

Maybe it was the killer's gum. Or maybe there was a harmless explanation for that piece of gum being there. Wouldn't it have been nice to know either way?

The implications for the prosecution were obvious. If the gum was Simpson's, it places him at Bundy within a week of the murders, contradicting his statement to Vannatter and Lange that he hadn't been there for a week. For the defense, the implications were even more apparent. Could this be a different suspect? Why wasn't the gum found during the initial investigation? Why would Fuhrman, who's supposed to be trying to frame O.J., come up with a piece of evidence that might point to someone else?

The gum was booked as evidence, but was never used in court. The defense never mentioned the gum, maybe because they suspected whose it was.

Focusing on detail is what being a detective is all about. All evidence is important, and you shouldn't judge it until you've collected and analyzed it. At the very least, you may then know conclusively that the evidence will not help you. You may walk down a few dead ends, but at least you know where those roads go. You have to follow up on every possible clue until you are certain you have learned everything you can from existing evidence. Very seldom do you find a smoking gun, or even a bloody fingerprint. Most murders are solved because of the little details, many of which were passed over in the Simpson case by the investigating detectives from Robbery/Homicide.

I would like to make clear that the last thing I want to do is tear down or discredit the work done by the LAPD in this case. The dilemma I have is that the department and the district attorney's office ignored these obvious errors and forced me to take the blame for the failure of this case. Below I have listed what I believe to be the most prominent mistakes made by Lange and Vannatter.

1. The bloody fingerprint was never recovered.
2. Lange never made a thorough inspection of the walkway gate at Bundy.
3. My return to the Bundy scene to compare the glove there with the one found at Rockingham was unnecessary.
4. Vannatter's search warrant was brief, and lacked sufficient detailed information about the investigation, opening up our legal search at Rockingham to legal challenge.
5. The Bronco was not impounded early on and taken to Parker Center. Instead the exterior and interior were needlessly contaminated.
6. Lange had a blanket from inside the townhouse placed over Nicole's body, furthering the defense's claim of crime scene contamination.
7. Vannatter carried a vial of Simpson's blood sample to the Rockingham scene instead of booking it as evidence.
8. Lange ordered Dennis Fung to test and recover blood on the back gate on June 13, but did not confirm that Fung had done so. As a result, the blood was not recovered until weeks later.

By the time we returned with the second search warrant on June 28, much of the potential evidence had been destroyed or removed. The Rockingham house had been cleaned and the carpets shampooed. Any visible blood evidence we hadn't retrieved the first time had been cleaned up.

Even though the premises had obviously been cleaned, we still could have found more blood evidence, or at least indications of such evidence, that would have gone a long way toward giving us an idea of Simpson's movements in the house the night of the murders. Luminol, a clear liquid, reacts to traces of blood that are not visible to the naked eye. If you spray Luminol on a surface and then black out the room or outside area (Luminol requires a complete absence of light), almost immediately the blood traces will show up as a fluorescent greenish-white glow.

Many of the questions which plagued the investigation and prosecution might have been answered had Luminol been used throughout the house. We possibly could have established Simpson's movements through the house on the night of the murders.

I am aware that Judge Ito established some major barricades against Luminol's use. But this only affected using the results in the courtroom. The aid Luminol would have provided was not as courtroom evidence but to the investigators in establishing many of Simpson's movements in the Rockingham estate. These procedures might have led to a better understanding of where evidence might be that could have been used in court. It's easy to second-guess any investigation, but this is not just hindsight. My suggestions were repeatedly ignored or dismissed by the RHD detectives.

Everyone makes mistakes, but the mistakes made by the investigating detectives seriously undermined what should have been an easy case. They contaminated evidence and mishandled the crime scenes themselves. In addition, their supervisory lapses allowed further mistakes. These were not just instances of inevitable human error, but serious blunders that any experienced detective should have avoided.

Even without important pieces of evidence, Vannatter and Lange had still seen enough to consider O.J. Simpson their prime suspect. But for some reason, they didn't treat him like one.

Chapter 5

THE INTERROGATION

LANGE: *There's blood in your house ...*
Is that your blood... ?

SIMPSON: *If it's dripped, it's what I dripped*
running around trying to leave.
... That was last night when I was... I don't know what I
was, I was in the car getting my junk out of the car. I was in
the house throwing hangers and stuff in my suitcase. I was
doing my little crazy what I do, I mean, I do it everywhere.

O N JUNE 13, 1994, AT 1:35 P.M., Detectives Lange and Vannatter were given the opportunity of a lifetime. During the investigation of a brutal double homicide, they were allowed to interrogate the only suspect, without his attorney present, and with a properly read constitutional advisement and waiver.

The suspect, Orenthal James Simpson, had an ego so large that he gambled his life on his ability to withstand the questions of two seasoned homicide detectives. What Simpson couldn't have known was that these two detectives would treat him more deferentially than any normal suspect, and as a result undermine their own interrogation. He would walk out of the interview room having learned more about the evidence against him than they had learned about his actions and movements the night of the murders.

The entire transcript of the interrogation is reprinted in Appendix A. To the layman, Simpson's statements might seem to indicate guilt. And it is a testament to just how vulnerable Simpson was that this interrogation, fraught with amateurish mistakes and missed chances, still showed the suspect in a guilty light.

Simpson offered many obvious clues that he was primed to make mistakes in the interrogation. His lawyer, Howard Weitzman, later claimed that he advised Simpson against speaking to the detectives, but could not convince him. Vannatter and Lange should have been able to take advantage of Simpson's willingness to talk. Instead, they gave him a preview of the case against him.

Criminal interrogation is a real challenge, and doing it right is an art. I have performed hundreds of interrogations, and each one was different. If you pay attention, you can learn something every time about suspects and about yourself.

One of the first rules of interrogation is to never underestimate the suspect. There are many different types of suspects. You must assess what kind of a suspect you are questioning before you go ahead with the interview. If the Bundy murders had been a robbery/homicide, as I first thought possible, and we had apprehended a violent career criminal, the interrogation should have been conducted a certain way. Violent career criminals are often sociopaths. They obey no rules and feel no moral obligations to anyone else, not to their families or to the society they prey on. Sociopaths feel no remorse, have no conscience, and are difficult to interrogate. You can't get any hooks into them. You can't play nice guy. You can't play tough guy. They just don't care.

O.J. Simpson was a different type altogether. He was not an experienced criminal. He was a successful and popular celebrity who had a great deal to lose. No doubt he felt guilty about the murders, but he would try to act nonchalant. Still it would not be easy for him to maintain his demeanor; he could be broken. All the interrogators had to do was play on his guilt, on his family and children, on his position in society, and his nearly universal adoration. Simpson was obsessed with his image, he was addicted to fame, and he always needed friends around him. These personality traits could have been put to advantage by an effective interrogator.

You want to start off interrogating a suspect like Simpson by treating him with respect. Ask him open-ended questions, and let him answer them. Lull him into a false sense of security. Get him to think that you don't suspect him, or that you don't want to suspect him. Say, "I don't want to believe you did it, but I just have to ask these questions in order to clear some things up." Let him think that he can talk his way out of it. Get him to tell a story. Then have him tell it again. And again. See if he contradicts himself. Lead him down the path, and then shut the door on him.

Perhaps Simpson would have folded, but even if he hadn't, he still might have provided corroborative and incriminating statements that could have been used later. In any interrogation, your goals shouldn't be too high. Sure, it would be great to get the suspect to give a full confession. But short of a confession, you can still learn a lot during an interrogation that can be used in court or in a subsequent investigation.

A second rule about interrogation is not to rush it. Be aware that if the suspect waived his rights and has no attorney present, he thinks he's going to be able to talk his way out of this. His goal is to make himself no longer a suspect. You have the opposite goal—solving the crime.

Simpson was obsessed with his image, he was addicted to fame, and he always needed people around him.

Lange and Vannatter spent a grand total of thirty-two minutes interrogating the only suspect in a high-profile double murder. I have interrogated vandalism suspects longer than that. There was no reason for the detectives to terminate the interview when they did. They should have interrogated Simpson until they got a confession, conflicting statements, or at least one clear timeline for his movements the night of the murder. They got none of these, precisely because they rushed through the interview. Both detectives clearly appeared uncomfortable interrogating the popular celebrity.

A third rule is to be prepared. There should always be two questioners in an interrogation. Before walking into the room, you and your partner should decide who takes what role. One of you should take the "in-charge" role, while the other takes notes, pretending to write down everything, when in fact you're just noting pertinent details about the suspect's story. Work out in advance at what point you're going to turn up the heat and become accusatory. You usually have strong evidence that this suspect committed the crime. Plan ahead when you are going to use it.

It appears evident that neither detective interrogating Simpson was prepared. They didn't seem to have a clear script for their roles. Neither one took over the "in-charge" role completely, and both seemed to dance around the questions, as if being careful to avoid offending Simpson.

A fourth rule is to get the suspect to stick with a story, any story. Let him build up your case by giving you what he thinks are harmless bits of information. He doesn't know what this information might mean to you. And don't let on if he says something important. With Simpson, the detectives needed to get him committed to a timeline, an alibi, and an explanation of where, why, and how he bled. He didn't have to know, or even think, he was a suspect. His ex-wife had just been murdered; he could be convinced that he's being asked questions because he's her ex-husband and the officers need to know some things in order to eliminate him as a suspect. They didn't need to get a confession from Simpson. All they needed to do was get him to commit to some details that they already knew were untrue. Then they could use his own statements against him.

A fifth rule is to take it easy. Interrogations are not conducted like Joe Friday questioning suspects in the old television show *Dragnet*. The questioning should not be accusatory *until it needs to be*. Relax yourself, and try to get your suspect to relax. Get a cup of coffee. Complain about the routine. Say how you want to get this over with and go home for dinner. Disarm him with small talk.

There's no need to ask specific questions. Just let the suspect ramble on. You don't have to be pointed or accusatory at this juncture, when you are still getting him to open up. Mix simple, or even meaningless, questions with the ones you really want answered. Once the suspect starts making enough mistakes you can turn the heat up. But be careful. You don't want the interview to become antagonistic. You don't want the suspect to invoke his rights. Get as much out of him as you can while you can. This might be the only opportunity you have to speak directly to him.

Before they even said a word, Vannatter and Lange had committed a huge blunder. Both of them left crime scenes they should have been overseeing. During the interrogation, the Rockingham estate was being searched, and Vannatter should have been there. Lange was supposed to be in charge of the Bundy crime scene, and he should have remained there until all the evidence was collected and the scene was shut down. There were perhaps a dozen detectives familiar enough with the case to perform the interrogation of

Simpson. In their questioning, Vannatter and Lange didn't use one piece of evidence that any other detective familiar with the case didn't already know. Instead of supervising their crime scenes, Lange and Vannatter decided to interrogate Simpson. Their having two active and open crime scenes obviously hurried the interrogation, which I will now discuss in chronological detail.

After the tedious but necessary preliminaries, Vannatter seemed quite uncomfortable. He didn't take charge of the interrogation at the beginning or at any time. Vannatter and Lange asked Simpson questions that they could easily have answered themselves. His office phone, Paula Barbieri's address, his wife's birthdate, the length of his marriage to Nicole, their custody arrangements. These are all facts that could be discovered from various sources. Instead of using familiar and non-threatening questions to lead Simpson where they wanted him, they wasted time and distracted themselves with irrelevant lines of questioning.

When they asked Simpson about his and Nicole's relationship, he launched onto the first of many convoluted answers to troubling questions. But instead of letting him ramble and perhaps say something pertinent, Vannatter interjected with "Okay, the two children are yours?" This question was completely unnecessary; they already knew about the kids. It only changed the subject and let him off the hook, just when he was beginning to show signs of discomfort.

Then Vannatter brought up Simpson's history of domestic violence. When he asked the first question concerning Nicole's crime reports, he sounded hesitant: "Uh huh. I understand that she had made a couple of crime...crime reports or something?"

Simpson then told his side of the story, that the incident wasn't a big deal, that she attacked him, and that he should have made a crime report himself.

> **SIMPSON:** Ah, we had a big fight about six years ago on New Year's, you know, she made a report. I didn't make a report. And then we had an altercation about a year ago maybe. It wasn't a physical argument. I kicked her door or something.
> **SIMPSON:** And she made a police report on those two occasions?
> **SIMPSON:** Mmm hmm. And I stayed right there until the police came, talked to them.

LANGE: Were you arrested at one time for something?

SIMPSON: No. I mean, five years ago we had a big fight, six years ago, I don't know. I know I ended up doing community service.

VANNATTER: So you weren't arrested?

SIMPSON: No, I was never really arrested.

LANGE: They never booked or…?

SIMPSON: No.

Suddenly, while Simpson was talking about the criminal charges against him, Vannatter asked, "Can I ask you, when's the last time you slept?"

Why did he ask that? Who cares when he slept? Why give the suspect sympathy or an excuse for his fragmented answers? You want the suspect to be vulnerable, and you want to take advantage of his vulnerability, whether guilt-ridden, distraught, in fear of being discovered, or even tired.

The questioning went on as the detectives attempted to establish a timeline for Sydney Simpson's dance recital, and Nicole and O.J.'s movements directly following. Then Vannatter asked about the Bronco. Throughout the rest of the interview, he and Lange constantly referred to the Bronco, making clear to O.J. that it was parked awkwardly and had blood on it. By doing this so obviously, they let Simpson know that the Bronco was a significant piece of evidence. So naturally his answers concerning it were purposefully vague and evasive. The detectives were unable to get a firm story of his actions in and around the car. They kept interrupting him while he talked, finishing his answers for him, giving him an out, and changing the subject.

They asked him when he last drove the Bronco the day before. His answer: "In the morning, in the afternoon."

The next question should have been, "Which is it, O.J., morning or afternoon?" Instead, they started asking about the recital again, information they had already established. They asked him where he went after the recital.

"Ah, home, home for a while, got my car for a while, tried to find my girlfriend for a while, came back to the house," Simpson answered.

Instead of pinning him down on specific times and movements, they asked who was home when he got there, without even making clear which time period they were asking about. Simpson responded that Kato was home. At that point in the investigation, Kato Kaelin was a material witness, possibly an accessory, or even a suspect. He was one of the few people who could corroborate Simpson's whereabouts. But the detectives weren't interested in Kaelin. Instead, they quickly shifted to Arnelle, even though they knew she wasn't home at the time of the murders.

By not following a line of questioning about Kaelin, the detectives indicated they did not suspect him, or thought that Simpson had already gotten to him. This was enormously helpful to Simpson, as he no longer had to worry about his permanent houseguest, so long as Kaelin kept his story straight.

Kato Kaelin and Arnelle Simpson had already been questioned. Vannatter and Lange could have used Kaelin's statements to contradict Simpson, or they could have made up something in order to trick Simpson into an admission or conflicting statement. The detectives could have said, "Well, we talked to Kato, and he said you were missing for an hour around the time of the murders, and when you returned you were bleeding like a stuck pig." True or not, such statements could have led Simpson to reveal important information, make a damaging statement, or even confess (a tactic universally approved by the courts). But the detectives didn't use any of their leverage against Simpson. They seemed awed by him, and too worried about how the interrogation would be seen by the department, in the trial, and in the press. Ironically, they didn't have to worry about how the interrogation was seen by the public, because it was never used in the trial.

Throughout the interview, Lange and Vannatter asked far too many irrelevant questions. They finished Simpson's sentences for him. And even though every time Simpson discussed a sticky issue he rambled on incoherently, instead of allowing him to ramble, the detectives kept asking him more questions, many of them irrelevant or on a different topic that Simpson gladly answered to avoid the more difficult issues.

One of the most important points of this interview, and what should have been one of the primary goals, was to establish how and when Simpson was cut, and where he bled. Simpson offered a variety of explanations, but the detectives never pinned him down to one story and they never used his own conflicting statements against him. He kept saying he did not remember how he was cut, then he offered possible explanations. But he never gave the detectives one clear answer about how or when he cut himself.

Vannatter asked: "How did you get the injury on your hand?"

"I don't know," Simpson answered. "The first time, when I was in Chicago and all, but at the house I was just running around."

Huh? Is Simpson saying he first cut it in Chicago? Or is he saying he bled in the house while he was getting ready to go?

Vannatter followed up, not with an open-ended question that would have allowed Simpson to dig himself a deeper hole, but instead with a specific question that allowed him to further develop his cover story.

"How did you do it in Chicago?"

"I broke a glass. One of you guys had just called me, and I was in the bathroom, and I just went bonkers for a little bit."

"Do you recall bleeding at all in your truck, in the Bronco?" Lange asked. Why not just ask: "Where did you bleed?" Lange's question told Simpson where his blood was found and where he would have to say he bled.

"I recall bleeding at my house, and then I went to the Bronco. The last thing I did before I left, when I was rushing, was went and got my phone out of the Bronco."

Later in the trial, the defense would argue that Simpson cut his hand getting his cellular phone out of the Bronco. Here he seems to be saying that he cut himself before going into the Bronco. Still, the detectives wouldn't or couldn't nail him down on a detail most people would find very easy to remember.

Let me ask you, the reader, a question. Do you have cuts on your hand now? How many? Do you remember how you got them? When was the last time you cut yourself badly enough that you dripped blood on the floor? Didn't you clean up the blood immediately? Didn't you put something on the cut? Or did you run around your house bleeding everywhere?

It simply isn't credible that O.J. Simpson couldn't remember how he cut his finger the previous night. How could he not remember a cut which surely must have hurt, and which bled enough to drip all over his car, property, and inside of his house?

But Vannatter and Lange failed to get him to commit to an explanation about the cut. At one time, he said it happened after he ate at McDonalds with Kaelin. Another time, he said it was while he was getting ready to leave for Chicago and the limo was waiting. Or he was in the kitchen, where he wrapped a napkin around it? Or did he cut himself in Chicago? What really happened, O.J.? The detectives never got him to give them an answer.

What about his actions the night of the murders? The detectives weren't asking him about a series of events in the distant past; they were talking about the previous night. People can usually remember what they did the night before, no matter how mundane. But except for the recital, the trip to McDonalds, and the limo drive to the airport, Simpson is either vague or self-contradictory about his movements throughout the interrogation. Still, Lange and Vannatter did not try to clarify his vague answers or use his self-contradictions against him.

A good example of how useful this interrogation should have been occurred during the civil trial. In Simpson's deposition, Daniel Petrocelli, the Goldman's civil attorney, did nail Simpson down to his movements and actions the night of the murder. Now, almost two years later, Simpson miraculously remembers that he was playing golf in his backyard, a rather leisurely and relaxing endeavor, which tends to contradict the description that he gave to the detectives of rushing around. And in the Superior Court trial, limo driver Allan Park testified that Simpson said he had overslept and was then just getting ready. Any one of those stories would have been difficult to forget, especially fifteen hours after the murders. But Simpson can't seem to keep his lies straight enough to remember what he said to the last person. He confuses himself, so one lie creates two more lies.

In the civil trial deposition, Simpson declared that he didn't believe he was cut before he left for Chicago and the injury to his left knuckle occured in his hotel room after he was informed of his wife's death. Yet, in his statement to Vannatter and Lange, Simpson did admit to cutting himself before he left for Chicago, and admitted bleeding in his house, in the driveway, and in the Bronco.

"Hmm, it was cut before. But I think I just opened it again. I'm not sure," he told Lange and Vannatter.

But in his civil trial deposition, he never admitted that he even saw a cut.

So what happened between the Vannatter and Lange interrogation and his civil trial deposition? Simple. Simpson hired attorneys.

It would have been easy for Vannatter and Lange to nail him down to one story, to go through all his actions and movements the night before, starting with the recital and ending with the limo drive. Every half hour or fifteen minutes, what was he doing then? They could have had him commit to a timeline.

There are many other specific questions that Simpson should have been asked. Did he go into the service entrance and laundry room? Did he usually put his clothes in the washer? Did he usually put his clothes away? What about his socks? Did he go behind the bungalows? What's his shoe size? Did he own brown leather gloves or a black knit cap? Did he own a knife?

Wouldn't an admission that he bought a knife just weeks prior while on location at a movie set have been helpful to the detectives at this time? The follow-up should have been: "Where is the knife now, O.J.?" If the knife was at his estate, he could have described where it was. Conversely, if he said, "No, I don't own any knives, except for kitchen knives," that would have eliminated the defense's miraculous discovery of the Stiletto and the mysterious envelope containing it, and brought up some interesting questions about the empty Swiss Army knife box that was sitting on the edge of the bathtub. A simple question— do you own any knives other than kitchen knives?— could have solved some of the mysteries in this case.

These are all specific and direct questions that should have been used to get Simpson tangled up in his own lies. But Vannatter and Lange never asked any of them. They didn't nail Simpson down to anything. Then they started telling him about the evidence they had on him. Almost apologetically, Vannatter recounted what they had found at the two crime scenes. "'We've got some blood on and in your car, we've got some blood at your house, and it's sort of a problem."

Simpson said, "Well, take my blood test."

Lange jumped in: "Well, we'd like to do that. We've got, of course, the cut on your finger that you aren't real clear on. Do you recall having that cut on your finger the last time you were at Nicole's house?"

"No," O.J. answered. "It was last night."

At that moment alarms should have gone off. Did Simpson say he bled last night at Nicole's house? But instead of trying to place a bleeding Simpson at his ex-wife's house, Lange gave him an out.

"Okay, so last night you cut it?"

Inexplicably, Vannatter jumped in, "Somewhere after the dance recital?"

Vannatter's question opened up the time frame again and allowed Simpson to give another amorphous answer with a one-word response.

"Yeah."

Finally, Vannatter tried to pin him down.

"What do you think happened? Do you have any idea?"

"I have no idea, man. You guys haven't told me anything," Simpson protested.

Wait a second. Weren't the detectives interrogating Simpson? Since when did they have to tell him anything? Then Simpson launched into a long and confusing digression about an incident that occurred a month prior while he was driving his Bentley and some "Oriental guys" appeared to be trying to rob or carjack him. Instead of getting the interrogation back on track, the detectives asked him more questions about the supposed incident.

Finally, Vannatter returned to the murders, asking if Nicole had been getting any threats or was concerned about the kids' safety. They talked about her being security conscious, and then Vannatter asked Simpson if he ever parked in the rear of the Bundy residence.

This question obviously tipped Simpson off that there was evidence in the alley behind Bundy. Simpson explained (in his rambling fashion) how sometimes he drove up behind the house, or in front of it, depending on the circumstances.

Vannatter went back to their relationship. Again Simpson rambled, and again the detectives kept interrupting him, asking irrelevant and distracting questions like, "How long were you together?" Then Vannatter asked, "Did you ever hit her, O.J.?"

Simpson launched into another meandering explanation and repeated his "battered husband" argument. Everything was Nicole's fault. She started it, he did nothing. Well, maybe he wrestled her a little. But he didn't hit her, and never touched her again after that incident which occurred five or six years ago, although the detectives never established which incident he was referring to.

Vannatter followed up by asking about Nicole's birthday and whether Simpson gave her any gifts. This was a potentially interesting line of questioning, because the relationship had to have taken a dramatic turn for Simpson to become violent. She had returned a bracelet and earrings Simpson had given her. Did this signal that the relationship was over for good? Just when it seemed that they were about to establish the return of these gifts as a significant event, Tom Lange changed the subject, bringing up the last thing you ever want to mention in a criminal interrogation: the suspect's lawyer.

"Did Mr. Weitzman, your attorney, talk to you anything about this polygraph we brought up before? What are your thoughts on that?"

What possessed Lange to mention Simpson's lawyer and risk his invoking right to counsel? Why would he talk about a polygraph? Why would he change the subject just when it seemed they were getting somewhere?

They discussed the polygraph, and Simpson eventually said that he would talk to his lawyer about it. At this point, the interrogation was effectively over, as it now could be argued that Simpson invoked his right to counsel.

However, Lange then became accusatory, telling Simpson that he was the suspect and giving him detailed information about the investigation and the evidence against him.

"Well, there's blood in your house and in the driveway, and we've got a search warrant, and we're going to get the blood. We found some in your house. Is that your blood that's there?"

Why did he ask Simpson this? Wasn't it already established that Simpson had been bleeding? What hadn't yet been established was when he cut himself, how, and what he did between visiting McDonald's and the limo drive. Why didn't either detective try to establish these crucial points?

After previously stating that he "kind of leisurely got ready to go," Simpson then said he was "hustling," "rushing," "running," "doing my little crazy what I do, I mean, I do it everywhere." Instead of using his own words against him, the detectives tried once more to get a firm answer when he was last at the Bundy residence. Once more, Simpson evaded them. Finally, the detectives decided they were through. Instead of interrogating him further, they started talking about bringing in the photographer, and they terminated the interview.

The interrogation was extremely important to the entire investigation, maybe as important as the physical evidence. It should have been well planned. The detectives should have taken the time to go over Simpson's alibi, his movements after the dance recital, the cut on his hand, the blood in his Bronco, and the glove found at his house. Any crucial statements should have been covered, over and over, to allow him to stumble on his lies. Simpson should have been forced to account for his time from the recital until Phillips called him in Chicago. He should have been locked into his story during this taped interview. Vannatter and Lange should have entered the interview room with just a few goals. Establish where and when he cut his finger and where he bled. Does he own any brown leather dress gloves? What size shoe does he wear? Is he right- or left-handed? Has he ever been behind Kato Kaelin's room before? What's back there, anyway? Confront him and let him explain why he never even asked the detective who notified him of Nicole's death how she was killed.

Unfortunately, he was never even directly challenged on any statement. Vannatter and Lange had their suspect right where they wanted him, but then they let him go, never confronting Simpson with the possibility of any participation in the murders. The interrogation seemed more an opportunity for Simpson to explain away areas in which he appeared guilty, and by not challenging his excuses, the detectives almost appeared to accept the answers.

The most shocking aspect of the interrogation was that Lange and Vannatter terminated the questioning to photograph Simpson's finger. An effective interrogation would have continued for hours, as long as Simpson didn't invoke his constitutional rights. If they wanted a photograph or blood taken, all the detectives had to do was write a search warrant and take the evidence later. There is no reason why they had to interrupt the questioning that could have slammed the door on Simpson.

Two people were dead. The suspect had waived his rights and was sitting right across the table from two experienced detectives. They had him where they wanted him, and they interrogated him for only thirty-two meandering minutes. They learned close to nothing. In thirty-two minutes, I could barely have begun to build a rapport with the suspect.

A good interrogator would have tried to establish a solid answer on Simpson's part, then used the evidence at the scene to begin to poke holes in his answer. Let him talk about the previous day without interruption, and then question him about his own statements. Allowing him to change his story would have confused him. After five or six hours of the game, he would have made mistakes, and then a smart interrogator would have gone in for a gentle kill.

Whenever Simpson appeared to be lying, he talked in circles and said almost nothing. They shouldn't have let him get away with it. They should have nailed him down to a single timeline, and then poked holes in his story. When was the last time he visited the Bundy residence? The recital ended around seven. What did he do from seven to eight? From eight to nine? From nine to ten? From ten to eleven? If he didn't remember when he cut himself, exactly when did he realize he was bleeding? What "stuff" did he get out of the Bronco? Why did he leave the shovel and package in the back?

In an effective interview, just as Simpson would begin to run out of excuses, the questioning would become more accusatory. No one is smiling anymore, and the pressure builds. Just before Simpson is about to ask for his attorney, the "in-charge" detective elevates his voice and says, "O.J., we both think you were involved in this murder.... We think you killed Nicole."

The inevitable pause is important. You read his eyes. "You left a bloody glove behind Kato's room. You screwed up.... You left evidence everywhere."

You throw a couple of Polaroids from the crime scene onto the table. You get graphic.

"How did it feel, O.J.? How did it feel to kill the mother of your children? How did it feel to have her warm blood running down your hands?"

Let him think about it a moment.

"What about your kids, O.J.? How are they going to feel, knowing their daddy killed their mommy? What's going to happen to them? How does your mother feel? Is she proud of you now? How about all your fans? Will they still cheer a murderer?"

If he declares his innocence, then offer a polygraph. But unless he wants to invoke his rights, you keep hammering away. Use your notes to once again go over his statements where he obviously was lying. This is the point where many cases are won or lost. Play on his love of his children and the brutal way their mother was murdered, left for his children to discover. Play on his ego. Only a coward would murder a defenseless woman.

Simpson's interrogation should have been easy. A strong line of questioning and intelligent interview techniques might have prompted him to confess, or at least provoked an incriminating statement or contradictory stories. But Vannatter and Lange's interrogation couldn't get Simpson even to admit that he had slapped Nicole during a documented episode of domestic violence.

At the end, the only result of the interview was that Simpson knew more about the evidence than the detectives learned about Simpson's involvement.

Here is what Simpson learned from the interrogation:

1. He was the suspect.
2. Nobody saw him in the Bronco about the time of the murders.
3. The police didn't seem to care about Kato.
4. The police found blood in the Bronco.
5. The police impounded the Bronco.
6. The police knew about the argument with Nicole at the recital.
7. The police are interested in his shoes.
8. The police found blood at Nicole's house that was thought to be his.
9. The police know that the Bronco was parked behind Nicole's at the time of the murder, or they think it was there.
10. The police want to give him a polygraph.
11. The police found blood in his house and on his driveway.

And what did the detectives learn from Simpson that they did not already know, or couldn't have found out elsewhere?

1. When he last slept and how much.
2. That he drives the Bronco, as do his maid, Arnelle, and Kato.
3. He always parks the Bronco on the street.
4. He tried to call Paula Barbieri the evening of the murders, time unknown.
5. He parked the Bronco at eight-something and went to get a burger with Kato Kaelin.
6. He cut his finger, but didn't know exactly where or when.
7. He bled in the Bronco when he got his cellular phone.
8. He felt that his relationship with Nicole was always a problem, but nothing was his fault.

Once Simpson realized he was the only suspect, he would no longer talk to the police. Lange and Vannatter had their only chance to interrogate the suspect, and they blew it. In a case filled with unnecessary blunders and missed opportunities, Lange and Vannatter's thirty-two-minute interrogation of Simpson was one of the most tragic. Instead of slamming the door on O.J. Simpson, they left it wide open, and he ran right through it.

Chapter 6

SLOW-SPEED PURSUIT

---

*I want to say something to the entire community. If you
in any way are assisting Mr. Simpson, ... Mr. Simpson is a
fugitive of justice now. If you assist him in any way, you are
committing a felony ... and you will be prosecuted as a felon.*

—LOS ANGELES DISTRICT ATTORNEY GIL GARCETTI

R EGARDLESS OF WHAT TURNS the investigation had taken up to
Simpson's interrogation, Vannatter and Lange still had more than
enough evidence to arrest him late on the afternoon of June 13. But
they didn't. Vannatter said he had to wait for test results on the evidence,
specifically the DQ-Alpha DNA tests, which would have provided preliminary
genetic evidence.

How did we ever arrest anyone before DQ-Alpha DNA testing? Let us
review the evidence we did have. There was blood on Simpson's Bronco, on his
property, and in his house, and a bloody glove had been found on his estate that
matched the one found at the Bundy crime scene. His interrogation statements
were self-contradictory, vague and evasive, and did not even establish a

consistent story about his actions the night of the murders, much less provide him an alibi. The time period he had the most difficulty accounting for was that surrounding his ex-wife's murder. He had an unexplained cut on his finger, and his several different statements to the detectives concerning the cut only made it appear more suspicious.

We could have typed the blood in the Bronco, at Rockingham, on the Bundy gate, and on the glove. We could have typed the blood of both victims and Simpson's sample. And we would have found that Simpson's blood type matched that on the Bundy walkway, and that the victims' and Simpson's types were both on the bloody glove and inside the Bronco. This would have been more than enough evidence to arrest Simpson. We didn't need any more scientific tests.

So, why wasn't he arrested the day after the murders?

First, I don't believe it was Vannatter or Lange's decision. The word had to come from higher up. The department probably was afraid to arrest a popular celebrity for murder and be second-guessed, or even wrong. The preferential treatment Simpson received indicated how uncommonly he was handled in otherwise common circumstances. After all, Los Angeles has hundreds of murders a year. The police usually don't release homicide suspects once they have sufficient evidence to arrest or detain them. But Simpson was not just any other suspect: he was "the Juice."

The media was all over this case from the beginning, and everyone was worried about how they would look in print and on television. So, the only suspect in the double murder case was released for four days, when there was more than sufficient evidence to arrest him. If it had still been my case, I would have just booked Simpson.

Simpson's arrest was inevitable. On Friday morning, June 17, the district attorney's office and the LAPD had their DQ-Alpha results, which confirmed their suspicions, and made the decision to arrest Orenthal James Simpson.

The previous night, Simpson's new lawyer, Robert Shapiro, had convinced the detectives to allow Simpson to surrender instead of arresting him. Lange called Shapiro at 8:30 on Friday morning and told him that the LAPD had issued an arrest warrant for Simpson. Lange gave Shapiro until 11:00 A.M. to bring his client in. Shapiro promised that he would do his best, but said he was worried about Simpson's mental state and that he might be suicidal.

Shapiro knew something that few others, including the arresting detectives, did: Simpson was not at his home in Brentwood, but was staying at his friend Bob Kardashian's house in Encino. Rather than calling his client to inform him about the impending arrest, Shapiro drove over to Kardashian's house and told Simpson in person. Shapiro called the LAPD regularly from Kardashian's, but he wouldn't say where he was or when the suspect was coming in.

Meanwhile, Simpson underwent a battery of physical tests and photographs by the medical experts Shapiro had already brought in on the defense team. Then O.J. had to write letters, he had to make phone calls, he had to say goodbye to people, he had to get ready (no doubt once again performing his "little crazy what I do, I mean, I do it everywhere"), and he had to spend a few moments alone with Paula Barbieri. Finally, he had to get dressed, and his good friend Al Cowlings went with him.

> **As a past member of the LAPD pistol team, I was considered one of the best shots, and Brad wasn't far behind. We were to be the shooters.**

More than an hour after the deadline for surrender had passed, LAPD officers arrived at Kardashian's house to arrest Simpson. They looked in the room where they had been told they'd find Simpson, but he wasn't there. In fact, he wasn't anywhere in the house. The celebrity suspect had escaped under the watchful eyes of his own attorneys, who had promised to bring him in. He was now a fugitive from justice.

Midday on June 17, I was having lunch in the San Fernando Valley with John Wright, a city attorney. John had defended me in a case involving a suspect, Joseph Britton, who was shot during a robbery. During the trial, John and I became good friends, but that day I did not divulge to him any particulars about the Bundy murders. I knew there was going to be a press conference about the case, so we sat in the bar within view of the television.

As soon as the press conference started, I knew that something was wrong. Nobody was on the stage. The press conference had been delayed. Then they said there was a bomb threat. I exclaimed, "John, I've got to get back, something's wrong!" I left without finishing my lunch.

I drove as fast as the Los Angeles traffic would allow me, which at some points was merely a crawl. When I finally reached the West LA station it was a little after 12:30 P.M. Ron Phillips and Brad Roberts were headed toward their vehicles. Ron yelled to me, "Simpson didn't show to surrender. They can't find him. Robbery/Homicide wants us up at the Rockingham estate; he might show there."

Brad Roberts and I drove there together, parked on Ashford, and waited. While sitting in the car, Brad and I remembered that the house directly east of Simpson's, bordering the tennis court, could easily be used to enter the estate without being seen. We approached the residents, who had just purchased the house, and asked to sit in their backyard. They were very cooperative, explaining that the house was still empty and we could use any part of it we needed. We both sat in lawn furniture that gave us a view of Ashford and the tennis court access from the two properties. We stayed there most of the afternoon, waiting for Simpson to return.

At 1:55 P.M., LAPD Commander David Gascon finally had his long-delayed press conference. After informing the press and public about the charges against O.J. Simpson, and the arrangement for his surrender, Gascon then said: "Mr. Simpson has not appeared. The Los Angeles Police Department right now is actively searching for Mr. Simpson."

An hour later, Gil Garcetti had another press conference, in which he said that Simpson was a fugitive from justice, and anyone assisting him would be committing a felony. One reporter asked him if he could explain how the LAPD let such a high-profile suspect escape. For once, Gil Garcetti did not have an answer.

Even though we were out in the field, we didn't know any more or any less than the people downtown. Information was scarce, but late in the afternoon Ron Phillips notified us that Simpson might have committed suicide, but they still couldn't find him. This news probably came from Robert Shapiro's 5:00 P.M. press conference, when he asked Simpson, wherever he was, to surrender. Shapiro then introduced Bob Kardashian, who read a suicide letter Simpson had left behind.

Later, Phillips informed us that Simpson was with Cowlings in the Bronco driving on the freeway in Orange County. The police were chasing him, but rather slowly. Ron didn't know where O.J. was headed, and said he'd keep us posted.

So, while most of America watched the now-famous slow-speed pursuit of Al Cowlings's white Bronco across the Southern California freeways, we were sitting almost in Simpson's backyard trying to figure out where he would eventually stop. Once Simpson declared that he was headed for the Rockingham estate, things started happening rather quickly. He was on his way with dozens of police cars behind him, and we needed a plan.

Ron Phillips, arriving less than an hour before Simpson, was the ranking officer at the Rockingham scene and immediately took charge. He met with Brad and me outside the estate and described the situation as well as he knew it. He had a heavy responsibility at the estate, having to plan a tactical operation to capture Simpson and Cowlings, hopefully without injury. Simpson's estate was now occupied by family members. When Ron realized that Rockingham was Simpson's probable destination, the estate had to be evacuated.

Ron ordered Brad and me to accomplish this immediately. We entered the house and quickly made it clear to the people inside that they had to leave. Finding everyone was easy, as they were crowded around the television watching Simpson and Cowlings in the Bronco. It was as if they were watching a Super Bowl game and O.J. was running for the end zone.

Everyone left without much discussion or problem except Jason, Simpson's oldest son. Jason stood at the top of the stairs and refused to leave the house, or even come downstairs. In a very calm but forceful voice Brad informed Jason that he was leaving one way or another, but one thing was sure—he *was* leaving. Jason, with as much bravado as he could muster, reluctantly came down and walked out to the street.

Phillips knew that SWAT had been notified, but he wasn't sure when they would arrive. Ron, having worked Metro division as a uniformed officer, was familiar with tactical situations and realized that this would be complicated even further if there were not a plan in place if Simpson arrived before SWAT did, so he developed a contingency plan. Ron briefed me, Brad, and another detective, Randy Fredrickson, on what he wanted as a tactical plan to deal with the situation as it might unfold. Randy had experience in SWAT, so he began analyzing the tactical options. We discussed the layout and decided to leave the Ashford gate open and force the Bronco into that location. Then we chose cover positions and decided what roles we would be responsible for upon the Bronco's arrival. As a past member of the LAPD pistol team, I was considered one of the best pistol shots in the department, and Brad wasn't far behind, if at all. We were to be the shooters, positioned on either side of the driveway.

Without speaking to Brad, I knew he must have felt what I did. An enormous burden had just been placed on our shoulders. A man who was desperate, suicidal, and with a hostage/accessory would be here in a few minutes. We would have to make split-second decisions that not only our department or a few lawyers, but also the entire world, would dissect. This was not a desirable situation. But I knew that Brad and I would never say we couldn't or didn't want to do this. It was our job, and we were as ready as we could be.

I have had many conversations with Brad about what might have happened, and we have yet to come to the end of the scenarios. The scene was too much like a cop movie in which we weren't sure of the script, and we didn't want to speculate on the one thing we were sure of: we were caught in a situation where we could do virtually nothing right. We were not negotiators; we were not SWAT officers; we were homicide detectives. Had we delayed too long and Simpson killed himself or Cowlings, we would have been crucified. If our handling of the situation resulted in a shooting between Roberts, myself, and Simpson, we would have been criticized no matter who took the bullets. And even if we talked Simpson out of the standoff and convinced him to drop the weapon, O.J. would get the credit, not us. We were in a no-win situation, so we were damned glad when SWAT finally got there.

SWAT arrived just minutes before the Bronco pulled in, and quickly took over the tactical operation. The SWAT sniper positioned himself in the children's playground, dressed in a Gurkha suit and armed with an AR-15 rifle. He was hugging the ground like a plant.

We watched the situation unfold from across the street. The scene was surreal. It was early evening and growing dark. Over our heads, some half dozen helicopters hovered. The noise was so loud I could barely hear myself speak, and had to plug one ear to hear anything on the radio. The street was blocked off with the media behind barricades to the north. One reporter tried to break away from the pack and was quickly stopped by the police. Hundreds of Simpson supporters had followed the pursuit and were now gathered on Sunset Boulevard. Some were throwing rocks and bottles. This could be the ignition point of a riot if something were to happen to Simpson.

The Bronco arrived with a long line of police vehicles. There were Highway Patrol and Sheriff's cars, all with their lights blazing and sirens blaring. Hundreds of camera lights combined to make the scene look like a movie set. Policemen often complain that cop shows are completely unrealistic, but this was more unreal than anything I had ever seen on television. As so often happened in the Simpson case, you could never have imagined events so bizarre as those that actually happened.

Just as the Bronco entered the estate, a Highway Patrol officer with gun in hand leapt from his car and tried to go through the gate. Luckily, a SWAT officer holding an MP-5 machine gun grabbed him and pushed him away from the scene.

Hostage negotiation teams began speaking on the cellular phone with Cowlings and Simpson. The helicopters continued to rotate around the estate, and cameras flashed while we waited and waited. At one point, Simpson's cellular phone battery went dead and we needed a replacement. Phillips asked a media anchor to donate his, but the anchor refused. Ron finally got another battery from a nearby resident who was glad to help. I'm sure that reporter feels cheated that he didn't donate his phone, because it could have been his one connection to the case. Once the battery was replaced, negotiations continued until Simpson finally left the Bronco to go into the house one last time to talk to his mother. He also wanted to drink some orange juice. When Simpson emerged, he was handcuffed and taken into custody. The standoff was over.

The tactical operation concluded, Ron, Brad, and I headed for the estate to assist Robbery/Homicide with the new evidence. As Brad and I approached the driver's side of the Bronco, Jason Simpson ran up to us. With great emotion he shook our hands and exclaimed, "Thank you for not killing my dad!"

Walking by the Bronco, I saw the six-inch blue steel revolver in the back seat area. We had risked countless lives to save Simpson from himself, which would have been avoided if he had been booked the first day after the murders. By giving him his freedom, we only delayed the inevitable, and made an already complicated and difficult situation even more so. We allowed him four days to brood, feel guilty, worry about his future, and grow more desperate. His flight and pursuit created a tactical nightmare involving two counties and several law enforcement agencies. The slow-speed pursuit was unlike any treatment of any other felony fugitive I have ever seen or heard of. The chase and confrontation at Rockingham endangered the lives of dozens of officers. Police negotiated with an armed suspect who did not have a hostage, only a possible accessory.

Even after he surrendered, Simpson was allowed to go into his house to make a phone call and have a glass of orange juice. Finally, the police put the cuffs on a man who was a fugitive, had avoided arrest, had been carrying a gun, and had almost incited a riot. What other suspect would have been given this kind of treatment? Was it fair? Was it worth it?

What would have happened if Simpson hadn't given himself up? He had a gun. His family was surrounded by spectators, countless members of the media, and a large police contingent. It would have been a real big mess. Luckily, he gave himself up, and Los Angeles was probably spared another riot. But having watched the pursuit and its conclusion, I wondered—how could anyone now say that Simpson wasn't guilty?

Simpson had eluded arrest before. In the 1989 domestic abuse case, instead of handcuffing Simpson on the spot, the arresting officers asked him to go back inside his house and get dressed (Simpson was wearing a bathrobe). Once inside his house, Simpson escaped out another door, jumped in his Bentley, and drove off. The police attempted pursuit but soon lost him. He was eventually brought in for a plea on the domestic abuse charges, but was never confronted about his flight from the arresting officers. After all, he was O.J.

The 1989 incident was an indication of how Simpson thinks. He knows he's going to be arrested, everyone knows who he is, everyone knows where he lives—it's impossible for him to escape. Still, he runs away. He's like a child who thinks that if he runs and hides for a while, everyone will forget he misbehaved, and he'll be able to go home again. By 1994, the stakes were higher and the crime was more serious, but Simpson still believed that if he ran it would all be okay.

As of 8:53 P.M. on the evening of June 17, Simpson had nowhere to run. He was in custody. His mug shot shows a man filled with confusion and remorse. But whatever guilt he felt was quickly replaced by the cocky and callous attitude of the man who sat at the defense table, surrounded by his high-priced attorneys, and said: "ABSOLUTELY 100 PERCENT NOT GUILTY."

Chapter 7

THE SCHEME TEAM

---

*For some time it has been open season on
African-American males... If it can happen to
Michael Jackson or O.J., it can happen to any of us.*

—JOHNNIE COCHRAN

T HE Bronco chase, the suicide note, the interrogation, and the
initial evidence all pointed to an apparently guilty suspect. But
Simpson had resources most other suspects don't. He was famous,
wealthy, and well liked. He was a sports icon. Soon, he was surrounded by
high-priced legal counsel.

Simpson's defense attorneys were quickly dubbed the "Dream Team" by
a media that never met a cliché they didn't like. The Simpson lawyers used
money, influence, and whatever tactics they could get away with to free their
guilty client. That's not to say that everything they did was unethical or wrong.
In fact, there was some pretty good legal work done by the defense.

Unfortunately, the good was obscured by character assassination, absurd theories, and baseless claims.

By the time of Simpson's arrest, Robert Shapiro, a lawyer who often handled high-profile celebrity cases, had already replaced Howard Weitzman. Shapiro was known in legal circles for his proficiency at cutting deals. Even at this early stage, he probably thought Simpson was guilty, or was at least implicated with the murders in some way. But there was no reason for him to start negotiating a plea bargain now, especially since his client claimed he was innocent. So, Bob Shapiro went to work building his case.

Armed with the information Simpson had learned from the detectives during their interrogation, Shapiro began putting together the defense team. Knowing that there was significant forensic evidence against his client, Shapiro hired a top medical examiner, Dr. Michael Baden. Knowing there was a great deal of blood evidence, Shapiro hired one of the best criminalists in the world, Dr. Henry Lee. Knowing that the prosecution would test the blood for DNA, he brought aboard two of the best DNA litigators in the country, Barry Scheck and Peter Neufeld. Knowing that his client appeared very guilty and the evidence was damning, Shapiro figured that there was a good chance Simpson would be convicted, so he hired the most famous appellate lawyer on television, Alan Dershowitz.

Simpson's defense was being formulated even before he was charged with the crimes. One of the first things Shapiro did was arrange for Simpson to take a polygraph test. But he failed the test so completely that the results were kept secret until well after the trial.

A couple of days later, on the morning of June 17, Simpson's surrender was delayed for no other reason than further preparation of his case. Shapiro summoned two medical experts to Kardashian's house, forensic psychiatrist Saul Faerstein and internist Dr. Robert Huizenga, as well as the two newly hired expert witnesses, Drs. Lee and Baden. That morning, the doctors performed a battery of tests and took several photographs that were later used to argue that Simpson was not extensively injured or cut. In the trial, Huizenga would argue that Simpson had no injuries other than a few small cuts on his hands. He would also claim that Simpson's physical condition had so deteriorated since his playing days that "although he looked like Tarzan, he was walking more like Tarzan's grandfather." But when cross-examined by the prosecution, Huizenga had to admit that Simpson was physically capable of committing the murders.

Faerstein's job was to keep Simpson sedated and monitor his emotional state. When Simpson was already past his surrender deadline, Faerstein told the LAPD that his patient was clinically depressed and could not come in. Then, claiming doctor-patient privilege, he refused to tell the police where Simpson was. Faerstein never testified during the trial, but his hiring does raise a question: Why do you have to worry about the mental health of an innocent man?

Dr. Henry Lee is a great forensic scientist. He knew who was paying for his testimony, and I'm sure the defense was pleased with the outcome. His scientific knowledge is considerable, but in court it was often overshadowed by his showmanship, a talent the defense used to great advantage. The courtroom demonstrations on blood spatter and evidence gathering that he conducted were no doubt entertaining, but they had little or no legal weight.

Simpson failed the polygraph test so completely that the results were kept secret until well after the trial.

Lee is very aware of his theatricality and its effect in the courtroom. As prosecutor Hank Goldberg reported in *The Prosecution Responds*, after finishing his testimony, Lee came up to Hank and said: "See, gave you a little and gave them a little."

Dr. Michael Baden is a highly skilled forensic pathologist, probably one of the best. I had once worked a case where he was brought in by the victim's family to give a second opinion. At first the case was deemed an accidental death, but Baden's review of the autopsy allowed the police to reclassify it as a homicide. Baden appears to be a scientist first and an expert witness second.

By hiring these and other expert witnesses, Shapiro was doing two things. First, he was lining up some of the best witnesses available. Second, he was making it impossible for the prosecution to use them. Both prosecution and defense have a right to use expert testimony. However, the defense has one significant advantage over the prosecution—they can pay for it. While the defense can use witnesses for hire, the prosecution has only the power of subpoena.

Expert witnesses make a living testifying in court. Some of them keep their day jobs, but others are solely professional witnesses. Professional witnesses may not alter the truth, but they certainly shade its implications in order to please the client. The defense attorneys don't have to say, "Look, we need you to say this and that, and make sure you don't say that and this." Instead, it is tacitly understood by all involved that the defense experts will do what they can to strengthen and reinforce the defense's case. They will put great emphasis on any evidence that is the least bit exculpatory. That is what they are paid to do. Right or wrong, this is how the legal system works today.

To anybody who would listen, and everybody on his payroll would, Simpson repeatedly proclaimed his innocence. Even when the DNA evidence started coming in and Simpson could not explain it away, he continued to insist he didn't do it. And he hired a team of experts who would spend the next year trying to find something, anything, that could prove their client's innocence. When they failed to find even a single shred of evidence that either implicated another suspect or offered an affirmative defense for their client, the defense attorneys gave up. Instead of defending their client, they focused all their firepower on the prosecution.

Although the Simpson defense team had more famous attorneys than most others, it was not unique. They didn't have any magical powers, aside from O.J. Simpson's bankbook. And even though the Simpson team was better paid than most defense attorneys, that doesn't necessarily mean they were excellent lawyers. Given the almost unlimited resources at their disposal, it's no wonder they mounted a vigorous defense.

On many issues, they were right. There were significant problems with some of the policework. The conduct of the police at the scene left the investigation and evidence vulnerable to charges of contamination. The prosecution made a lot of mistakes. Had the Simpson defense team just stuck to the material issues in the case, they would have done a good job. Unfortunately, they went over the line, particularly in their use of race and racial issues.

The race card was dealt from the beginning. Days after Simpson's arrest, several black leaders met with Gil Garcetti at Urban League headquarters to express their concerns that Simpson might not get a fair trial. These leaders insisted that the jury be racially mixed and warned that an unpopular verdict might result in another round of riots. Chief among the leaders was Johnnie Cochran, who took the opportunity to remind Gil Garcetti that the black community would be watching. Meanwhile, he was talking with Simpson about handling his defense.

Even if he thought Simpson was guilty, Shapiro wanted to defend his client to the best of his ability. But he also knew that there was little he could do that reason, honor, and the law would allow. Shapiro is a decent man. He slammed me in court and in the media, but that's to be expected. On a personal level, he has always treated me with respect. Shapiro was the only defense attorney who would greet me every morning when I appeared. Had Shapiro remained in charge of the defense, he would have done everything in his power to make sure that Simpson received a fair trial, and he would have done all he could to get Simpson off. Shapiro would have fought hard to exclude evidence that he didn't think belonged in the trial, and he would have fought hard to introduce evidence that he thought was relevant. But he would have kept the trial within the bounds of reason and integrity.

When Johnnie Cochran joined the defense team, it lost a little class. The defense's posture and attitude changed overnight. There was a no-holds-barred atmosphere that infected almost every aspect of their case. This new attitude even affected the client. Simpson was no longer the guilt-ridden and morose character of the Bronco chase and his subsequent booking. Giving his plea in the Superior Court trial, he would later say, "absolutely 100 percent not guilty."

We don't know how much Simpson spent on his defense, and we will probably never know. There are rumors and estimates and speculation, but only a few known facts. Shapiro was put on a retainer of $100,000 a month, although he hasn't been paid in full. We know that Dr. Michael Baden was paid $100,000 for his services, and that the defense hired several other expert witnesses at about the same rate. We also know that a team of private investigators flew all over the country trying to dig up dirt on people, including me. This last investment may have been their best.

The defense team had talent. But more importantly, it had substantial financial resources. Those resources allowed the defense to spend a great deal of time, effort, and expense making legitimate arguments about the problems in the case. But they also used those same resources to second-guess evidence and witnesses that should have been unassailable. And they used their considerable assets, in both personnel and cash, to conduct a smear campaign against me and others.

There's an old legal saying: If the evidence is with you, pound on the evidence. If the evidence is against you, pound on the law. And if the evidence and the law are against you, pound on the podium. The Simpson lawyers didn't have any credible defense, so they started pounding on the podium, and anyone else who happened to be nearby. Unfortunately, I walked right into the middle of it.

Chapter 8

WITNESS FOR THE PEOPLE

As I watched the six-day preliminary hearing ...
I was mystified at some of what the defense did. It seemed
ill prepared to really examine Mark Fuhrman.

—JOHNNIE COCHRAN

J UST PRIOR TO SIMPSON'S ARREST, District Attorney Gil Garcetti decided to present the case against Simpson before the grand jury. In my opinion, this was a well-calculated move to limit the exposure of his case before trial. Grand jury proceedings are secret, and defense counsel are not present to hear the prosecution's case. A preliminary hearing, the alternative to a grand jury, would have made public any items of evidence, witnesses, and the prosecution's theory of the crime and motives which would make jury selection even more difficult.

I was subpoenaed to appear before the grand jury and went to the criminal courts building at 210 W. Temple the week of June 20. I sat in the grand jury witness waiting room with Phillips, Vannatter, Lange, and others all day, talking, drinking coffee, and reading three-month-old magazines. But we were never called to testify. When Simpson's defense challenged the grand jury on grounds that its members had heard excerpts from the tapes of the 911 call Nicole made in 1993, the district attorney's office went along with the motion, and the grand jury was dismissed. Although we were never told by the prosecutor's office, we wound up hearing in the news coverage that the Simpson case would not be heard by the grand jury.

With the grand jury hearing blown, the only alternative was a preliminary hearing. A preliminary hearing is normally a skeleton case, with the prosecution using only enough witnesses and evidence to hold the suspect over for a Superior Court trial. In a preliminary hearing, the defense can cross-examine witnesses and all evidence used is made available to them, so it is in the prosecution's best interests to keep everything to a minimum.

Having not been notified or subpoenaed for the preliminary hearing, I never gave it a second thought, figuring that they didn't need me as a witness. I knew that the evidence I found was no doubt important and my presence would be needed at the Superior Court trial, but considering what I knew of the case, I wasn't sure that it would even get that far. With as much evidence as I thought we had against Simpson, there could have been a plea bargain.

Before the preliminary hearing I already knew the importance of the glove I had found at Rockingham, but I didn't yet realize how central it was to the case. Although Lange and Vannatter were told not to divulge the results of the preliminary DNA tests on the glove to anyone, within hours of the results Phillips and I were told that the Rockingham glove was stained with blood from Ron, Nicole, and Simpson.

Then on July 5, sometime around noon, as I was just sitting down to eat a sack lunch at my desk, the district attorney's office called and told me to be in court at 1:30 P.M. Our normal homicide vehicles needed to be used that afternoon, so I borrowed an older car from burglary and drove to the Criminal Courts building.

Eating my tuna fish sandwich as I drove to court, I realized that the Rockingham glove proved one irrefutable fact if nothing else: Because it had the blood of all three people, it was the one piece of evidence that linked Simpson with the two victims. And it also connected the crime scene at Bundy with the Rockingham estate. No wonder they needed me to testify.

I arrived at the Criminal Courts building shortly before 1:00 P.M. When I got there, I met Marcia Clark for the second time, although we didn't have a chance to say much more than hello. She told me I was going on in a few minutes and that was all. We didn't have any time to talk about my testimony.

It's weird what you recall two years after an event. I remember thinking that I had a small hole in my rear pants pocket, my jacket was wrinkled in the back, and I had a sport jacket on, not a suit. I had played basketball at 6:00 that morning, and I had a bad hair day after my shower. These details seemed important then.

Once I took the stand and was sworn in, Marcia led me through my actions and conclusions at the crime scenes in some detail. Then defense attorney Gerald Uelmen conducted my cross-examination. Early in the questioning he focused on the events leading up to our arrival at Rockingham. Although I didn't think that the investigating officers should have left the crime scene, I went through the reasoning that Vannatter and Lange had for going to notify Simpson at his home. Whenever possible, the families of murder victims should be notified in person. It was the Robbery/Homicide detective's job to make the notification; Phillips and I were there for support. Vannatter and Lange instructed me to show the way. Even though I had been to the estate before, I didn't remember exactly how to get there and had to ask Officer Riske for directions.

The reason for Uelmen's line of questioning was simple. The defense was making a 1538.5 California Evidence Code motion to suppress the physical evidence we collected at Rockingham on the grounds that our entry of the estate was an illegal search and seizure. The motion to suppress was the first major legal challenge by the defense of the policework done on June 13. In California, the defense has only one chance to exclude evidence on such grounds, and Simpson's lawyers took a big gamble by bringing in Professor Uelmen to argue the motion. They may have thought that because Judge Kathleen Kennedy-Powell was a former student of his, she would favor her old teacher. Personally, I think Robert Shapiro would have been more convincing, but they went with the professor.

Uelmen's strategy was to question our reasoning in deciding that we had probable cause to enter the Rockingham estate. He argued that we had violated Simpson's Fourth Amendment rights. I knew we had not.

A cop has to understand search and seizure. It's not a sixth sense or a hunch. You need a knowledge of the law, attention to the evidence, and the experience and judgment earned only through years of policework. The crime scene provides you with clues, and as you connect the clues together, they begin to paint a picture. But you can't make the picture fit your own preconceptions. You have to be reactive, not proactive, and make only the judgment calls that the evidence allows you to make.

Under the law, if you are at a scene and confronted with exigent circumstances—unexpected conditions that you must react to—you have probable cause to investigate further in order to protect lives or pursue suspects. Sometimes it can be a life-and-death situation, so you must act both quickly and within the law.

When we arrived at the Rockingham estate, we were presented with pieces of evidence that, once compiled, resulted in obvious exigent circumstances. We had just been at the site of a brutal double murder. There were footprints and blood drops leaving the scene, and the suspect appeared to have been bleeding. But the blood stopped in a back alley, where the suspect probably entered a vehicle, which then left the crime scene.

At Rockingham, there was blood on a Bronco, which was parked haphazardly. Another car, the Nissan 300Z, did not fit the neighborhood and was registered to a Hollywood resident, a neighborhood some eight to ten miles away. We knew two people were dead, but there could have been a third victim at Rockingham. The scenarios were countless, due to our inability to even speculate on the male's identity, and the fact that we didn't know the movements of either victim before the murders. Although we believed the female to be Nicole Brown Simpson, we were not yet sure. As far as I knew, the female victim could have been her sister, a babysitter, or someone staying at the house.

A chain of circumstances was beginning to build. Any one of them separately might have been easy to explain. But taken together, they suggested something had happened at Rockingham as well. The blood on the Bronco was located where someone would put a hand on the door to open it. The brush marks on the doorsill looked like blood from shoe soles. The Bronco was owned by Hertz, a company we all knew Simpson worked for. Inside the Bronco was a package with his name and address on it. There was also a shovel and what appeared to be plastic sheeting inside. An unexplained piece of wood lay on the parkway by the Bronco; it didn't seem to come from anywhere in the immediate neighborhood. Simpson had not notified his security service, Westec, that he would be out of town. A maid was supposed to be there all the time, and there were lights on in the main house, both upstairs and down. Yet, no one answered the door or the phone.

There was a level of urgency here that made it necessary for us to investigate inside the Rockingham estate. What if we had not gone in, and O.J. was lying inside somewhere bleeding to death? If you went to the house of a friend or family member, seen what we had at Bundy and then at Rockingham, would you have simply rung the doorbell a few times and gone home? No, you'd call the police and want them to do something, or you would go in yourself. And that's what we did.

Still, sometimes when the police take action and do exactly what they're supposed to do, they get raked over the coals for it. That's what happened in this case.

A detective is paid to make decisions. Here were four detectives with almost one hundred years of combined experience. A policeman's job is to make split-second decisions that legal experts spend decades analyzing. It's not fair, but that's the way it is.

> **When I found the glove behind Kato's bungalow, I was looking for a suspect or victim, not evidence.**

We entered the property because we were presented with circumstances over which we had no control, and we were obligated to investigate further to make sure that no one else was hurt and that the suspect was not hiding somewhere nearby. That's all we did. Once we entered the Rockingham estate and found that everyone was safe, we did not conduct any further search until we got the warrant. When I found the glove behind Kato's bungalow, I was looking for a suspect or victim, not evidence. I believed we had probable cause in entering the Rockingham estate.

Judge Kennedy-Powell agreed, ruling on July 7 that our judgment was sound and the evidence would be allowed. In her decision, the judge commented: "This would be a very easy decision for me if in fact these officers went in there like storm troopers, fanning out over the property, examining every leaf, every car, every closet, every nook and cranny of this location. But the testimony...shows this did not happen." Not only did she rule that we had made a lawful decision, but she also praised our efforts to notify Simpson in person and make arrangements for his children to be reunited with him. "The place for two small children whose mother has been murdered is not at the police station, sitting in a corner drawing pictures on a tablet," the judge said in her ruling. "The place for those kids is with their family."

In their arguments, the prosecution did not use *People vs. Cain*, the 1989 California appeals case that Kennedy-Powell cited in her ruling. Because I dealt with so many search warrants, I kept up on case law, particularly in the area of search and seizure. In fact, just weeks prior I had read *People vs. Cain* myself, and while I can't say that I was thinking about it as we decided to enter the estate, I certainly was familiar with the case. In *People vs. Cain*, the police had even less dramatic exigent circumstances than we did at Rockingham. Sheriff's deputies investigating an assault and attempted rape came to the victim's apartment. They saw lights and heard music in the apartment next door, even though it was early in the morning. So they knocked on the neighbor's door, but no one answered, which made them think there might be an additional victim inside. When they entered the unlocked door, they found a man passed out. In that apartment they recovered evidence that tied the man to the crime and eventually convicted him. The appeals court ruled that experienced police officers can use "reasonable inference," but the search "must be strictly circumscribed by the exigencies that justify its initiation."

Judge Kennedy-Powell's ruling was a big victory for the prosecution and a setback for the defense. But while the judge made it clear that we had acted reasonably and responsibly, the defense continued to question our motives for entering the estate. Even though these arguments had no legal bite after the ruling, the defense's repeated assertions that our actions were somehow questionable served as prologue to the bizarre conspiracy theories they would spin throughout the trial.

My testimony did not cover only the search and seizure challenge. I also described all my actions from the initial call at 1:05 A.M. the night of the murders through the discovery of the glove at Rockingham. I talked about the crime scenes and evidence. I had testified hundreds of times and was not intimidated by defense attorneys. I did well that day, and I think I made the defense nervous. If it was a bad day for the defense, it was partly their own fault; they were unprepared.

Early in his cross-examination, I realized that Uelmen did not appear to know anything about what had happened during the investigation. He broke the cardinal rule of a litigator: asking questions he did not know the answers to. The second miscalculation he made, I think, was assuming that I was legally misinformed, easily intimidated, or did not have a high level of professionalism in my work. Uelmen approached the cross-examination not giving me credit for nineteen years of service, having testified in hundreds of trials, and having been confronted by countless defense attorneys who had tried the same tactics he himself was now attempting. He tried to rattle me by questioning my judgment. He waited for me to falter or stumble on my words. But he walked away disappointed. The following excerpt from the hearing is a humorous but telling example of Uelmen's unsuccessful attempts to raise questions about my policework:

> **UELMEN:** Now, you indicated that you believe these stains [on the Bronco] to be blood?
>
> **FUHRMAN:** Yes.
>
> **UELMEN:** Could you explain why you came to that conclusion?
>
> **FUHRMAN:** Just the appearance of the stain. It looked like a red translucent stain that when you see dried blood, that's what it looks like.
>
> **UELMEN:** Well, does dried blood look any different than dried taco sauce?
>
> **FUHRMAN:** I don't take much note of dried taco sauce too often, so I wouldn't know.

After my first day of testimony was over, Marcia and I walked together to the elevator. Standing there staring at the closed doors, Marcia turned to me and smiled.

"You're one of the best I've ever seen," she said.

I didn't know what to say other than thank you. I was a little embarrassed. I was just proud that I had been able to do a good job for the prosecution.

The prosecution now considered me a star witness, while the defense now considered me a prime target. The defense had barely been aware of me until my testimony at the preliminary hearing. My name wasn't on the search warrant, and I was not in charge of the case. But I believe that once the defense lost their motion to suppress, largely because of my testimony, I became a target.

The fact that the hearing was on television didn't really hit me until I returned to the West LA station. As I walked up to my desk, Ron Phillips smiled and said, "I should give you a big kiss!"

"What's up?" I asked.

Ron told me that ever since my testimony that afternoon, the phone had been ringing off the hook with positive comments and reactions. I thought he was pulling my leg. Then other detectives jumped in, describing some of the calls they had taken. I was shocked at the compliments: "That's what a detective is supposed to be"…"LAPD should be proud of Fuhrman"…"What a cop!"

I thought this would all pass by the next day. Boy, was I wrong.

The next day in court, Uelmen asked me, "Do you remember taking some notes that morning—would you like to look at them again to refresh your memory?"

"No, I don't need to."

The day before, as I came off the witness stand and walked past Uelmen's desk I saw his notebook folded open to my crime scene notes. Although he had discussed them in the beginning, I guessed my notes would once again be the subject of his cross-examination. So I knew I'd better review my notes to be ready for his questions.

As it turned out, this minor error on Uelmen's part probably eliminated his planned challenge to my notes, for he never went into them in detail later. He knew I was prepared. Here's one lesson the professor didn't learn in law school and probably doesn't teach his students: Don't have the questions you're going to ask your witness the next day on your desk in plain view.

Uelmen had already brought up my notes. On the first day, he opened his cross-examination with a line of questioning that puzzled me at the time:

> **UELMEN:** Detective Fuhrman, did you ever prepare any reports regarding your participation in this investigation?
>
> **FUHRMAN:** No. I just took some preliminary notes while I was still at the scene before Robbery/Homicide detectives arrived.
>
> **UELMEN:** All right. And what did you do with those notes?

FUHRMAN: I gave them to Detective Phillips, and they were in turn given to Detectives Vannatter and Lange.

UELMEN: And what did Detective Vannatter do with them?

MS. CLARK: Objection, calls for speculation.

Why did Marcia object to this, I wondered. The defense attorney rephrased his question.

UELMEN: Were they utilized in preparing any reports by Detective Vannatter that you're aware of?

FUHRMAN: I have no idea, sir.

UELMEN: Did you review any reports prepared by Detective Vannatter?

FUHRMAN: No, none.

The questioning quickly moved away from the subject of my notes. I wondered why Uelmen did not mention my notation of the bloody fingerprint on the rear gate, or perhaps my initial speculation that the blood apparently coming from the suspect could have been the result of his being bitten by the Akita. Particularly since this was his first line of questioning, I was very surprised that he did not follow up on these details. I was also surprised by Marcia's objection. But the full significance of that was lost on me at that point.

The second day of testimony concluded without incident. I did my job, Uelmen remained clueless, and the public seemed to like me. The media at the Criminal Courts building took notice, and reporters began hounding me for interviews. I said nothing.

That evening, my face was plastered on the television. I received compliments from many attorneys, but the most memorable was from Johnnie Cochran, who at the time was not yet on the defense team and was serving as a TV commentator on the case. Cochran described me as a "great witness direct from central casting." The attention embarrassed me; I didn't understand the media frenzy. That night the phone started ringing. By the next day, even at work, I received many phone calls from old friends, retired partners, and many cops, all praising my performance. The letters started coming in, eventually numbering a dozen or more a day, from people all over America. I heard from ex-Marines, school children, elderly women, families, cops, and police widows. They all thanked me for a job well done. I was overwhelmed. Maybe I had done a good job, but I didn't think I should have generated that much attention.

The media attention increased with requests for telephone or in-person interviews, all of which I politely declined. For the next two weeks, my work day consisted of half public relations and half police work. My fellow detectives had to answer the phones, and my buddies in patrol helped me sneak out of the station so I could avoid the reporters and cameras. People stopped, stared, pointed, and spoke to me all over town. Crime scenes, restaurants, stores, and even stop lights became showcases. The contacts were always positive, but I did not like my celebrity status.

As uncomfortable as even the positive press was for me, I had no idea that celebrity would quickly turn to notoriety.

Chapter 9

THE DEFENSE CARD

*I find the issue of racial animosity to be something that
[the defense is] entitled to cross-examine on.*

—JUDGE LANCE ITO, OVERRULING THE PROSECUTION'S MOTION
TO EXCLUDE THE ISSUE OF RACIAL EPITHETS FROM THE TRIAL

FOLLOWING THE PRELIMINARY HEARING, I tried to get back to my other cases, but on July 16, 1994, at about 4:00 P.M., I received a call from Jeffrey Toobin of *The New Yorker*. Toobin asked bluntly about a petition for pension I had filed in 1982. I told him I had no comment.

"I've spoken to the defense," Toobin continued. "They claim that you planted the glove at Rockingham."

"That's ridiculous!" I exclaimed.

Toobin asked if I wanted to make a comment because an article with this allegation would be in the issue hitting the stands on July 19.

Again, I had no comment.

It was a ludicrous charge. There was not a shred of evidence that I could have done anything like planting the glove. In fact, it could be proved there was no way I could have done so. But the defense would never even try to prove their planted glove theory. Instead, they would try to smear me as the type of man who would be willing to plant evidence. The first weapon they would use, and which Toobin used for his article in *The New Yorker*, would be carefully chosen excerpts from an application for a disability pension I filed in the early 1980s.

The Jeffrey Toobin I know is a person I've seen on talk shows and a writer whose articles and book I have read. He seems to be articulate and intelligent. And he truly believes that O.J. Simpson murdered two people. But he was too torn by his connections to the defense team to come out and say so until well after the trial. Toobin might have thought of himself as an independent, objective journalist, but in effect he was a stooge for the defense. He took the defense's position from the beginning, and then after doing enormous damage to the truth, slowly tried to slither back into the prosecution camp. As the first media purveyor of the planted glove theory, I have to wonder, did Toobin believe it? No. Did he compromise himself by reporting it? Yes. Did he wish that he hadn't? I'd like to give him the benefit of the doubt and say yes. Still, Toobin was the messenger of the absurd defense claims. But if Toobin hadn't been the messenger, the defense would have found some other journalist looking for a scoop.

The defense's racial strategy was quickly leaked to the press and the disability claim was just the initial step in their campaign against me. First, they would try to prove that I was supposedly a bigot, then claim I planted the glove because I supposedly hated black people. These accusations didn't need any facts to substantiate them because they involved race, the most sensitive issue our nation faces, and one which is rarely dealt with honestly.

My application for a disability pension in 1982 has been scrutinized at length in the media. Conveniently excerpted portions of my file have been publicized, and I consider all discussion of the contents of that file to be a breach of confidentiality. While I refuse to discuss the specifics of that file, I will, however, speak candidly about my life at that time.

The period in which I applied for disability could only be described as a time I felt lost. I know that my personality and inability to cope with job pressures broke up my first marriage. The immaturity of youth, stress of policework, and lack of a stable family life drove me in a direction I never wanted to travel. I was confused, depressed, and suffering nightmares. I sought help, taking well-meaning advice from friends, but that only complicated my life even more.

When the pension board refused my petition, I actually felt relieved. My attorney, Seth Kelsey, wanted to take the decision to Superior Court in hopes of overruling the pension board. As we stood on the steps of City Hall South, I told him, "No, I'm going back to work."

But Seth took the case to Superior Court anyway. My claim was refused, and my medical records became public record. I'm sure Seth felt he was being helpful, but his concern caused me to relive this painful part of my life over and over again, unfortunately with the whole world watching.

The only redeeming feature of this period was that I was able to take a break from the job and take a long look at myself. I didn't like myself then. But I realized that nobody was going to fix me but me. I got control of my emotions and learned to cope with stress.

By claiming victim status, the minority or advocate immediately puts the accused in a position of guilt, a charge that sticks regardless of any evidence to the contrary.

During the media frenzy surrounding the initial charges, Janet Hackett, my ex-wife, described to the press the change I underwent: "Mark got some counseling, *became a detective*, and turned his life around. Now he's getting screwed for it."

Picking myself up by the bootstraps, I began to make something of my life. I worked hard at my job and got my personal life in order. By the time of the Simpson case, I had a citywide reputation for being a very good detective. People are always willing to kick you when you're down. But they rarely give you credit when you pull yourself back up. I had problems, and I learned how to deal with them. It made me a better person, not perfect by any stretch, but I rose above my failures and eventually made a successful life.

Sometimes I wonder how my professional life would have evolved had I met Ron Phillips early into my career. Ron is more than a friend—he is like the big brother I never had. Ron had a way of teaching me things without saying, "Come here, let me teach you something." He has a personality that demands respect. He made me a better policeman and a better person.

Ron is the reason I became the detective I was the morning of June 13, 1994. We were a team—two "Type A" personalities who worked too hard, took our jobs very seriously, and loved what we did. We were so much alike that it scared even us. When we first worked together we found that we both cut our spaghetti and both put potato chips on our tuna sandwiches. I'll miss not working with Ron on another case. It was the best time of my career.

I had never told my wife, Caroline, about my emotional problems in 1982 because I was embarrassed. In my eyes, I had failed, and I didn't want to become a failure in hers. But after talking to Toobin, I called her immediately and told her all about it. Caroline remained calm. She said she understood, and it was no big deal. I was relieved to have her by my side.

That same day, I drove to Marcia's office and laid it on the line, telling her all about my problems back then. Marcia smiled and told me, "It will never come in, it's remote and irrelevant. Don't worry about it."

But of course I did. Now I had to think of something to head off Toobin's article. I remembered an ABC reporter whom I had met outside the Simpson estate a few days after the murders. A different sort of journalist, she was not caught up in the O.J. frenzy.

The next morning I phoned her. First, I explained enough of the situation to get her interest, then I asked for her help. She was interested and made arrangements to meet with me in a hotel near my house. There, I gave her a quick outline of my current problems. In addition to the Toobin piece in *The New Yorker*, *Newsweek* was also going to run a similar article. Both magazines were coming out Monday morning.

The ABC reporter used her contacts to obtain the rough drafts of both articles and to have them faxed to the hotel room. Once she read the articles, she thought they were not that bad. I disagreed—to me, they were devastating. We discussed the situation and agreed that a preemptory strike would take the sting out of the story, at least somewhat. She notified her boss and had a crew ready to do an interview in an adjacent room as soon as I gave the word.

Before I would submit to the interview, I wanted to clear it with my superiors. While there was nothing to keep me from talking to the media, I wanted to have the department's blessing and support. I began by calling Ron Phillips, who notified Captain Kurth, who in turn notified Chief Frankel. Quickly, the word came down that I would not be giving any interviews, and that was an order. I felt worse than before. My hopes of defending myself were gone, but I did what I was told.

The clock was ticking. I knew that on Monday the whole media world would be at my doorstep. I had to get my family out of town before the story broke. My sister-in-law Didi is very close to Caroline, and I wanted to bring her in to help move my family. On the Sunday night before the story appeared, I loaded my wife and children into Didi's Landcruiser and sent them away to stay with a friend in Ukiah, California. Thus began a game of cat-and-mouse with the media that continues to this day.

Monday morning, I awoke to an empty house. I made coffee and stared at the blank television screen. Although it was the middle of summer, the house seemed cold and lonely. I wanted to see the news coverage, yet at the same time I didn't. Finally, curiosity overcame me and I turned on the television. It came as no surprise that the media were in a feeding frenzy over me.

I phoned Ron at the station. He told me that Captain Kurth wanted to have lunch with Ron and me to discuss our options. Brad Roberts would come by my house just before noon to pick me up.

When Brad arrived, the media had not yet shown up. We escaped undetected in our four-door plain police car. Brad was sympathetic; I was embarrassed. We talked briefly about the news about me, but Brad was a good friend, and soon we were cracking jokes and laughing.

Captain Kurth was also sympathetic. Although I did not want to go out to lunch, his rank and personality won me over. Ron, the captain, and I went to a Mexican restaurant in Santa Monica and discussed the current problems over lunch. Kurth flatly asked what I wanted to do, and I quickly told him, "Get out of town and join my family."

The conversation went in circles, with me wanting to make the whole mess just go away and Kurth trying to protect the department, me, and the case all at once. Finally, he agreed to let me go to Ukiah for a week, and we would evaluate things when I returned.

I felt somewhat better, but still not relieved. Brad won the job of driving me home to await my evening flight to Santa Rosa and then on to Ukiah. When we got back to my house, we cracked a bottle of twenty-five-year-old Chivas Regal. The scotch eased my anxiety, and my sense of humor resurfaced. Before long, I was making fun of myself and the situation. Brad and I had some good laughs while we polished off the better part of the bottle.

Normally I enjoyed airports, especially LAX. I liked getting there an hour before the flight, or even earlier, so I could drink a cup of coffee and watch people. I analyzed their dress, walk, grooming; I tried to estimate their income, profession, or destination. Airports had been fun, but not anymore. Now I arrived just before departure, and I had to stay aware of anyone staring or media trucks parked in the area.

Checking in with only carry-on items, I discovered that my flight was half an hour late, so I had to kill some time. At first, I sat in my gate's waiting area. Within minutes, a lady asked if I was Mark Fuhrman. I responded that I was not, but thanked her for the compliment. The scotch still had ahold of my humor, but I had to take my bag and walk deeper into the terminal. Going past a small airport cocktail lounge, I saw that there was no one inside. Even though I really didn't need a drink, I thought I could sit there without being recognized. At the bar I ordered a Chivas. The bartender nodded at my request and poured me a tall double.

"There you go, detective," he said.

So much for traveling incognito.

The flight was short, but full of some people who thought they knew me and others who knew exactly who I was. After arriving in Santa Rosa, I almost walked right by my old partner Kevin Devries. It was great to see Kevin, and he immediately informed me that my family arrived safely after driving all night.

Kevin tried to reassure me that everything would work out. He knew me well enough to know that I was down, but not beaten. We stopped in Hopland at the brewery for a burger, a beer, and quiet conversation. Because we were such good friends, I felt obligated to try and explain everything they were saying about me, but he didn't need to hear it. Kevin obviously planned to take my mind off of all matters not related to wine tasting, skiing, basketball, and beer.

The week was very long for me. Even though Kevin kept us busy, media reports about me slipped into our day at every turn. My childhood, military service, police career, and two prior marriages were now nothing more than daytime talk show chatter. I was being tarred and feathered, and I couldn't speak in my own defense.

One day while I was away from Kevin's house, my wife heard about a plug for an upcoming *Geraldo Rivera* show that—no great surprise—was about me. Evidently, Geraldo was going to interview an officer on the LAPD who supposedly was head of a secret hit squad on which I was allegedly a member. The officer's identity was going to be kept secret, but his allegations weren't. Caroline was beside herself with anger. A person who is not normally confrontational, Caroline called the *Geraldo* show, identified herself as Mrs. Fuhrman and said that what Geraldo was claiming was not true. Within seconds, Geraldo himself got on the phone.

Caroline no doubt read Geraldo the riot act considering these silly allegations. Then Geraldo asked a few questions of his own concerning "Men Against Women" and my supposed leadership of the group. Caroline heatedly explained that "Men Against Women" was just a screenplay.

Of course, Geraldo wanted to have my wife speak to him live on the show, but she refused. But he immediately informed the world that he just spoke to Mark Fuhrman's wife, and "Men Against Women" was just a joke turned into a screenplay. When I found out what she had done I was furious, but as my anger subsided I became very proud of her, even though I never told her. This innocent gesture, my wife's defense of me, might have been the clue that the defense later followed, leading them to Laura Hart McKinny and her infamous tapes.

While I stayed at Kevin's, some strange things happened. First, Kevin received a call from someone representing himself as an employee of the phone company. This person tried to convince Kevin that the company was having some trouble with the phone service and they needed some personal information to verify the phone number. Of course Kevin refused, as his number is not listed or available; he is a Ukiah police officer. Later in the day, Kevin once again answered the phone and a man with a British accent stated that he was from the *National Enquirer*, and he wished to speak to Mark. Kevin refused to give away any information or even acknowledge that I was there.

The next day, this same man called the house across the street, which is owned by someone I had met just days prior. Later he called Kevin's home once again, and I took the call. The offers to tell my side of the story were spoken in a tone meant to resemble sincerity, but I declined. When sincerity fails, the offer of money usually works, which was described as "name a price," but my comment to it all was, "Common sense dictates that I remain silent."

Like so many others involved in the trial, I had countless opportunities to sell my story for cash. But I felt I had a professional obligation to the district attorney's office, the LAPD, and the victims' families. So, while I was being attacked in the press with charges that were inaccurate, unfair, or simply untrue, I had no means by which to defend myself.

A week passed, and my family was ready to go home. Kevin made me laugh and showed me a good time, considering the obstacles, but I had many things to confront in Los Angeles. Although I didn't look forward to it, I had no choice but to get back in the game.

Without my asking, a West LA civil attorney by the name of Robert Tourtelot offered his services to help me fight the libelous accusations being made against me by the defense and spread in the media.

I had met Bob before when Ron Phillips and I worked on a robbery case in which Tourtelot's wife was the victim. Ron and I solved the case and sent the suspect to prison. When Bob read the allegations about me published by The New Yorker and Newsweek, he was furious. He offered his services on a contingency basis, and I hired him as my attorney. Bob came out swinging, defending me on any talk show that would have him. He also sued everyone who was responsible for the accusation that I planted the glove.

Soon, the famous private investigator Anthony Pellicano offered his services pro bono. Anthony is an investigator for the stars, having worked for Michael Jackson, Sylvester Stallone, Roseanne Barr, Don Simpson, James Woods, and many other celebrities. He pledged his total support and services. Anthony was and remains a loyal friend and great investigator.

Week after week, the press continued its relentless campaign. Radio and television commentators still kept spinning the planted glove/rogue cop theory, and Tourtelot kept defending me in the media. Tourtelot no doubt enjoyed the media attention, but at one point I told him that we had to back off a little. We were too exposed; we needed to be more out of sight, and then hopefully out of mind. As much as I tried to stay out of the media spotlight, giving no interviews or photo opportunities, the pressure continued. My ignoring the media seemed to motivate them to find new dirt, new angles, and new theories on how and why I supposedly planted the glove.

Although I functioned normally on the outside, I was devastated on the inside. The world that I struggled to become part of was slowly drifting away from me. The desperation I felt made me remember movies I had seen where the shipwrecked survivor watched the ships pass, time and time again. Just as I seemed to recover from one onslaught, another ship passed over the horizon. There seemed no way that I would be saved. Nevertheless, I kept putting one foot in front of the other and did my job.

Not all of the attention was negative. I was invited to lunches with commanders, deputy chiefs, and assistant chiefs. I received promises of another promotion when the case was over. Department personnel I never got along with were suddenly my friends. Still, it was a distraction. And many of those supporters began to desert me as the defense continued to play up the race card.

Race is a difficult issue, one that America still tiptoes around. After all, many times when racial accusations are made, they are used as a satellite issue to accomplish another goal. By claiming victim status, the minority or advocate immediately puts the accused in a position of guilt, a charge that sticks regardless of any evidence to the contrary. I understand racism, and I understand the inequality that it produces. But I also understand history, and as history has evolved, so have we. History is a learning tool that we use to make ourselves better, in hopes of not repeating the same mistakes. Without becoming too philosophical, I am trying in very few words to express that I understand the sensitivity, the feelings, and the pain of racism, but the hypocrisy of its use sometimes turns the tragedies of history into the tragedies of today.

In addition to playing on racial sensitivity, the defense also hoped to take advantage of their client's immense popularity and people's reluctance to think of him as a murderer. The defense card would be accepted by many in Los Angeles and throughout the country despite the lack of proof, because many did not want to accept the fact that Simpson was capable of this brutal crime.

I kept thinking that all this would soon blow over and we could get back to the central question of Simpson's guilt or innocence. But even before it began, the trial was already careening out of control.

During the period between the preliminary hearing and the Superior Court trial, one district attorney, Cheri Lewis, wrote all of the motions to suppress the defense attacks on my police and Marine records, charges of racism, and the planted glove theory. Cheri knocked herself out for me and the case. I don't think I will ever thank her enough.

Cheri is a very diligent, competent attorney who is also very likable. She worked hard to keep the case on the right track. But between the defense, the media, and Judge Ito, doing so was an uphill battle. And often her own colleagues in the prosecution were obstacles.

Just before opening statements in the Superior Court trial, prosecutors Cheri Lewis and Chris Darden argued a motion attempting to prevent any cross-examination on racism and use of racial epithets.

Chris told the court that the introduction of racial issues and use of epithets "will do one thing. It will upset the black jurors, it will issue a test, it will give them the test, and the test, will be 'whose side are you on?' The side of the white prosecutors and the white policemen or on the side of the black defendant and his very prominent black lawyer? That is what it is going to do. Either you are with the man, or you are with the brothers."

Whether or not the jury eventually saw the case in these stark alternatives, this is certainly the way Chris looks at things, especially when race is involved. He later said, "The next white police officer takes the witness stand—the jury is going to paint that white police officer with the same brush."

So Chris Darden drew the line, and then Johnnie Cochran placed him on the other side. As he would do throughout the trial itself, Cochran baited Darden with a mixture of racial politics and simple intimidation. He stated that Darden's "remarks this morning are perhaps the most incredible remarks I've heard in a court of law in the thirty-two years I have been practicing law. His remarks are demeaning to African Americans as a group. I want…to apologize to African Americans across this country…. It is demeaning to our jurors to say that African Americans who have lived under oppression for two-hundred-plus years in this country cannot work within the mainstream, cannot hear these offensive words…. I am ashamed that Mr. Darden would allow himself to become an apologist for this man."

Gerald Uelmen took up the defense's argument, saying that if the prosecution didn't call me as a witness, "he will make another appearance in this case, being called as a hostile witness by the defense, because he has a lot of relevant testimony to offer with respect to the Bronco automobile.... Lots of questions that are going to come up with respect to how evidence was contaminated in terms of the parade of officers who went from one scene to another."

After the trial, Uelmen commented, "Keeping the issue of race out of the trial of *People vs. O.J. Simpson* would have been like keeping the issue of slavery out of the Civil War." Uelmen's analogy is mistaken. The Civil War was fought because of slavery. The Bundy murders had nothing to do with race. They had everything to do with O.J. Simpson. A better analogy would be this: Trying to keep Simpson out of the case was like trying to keep Babe Ruth out of baseball. But that's exactly what the defense tried to do by injecting race into the trial.

Judge Ito finally ruled that if the epithet was used in a relevant incident it could be introduced in court. That should have meant that it would be relevant only if it somehow proved I manufactured or planted evidence. The word by itself could not have any relevance under Ito's ruling.

First, Ito ruled that the defense would have to show some evidence that I planted the glove before they could elicit testimony about racism or epithets. Then he changed his mind and decided: "I find the issue of racial animosity to be something that [the defense is] entitled to cross-examine on."

The defense played the race card, and Ito allowed it. Now the trial, and my life, would take a turn for the worse.

Chapter 10

THE ALLEGATIONS
AND THE FACTS

*The jurors come from the same public that would be
watching the preliminary hearing on television. And judges,
too, are human beings who are influenced by public opinion.*

—ALAN DERSHOWITZ

FOR TWO YEARS I HAVE BEEN READING about somebody in the papers
and hearing about him on the television and radio. The person is an
LAPD detective who is a rogue cop, a racist, a Nazi, a liar, someone
who beats up suspects and frames innocent people. Although they call him
Mark Fuhrman, I don't know who this person is. It certainly isn't me.

When the Simpson trial started, I had been a street cop for nearly twenty
years. During that time, I had made thousands of arrests and had contact with
tens of thousands of suspects. In my twenty years living in Southern California,
I had come into contact with countless people, both socially and professionally.
A lot of them liked me. Some of them didn't. And a handful of them wanted a
part of the action, or a little money, or else they just wanted to see themselves

on television. While the defense liked to use these questionable sources together to create a pattern of racism, none of their charges had any validity or relevance. Here I will answer all of the allegations separately and honestly.

There was no standard tactic for the defense's charges against me. They floated rumors, leaked "stories" to the media, and talked about supposed future witnesses, many of whom never appeared. The defense used the shotgun technique, firing everything at me and hoping that something would hit the target. There was no master plan, no rhyme or reason why some charges seemed to stick while others didn't. Too many people wanted in on the trial. There was too much media attention, too much money. The possibility of being associated with celebrities, or even becoming celebrities themselves, proved impossible for many to resist.

The defense needed to portray me as a racist in order to float their bizarre conspiracy theories. And the media was much more interested in the story of a rogue cop (which I wasn't) than a good detective (which I was). As the hysteria grew and attention increased, people came forward with lies and allegations about me. Unfortunately, they were given the benefit of the doubt, while those who told the truth about me were either shouted down or simply ignored.

The process was long and murky—Toobin's first story was published on July 19, 1994, and I did not testify until March 9, 1995. The true story of how the defense team floated its theories would be a fascinating study, if anyone could ever get to the truth. What's more important is how rumors, innuendo, and lies were interwoven into the trial itself. The charges against me supplied much of the spice and gossip in what otherwise should have been a fact-filled and solemn proceeding.

Toobin got his planted glove story from Bob Shapiro, but former LAPD officer turned criminal defense investigator Bill Pavelic was the source of the disability claim allegations. Pavelic worked for Robert Deutsch, an attorney on another case involving me. At about the same time of the Simpson case, I was being sued in a federal court for shooting Joseph Britton, a suspect involved in a robbery in progress. During that trial, Pavelic obtained medical records on my disability claim and thrust them into the suit brought by Britton.

The Britton shooting occurred in 1987, where we had reports of two robbers who sat and watched ATM machines at two locations across the street from each other. On at least three prior occasions, they had robbed people, threatening to shoot or kill them. The suspects' descriptions were unique, their modus operandi was clear, and the time and dates of the robberies had a pattern. I analyzed these crimes, and realized that a stake-out might produce the suspects in the act of committing a robbery. On April 7, 1987, at approximately 11:20 P.M. this in fact did happen.

While I was watching the ATM at the Sumotomo Bank on Olympic Boulevard through binoculars from across the street, a male approached the ATM machine. A male suspect, later identified as Joseph Britton, confronted the male and attempted to rob him. I and two other officers went to detain Britton, which led to a foot pursuit by the three of us. Britton hid in some bushes, refused to give up, and although ordered to surrender, instead acted aggressively to another officer who was completely exposed to Britton's possible gunfire.

If I were a racist, why would I work so hard to free a black man whose guilt seemed obvious to so many others?

Joseph Britton was shot several times and fell to the ground. Some of the wounds came from my weapon. Britton was handcuffed, and medical personnel were summoned immediately. A few feet south of him was the large butcher knife that he had been holding while hiding in the bushes. At the time of these crimes, Joseph Britton pled guilty to four counts of robbery, including the one after which he was shot. At no time during his plea did he express any claim that the knife that he dropped was planted by the police or that he was called any name or racial epithet. Only after he obtained a civil attorney, Robert Deutsch, did these charges surface. Even then, Britton said that an officer with red hair and a mustache (I have neither) called him an epithet. The first trial ended on a hung jury on one of the five counts, and it was set for retrial sometime in the near future. Then the Simpson case began, and the city settled out of court to eliminate my having to take the stand on the Britton case during the Simpson trial, regardless of the merits of Britton's charges. Britton eventually admitted on the *CBS Evening News* that I had never said anything racially oriented to him.

After my face was on television in the preliminary hearing, Deutsch contacted Robert Shapiro about my medical records, and Pavelic was used as the go-between. Pavelic spent a great deal of time, money, and energy to find witnesses against me. He also came up with a variety of witnesses willing to testify to all sorts of different things. He had witnesses who claimed to have seen a gang of Hispanics, an Oriental suspect, and some white guys, all at the murder scene around the time of the killings. Where was he finding these people—Witnesses 'R Us? Of course none of them ended up testifying.

While the first issue that surfaced was my 1982 disability claim, the onslaught continued when Johnnie Cochran received a letter written by a woman named Kathleen Bell. She claimed that she met me in a Marine Corps recruiting station in 1985 or 1986. During this encounter when I supposedly met her, I also supposedly made horrible references to blacks, which reduced her to tears and sent her fleeing to her upstairs office.

The next time Bell supposedly saw me was at Hennessey's Tavern in Redondo Beach, where she tried to introduce me to her girlfriend, Andrea Terry. Being a former Marine who lived in the neighborhood, I visited the recruiting office on occasion, and I went to Hennessey's frequently. While I remember a female in the office, I do not recall the faces of Bell or her friend. And if she was so hurt and offended, why would she play matchmaker and try to set up her friend with such an evil man? I find it uncanny that she could remember these ten-year-old incidents so clearly, particularly since one of them purportedly occurred in a bar where she probably had been drinking.

This was not simply a matter of Bell's word against mine. When Bell supposedly came into the recruiting station, I was seated with a recruiter named Joe Foss, who was eventually interviewed by the district attorney's office and my private investigator, Anthony Pellicano. Joe remembered Bell coming into the office and then trying to edge into the conversation. Joe described her introduction to me, but he recalled that I barely turned at all and basically kept my back to her. Joe was asked about the reported racial comments, and he responded that he never heard anything of the kind. Two other Marines who worked in the recruiting office said they hadn't witnessed or heard about the incident.

Staff Sergeant Max Cordoba was also assigned to this recruiting station and was present when Bell supposedly heard these remarks. Pellicano also interviewed Max, who stated that he did not hear anything that Bell described.

While Bell's statements were made public and became part of the trial, one of the tabloid news programs caught up with Max Cordoba. Max told them that

I was a nice guy and that he never heard me make any racial comments. But just as my testimony in the trial commenced, Cordoba claimed he had a dream about me in which I called him a racial epithet. This miraculous dream triggered a recollection, and Max then claimed that I made those remarks. Of course by then he was already talking to the defense.

The entire country was engulfed by Simpson frenzy, with people everywhere trying to exploit some attachment to the "trial of the century." So, why would my home town be any different? Two brothers named Darrell and Dan Blue lived in Eatonville at the same time as I did, and I knew them both. They were members of the only black family in our town of 952 people.

Dan and Darrell got their fifteen minutes of fame at my expense by claiming that I drove by their house yelling racial epithets. They said they were called such names repeatedly in Eatonville. Dan Blue even described how he observed my racist conduct when we supposedly played high school football together.

The truth is, I never heard either brother called anything other than their name, by me or anyone else. I never drove by their house yelling anything, let alone a racial slur. Darrell was something of a knucklehead, but harmless. Dan was a star high school athlete who dated one of the cheerleaders. Dan graduated from high school in 1974 with my brother Scott. Not only did I never play high school football with him, but I was in the Marine Corps during his four years of high school. Dan also forgot that I attended a different school, Peninsula High School in Gig Harbor, Washington.

The defense dug up two more witnesses, Natalie Singer and Roderic Hodge, to claim I was a racist. Later in the trial, after the screenplay tapes were admitted, they both testified.

I met Natalie Singer in 1987 because my partner was dating her roommate. I can't recall exact incidents, but I won't say we didn't argue. I do remember that we did not get along, and I tried hard to irritate and anger her.

I came to know Roderic Hodge while working a gang/narcotics unit as a uniformed officer in West Los Angeles from 1985 to 1987. Hodge was under investigation for dealing narcotics. I had many contacts with Hodge and arrested him twice. During both arrests, he made complaints about his handling by both arresting officers and wanted to speak with a sergeant. There was no merit to his charges, and he never claimed I used racial epithets. He was just complaining in an attempt to draw attention away from his own arrests.

Around that same time, I worked with Officer James Purdy, who eventually told the defense that when he married a Jewish woman, I supposedly painted a swastika on his locker.

I never touched Purdy's locker, nor would I have done anything so hateful. Purdy was hardly popular in West LA. There were so many people in the division who either didn't care for him or flat out couldn't stand him that it would be difficult to speculate who might have defaced his locker, if that incident really ever occurred.

Another ridiculous allegation concerned a newspaper cartoon I had in my desk. Yes, I did have a cartoon by Paul Conrad that had a swastika in it. My friends knew that I appreciated political satire, and even drew myself. They also knew that I liked Conrad but didn't read the *Los Angeles Times*, where he was the regular political cartoonist. So, when they saw a cartoon they thought was powerful or thought-provoking, they'd often clip it out and give it to me. I had about fifteen such cartoons in my desk. The cartoon in question is a single-frame drawing of a swastika rising out of the ashes of the newly fallen Berlin Wall. Conrad was asking whether we were making a mistake by allowing a country with the power and the history of Germany to be reunified. He was asking if we had awakened a sleeping giant, and whether we might have been better off leaving the giant alone. The fact that a single image can provoke such subtle and disturbing thoughts shows Conrad's great artistry, and that is the only reason I saved the cartoon.

I was also attacked for collecting war memorabilia, some of which happened to be German. In fact, I'm something of a history and military buff and collect all sorts of memorabilia. Decorations, daggers, and sabres are about the only artifacts from World Wars I and II which are neither too expensive, nor too rare for me to collect. British and German war decorations are recognized for their superb craftsmanship, many of these pieces are documented and engraved, and their makers took great pride in their work.

The defense claimed that because I had some German war memorabilia I was therefore supposedly a Nazi. That's like saying because I collect late 19th century American cavalry items, I approve of the slaughter of Indians. When I could still own weapons, I also collected old Winchesters and single action Colts.

Does this mean I'm an outlaw? I'm not obsessed, only extremely intrigued by holding a piece of history, no matter what period it might come from.

While the defense combined these imaginative leaps with the statements of a few disgruntled or attention-seeking witnesses, the district attorney's office thoroughly checked out my background, as well as the backgrounds of those who were making claims against me. The district attorney's investigators told me that they had stacks of impeachment evidence on every witness against me, but they never used any of it.

Not only did the prosecution have impeachment material on the defense's witnesses, they also had plenty of credibility witnesses ready to testify on my behalf. None of these were used, either. The defense was allowed to slander and defame me and turn the trial into a racially charged sideshow.

My ex-wife Janet told a reporter, "There's no way I would have married somebody with that agenda. I'm very sensitive to that [racial] issue. I teach kids of all ethnic groups. I don't even like [racist] jokes."

Danette Myers is a black district attorney and very close friend of mine. She was ready, at the drop of a hat, to do anything for me. Gil Garcetti repeatedly refused to give Danette permission to be interviewed by the media. He also kept her from testifying at the trial, claiming she had a conflict of interest. Danette knew me personally and professionally. She became close to my wife, played with my kids, and visited my home. We shared stories, secrets, and lunches. We tried cases together, and once in a while I'd protect her from the irate family or friends of a suspect she had put away. She is still my good friend. In one of her few statements to the press, Danette said: "Mark saw a lot of negative stuff, and maybe it got to him. But the person I know isn't a racist."

Patricia Foy is a black woman, the victim of a robbery, who chased the white man who had just robbed her. I solved the case by catching the man who did it and told her, "You were incredibly brave, but incredibly foolish to chase him. You could have ended up dead." When interviewed on CNN by Art Harris, Patricia said, "He's not a racist. They're just trying to hang something on him so they can cover up for the defense, that's all they're doing."

Harris also interviewed Connie Law, a black female whose uncle was bludgeoned to death with a hammer and dumped in Los Angeles. The victim, a retired Army master sergeant, was a resident of Las Vegas, so Brad and I went out there to investigate. The investigation began at the victim's home, which we searched with Las Vegas Metro homicide after obtaining a search warrant. We discovered evidence that the victim was killed in his own home, put in the trunk of his car, driven to Los Angeles, and dumped in an alley. Las Vegas police took over the case, as he was killed in that city, with the investigation focusing on three suspects, none of whom have at this writing been charged.

At the end of the investigation, Connie Law and several concerned members of the family arrived at the victim's home. They asked what we had found and we described our findings with as much delicacy as possible. Connie was standing next to me. Overcome with emotion, she began crying. None of the family seemed to come to her side, so I placed my arm around her to comfort her. I can't remember what I said to her, but I felt her sorrow.

Connie later told Harris, "As far as O.J. Simpson goes, I think he's innocent. As far as Mark Fuhrman goes, I think he's a great detective. He was great with us. He didn't show any signs of racism toward me or my family."

Many ex-partners, black, Hispanic, and white, came to my defense. Bob Alaniz, a Hispanic police sergeant, stood up for me on *Geraldo*. I talk with Bob on a regular basis, and he has visited me in Idaho with his daughter Lori, where I even got Bob on a horse.

Carlton Brown, a black detective whom I trained and worked with in West Los Angeles Robbery, also stood up for me. He told *Parade* magazine, "I never heard Mark refer to anybody in racist terms. I'd absolutely count on Mark to save my life."

Carlton was one of the guys I played basketball with early every Monday, Wednesday, and Friday morning. One time, Mark Brown, a black news anchor from Channel 7, showed up at the gym with a camera crew. Mark was a nice guy, so we allowed him to film the game.

Carlton went to the University of Arizona on a basketball scholarship. The man can play hoop. Meanwhile, I'm just a second string player with a decent touch in the corner. I can't go left effectively, and my foot speed is very slow. But I still love the game.

As the game started I was matched up against Carlton. From the first time I held the ball I was faking him, shooting over him, and driving around him. I was looking hot, but I always knew that Carlton pulled back to let me shine.

Walking to pick up my sweatshirt, Mark Brown smiled and said, "You got a pretty nice jump shot." I told him, "If the Lakers want to talk to me, I'll be in the office until five."

We both smiled, shook hands, and went our separate ways. The piece showed that night on the news, but as everyone can probably guess, the Lakers never called.

But stories like the early morning basketball games are good news, and most of the media aren't very interested in that. For every tidbit of truth about me, the media served up a five-course meal of slander and distortion.

While the defense brought up race at every opportunity, I still had to work in Los Angeles handling murders. One case was cited by Vince Bugliosi in his book *Outrage* as an example of my work and racial ethics, but because it is still an open case, he was not privy to all the details. I can now share the full story here.

Between my testimony in the preliminary hearing and the Superior Court trial, Brad Roberts and I were trying to solve the murder of Shawn Stewart, a white man. At first, all the evidence—including witness reports, a vehicle description, tentative identification, and a reported nickname—seemed to point to a black man, Aarick Harris. I obtained a search warrant for his residence, but found nothing except verification of his nickname, "Bo," embroidered on a hat. Harris then called me at the West LA station and said that he heard I was looking for him.

I talked Harris into coming to the station for an interview. When he arrived, he waived his rights and agreed to talk to Brad and me. As the lead detective, I set the pace and direction of the interview. After the first hour or so of the interrogation, Brad and I stepped out into the hall. I immediately told Brad that I didn't have the right feeling about this guy. Brad agreed.

The interrogation became more direct and accusatory. I watched Harris closely, trying to key into his body language. After a long session Brad and I once again stepped outside the interrogation room for a discussion. We didn't think Harris actually shot Stewart, but he definitely knew who did.

I had sufficient evidence to file a case on Harris and hold him for trial. But my gut feeling was that he wasn't guilty. If the crime had been anything but murder, I could have simply continued investigating leaving Harris at large.

But if my gut was wrong and someone was hurt or killed by Harris, the burden would be on my shoulders. I booked Harris and filed the case.

I could have just let the court system either convict or clear Harris, but this was my case, and I planned to see it through. We needed an informant, so I began circulating the rumor around the neighborhood that I wasn't so sure Harris committed the murder.

Within a few days, I received a call from an informant who claimed to have seen someone murder Shawn Stewart, and it wasn't Aarick Harris. Brad and I worked very hard to verify the informant's story and even gave them a polygraph. This person was telling the truth.

But before releasing Harris, I needed to obtain a continuance on the preliminary hearing to try and apprehend the true murderer. To accomplish this I needed to have Harris's attorney agree to a one-week delay. But his attorney, a seemingly inexperienced black female, was trying to play hardball. She demanded either a preliminary hearing or a dismissal. I tried to explain that I was working to clear Harris, but she wouldn't listen.

After overhearing my conversation with Harris's attorney, Ron Phillips interceded, telling the lawyer, "Listen to me. This detective is trying to clear your client, and to tell you the truth, I don't see many detectives working this hard on cases to arrest suspects, let alone let them go. Give him the continuance or we'll just go through the preliminary hearing and then try and clear him, but he'll be in jail a lot longer than one week. We are done talking to you. Goodbye."

Harris's attorney was in shock. Her mouth hung open, but she didn't know what to say. I looked at Ron and said, "You took the words right out of my mouth." She walked out of the station and straight to the court house. We got the continuance.

I knew of the actual suspect; I'd come in contact with him during a separate murder investigation. Brad and I spent a day gathering intelligence information on him and calling state parole. The next day we did a parole search of his residence and arrested him. Unfortunately, we did not find the gun. The case now pivoted on getting a confession, or at least conflicting statements. The suspect would give up nothing.

Although we had an eyewitness, I had given my word that the witness would not be identified. I wouldn't even give the name to the district attorney. The only people who knew the eyewitness's name were Ron, Brad, and me. There are probably many people, even policemen, who think detectives should burn an informant for a murder case. I do not. My word to suspects, informants, and citizens has got to be held as sacred as the oath I took when I became a policeman. In twenty years, I never violated the trust of any person on the street. There exists a mutual respect between street policemen and suspects. Even though we are on opposing sides, we understand the value of a man's word.

I was able to set Aarick Harris free; however, I was never able to bring Shawn Stewart's killer to justice.

If I were a racist, why would I work so hard to free a black man whose guilt seemed obvious to so many others? Why would I work harder than even his own defense attorney to get him off? The Shawn Stewart murder is only one of countless other cases throughout my career that shows it's impossible to be a racist and a good cop at the same time. And I was a good cop, at least when people let me do my job.

I didn't want to admit it, but once the allegations began, my professional life was over. The trial, the media, and even my own department paralyzed my effectiveness as a detective. I loved being a detective probably only second to loving my family, but I knew it was over. I miss policework more than anyone can imagine. I had to leave the force, and several cases I was working on, including the Shawn Stewart murder, remained unsolved.

Racism is the scarlet letter of today's society. A criminal suspect like O.J. Simpson gets presumption of innocence in the court and in the media. But a person who is charged with racism is considered guilty until proven innocent. Since you can't prove a negative, it's almost impossible to convince people that you aren't a racist. Therefore, the charge often sticks. Even for those who refute it, the stigma remains.

For the rest of my life, and even after I am gone, there will be people who believe that I am the horrible person they have heard about through the media. Because they don't know me, or because they refuse to listen, they will think the worst of me.

I can live with that; I don't have any choice. The tragedy is that beneath all the accusations and rhetoric, the world's real racism continues to fester. And in this murder trial, the side issue of race diverted attention from the question of whether O.J. Simpson killed two people.

Chapter 11

LIVING IN A FISHBOWL

Not one of the "Talking Heads" on television . . .
had one good word to say about [Mark] Fuhrman.

—VINCENT BUGLIOSI

THOUGH THE ALLEGATIONS AGAINST ME were all either weak or untrue, the controversy continued. My situation only became more complicated and more difficult. I wasn't desperate or without hope, but I realized that as the trial progressed, the attention and the controversy would only increase.

With the media constantly hounding me at the station, at crime scenes, and everywhere else I went, my detective work was compromised. The media harassed me on the phone, hid outside the station to take my photo, and even tried to follow me in vehicles. Desk officers would call upstairs to warn me that the media had arrived and that I ought to go out by the back of the station.

Although I had previously planned to retire after my twenty years and move out to the country anyway, I now decided to move up the timetable. My retirement would still commence August 4, 1995. But I wanted to get my family out of Los Angeles, away from the media attention, and out of possible harm before that time. In November 1994, we started planning to move.

My family and I were living in Redondo Beach in a house three blocks away from the ocean. We had lived there for seven years, and I spent that whole time renovating our house. We had great neighbors and close friends. And I loved my job. But I had always planned eventually to work in the private sector. I wanted to go into security consulting, or work as a bodyguard, or an insurance investigator. Our two young children were getting close to school age, and we didn't want to send them to the schools in Southern California or have them grow up in the city.

Having grown up in western Washington State, I wanted to move back to the Northwest. But we decided we wanted to live in a town that was slightly larger than my hometown of Eatonville, and I didn't want to go back to the place where I spent the majority of my youth. We wanted to live in a small town in a rural environment, close to nature but with some culture. A friend of mine recommended Sandpoint, Idaho.

We finally put our house on the market in October 1994. I went ahead alone to check out Sandpoint, and it was all that I had hoped. Visiting the town with a good friend of mine from Spokane, I met with a realtor named Rose Chaney. She turned out to be the wife of the mayor, Ron Chaney, and we quickly developed a friendship that continues today. Rose showed me around the area, and I loved it on sight.

By January 1995, we had sold the house in Redondo Beach and bought a house in a nice neighborhood in Sandpoint for less than the price of a one-bedroom condo in Los Angeles. I prepared to move my family to Idaho.

By this time I had already testified in the preliminary hearing. Stories about my supposed racism had been out for months, and the media was engaged in a nonstop feeding frenzy, particularly since I refused to talk to them. In Redondo Beach, the phone had never stopped ringing; reporters camped out in front of our house or left their cards at our door. As long as it was only me they were bothering, I could deal with it. But when the media started bothering my family,

I wouldn't put up with it. I thought that moving out to Sandpoint would end the media harassment of my family. I was wrong.

On a trip, coming back through the Spokane airport for our flight back to Los Angeles, my wife and I went into a waiting area near the gate and a man came up to me. He identified himself as a reporter with the Spokane *Spokesman-Review*. I told him I did not want to talk to him. My wife went off to buy a magazine. The reporter said that he had heard I just bought a house in Sandpoint.

"Why is that news?" I asked. If I had bought a palace in Cancun, maybe that would have been news, but a modest house in a small town in northern Idaho?

My wife came back from the newsstand. She saw me talking to the reporter and signaled to me that he had a microcassette recorder going underneath his notebook.

The reporter asked me a few more questions, which I refused to answer. Then I asked him a question.

"Where do you live?"

"Spokane," he answered.

"How would you like it if I came out to your house, bothered your wife and children?"

Self-promotion or self-preservation appeared to be the dominant motivation of the actors in the Simpson trial, all the way up to Judge Ito himself.

"I wouldn't."

"So, now you understand."

Obviously, he didn't. He asked if his photographer could take a picture. I said no; I didn't want anybody taking a picture of my wife. (For security reasons, obviously.) I don't even know why he asked, since it was clear they were going to do it anyway. The photographer ran ahead and stood in front of my wife and me as we made our way toward the gate. As he snapped several pictures, I held my briefcase out and kept walking straight ahead. The photographer ran into my briefcase, but wouldn't get out of my way. My wife walked off to the side.

"You've got your pictures, now leave us alone," I said.

But he kept shooting.

"Get out of my way," I said, and kept walking forward.

"No." The photographer refused to move.

So I reached up to grab his jacket and as soon as I touched him he collapsed like he was shot. As I stepped over him, I felt embarrassed for him. He got up and called for security. There were eight or nine witnesses who had seen the entire incident and agreed that it was the photographer's fault and he was a jerk. I felt it was a setup; the photographer wanted to provoke me into an altercation so he could have a dramatic story and maybe a lawsuit.

And he got one. The incident played big in the media. The managing editor of the newspaper the photographer worked for wrote a letter to LAPD Chief Willie Williams, which ran in the *Los Angeles Times* and is reprinted here in full:

Dear Chief Williams,

In the heat of the moment, a true professional keeps his cool. Unfortunately, Los Angeles police detective Mark Fuhrman lost his cool in Spokane on Wednesday, January 25.

During the course of a routine interview that evening at Spokane International Airport, detective Fuhrman grew enraged, then hit a Spokesman-Review photographer in the chest with a metal briefcase and proceeded to grab the photographer and force him to his knees, ripping the buttons off the photographer's shirt in the process.

This lapse of professional conduct and show of temper needs to be investigated by your office.

As an editor, I expect my reporters and photographers to keep it together, maintain a professional decorum and treat people with respect. The public expects this of the media. The same should be expected of LAPD officers.

I know Detective Fuhrman has been the center of much attention in relation to the trial of O.J. Simpson. Perhaps he is under stress. Probably he was hoping to find some serenity on his house-hunting trip to Idaho.

But all of this doesn't, in my view, excuse the shoving, yelling and ripping of buttons.

The Spokesman-Review's reporter Bill Morlin and photographer Dan McComb had a job to do Wednesday night. Their job was to interview a police officer who finds himself in the midst of a very big story. Reporter Morlin and photographer McComb maintained a high professional standard of conduct that evening. Upon first recognizing detective Fuhrman and his wife, they let the two finish dinner before approaching them. They identified themselves right away as working press. Witnesses will confirm neither reporter nor photographer raised his voice.

For this, McComb was subjected to profanities and then forced to the ground with a ripped shirt at the hand of detective Fuhrman. I hope you will agree this is conduct unbecoming a police officer. I would urge you to investigate these events and I await your response.

And one more thing. Dan McComb makes $455 per week. He could use a new shirt.

Editorially yours,
Chris Peck
Managing Editor

I've been accused of a lot of things in my life, but ripping buttons has got to be a first. Considering the circumstances, I thought I used incredible restraint and professionalism. But though I am a professional, I'm also a human being. I was in civilian clothes and with my wife on the tail end of a four-day vacation to buy a house. I understand that journalists have rights, but where do our rights come in? Don't we have a right not to be harassed by journalists? I had already given the reporter as much of an interview as I was going to give. And I had allowed the photographer to take photos. Everything beyond that was simply harassment.

Peck got what he asked for. Internal Affairs pursued an exhaustive investigation of the incident. After countless interviews and a report hundreds of pages in length, Internal Affairs completely exonerated me. Eyewitnesses in the airport complained about the two journalists and thought I did nothing out of line. They stated that any physical contact was the photographer's fault, not mine. There were no charges against me and no legal fallout in the trial, because Judge Ito for once ruled that any mention of the incident was not relevant. Oh, and I'm no longer bothered when I go through Spokane Airport.

One last thing: McComb will never get a new shirt from me.

The fact that I retired to Northern Idaho unfortunately dredged up the media stereotype of the area as a hotbed of militia freaks and Nazis. That is completely inaccurate. Sandpoint is less racist, less opinionated, and less plagued with human weaknesses than Brentwood. It's also more tolerant and more diverse than Brentwood. In Sandpoint, people of all races, religions, backgrounds, and economic classes live and work together. Brentwood could learn a lot from the people of Sandpoint.

The headquarters of Aryan Brotherhood is thirty miles south, in Hayden Lake. Thirty miles is a pretty good distance in northern Idaho, but the people of Sandpoint wish the Aryans were even farther away. In the two years I have lived in Sandpoint, I have never seen a Nazi, never talked to one, don't know anybody who has, and don't know anybody who has ever seen them in town. Most of the time, they stay on their compound, but once in a while they come into town in the middle of the night and drop literature, which nobody wants to read and everyone resents, but it starts nice fires. If the people of Sandpoint hate anybody, it's the Aryans. No doubt there are Aryans and other crackpots in Los Angeles or New York, probably more proportionately than there are in northern Idaho. But the media doesn't ever characterize those places as bastions of Nazism.

Our house cleared escrow in late February 1995, and we all drove up to Sandpoint. The moving company was due to arrive a day after us, so we spent our first night at Ron and Rose Chaney's house. The next morning, my wife and kids began settling into the new house. I flew back to Los Angeles to take the stand.

Around the same time, my mother received the following letter from Daryl Gates, former chief of the LAPD.

Dear Mrs. Fuhrman,

Thank you for your thoughtful letter. For some unknown reason I just received it today, obviously it came by way of China. At any rate, I deeply appreciate your kind comments. I, too am very proud of Mark and I know he has done his job "proudly and properly" and very effectively, perhaps too effectively for the O.J. defense lawyers!

Now that the trial is beginning there will be more accusations. You can be assured that I will continue to make my voice heard in support of Mark and other LAPD detectives.

Best always,
Daryl Gates

Chief Gates was right, but I don't believe even he could have predicted that the accusations would be so numerous and so outrageous.

As I flew back to Los Angeles, I did not welcome what awaited me. For months, the defense had painted a picture of me that was at the least not accurate, and most times completely false. Had I been able to address some of these issues and defuse them as they came up in the media, I would have had less of a burden to bear during my testimony. But that was not possible. Although my personal life was being attacked, I had to agree with the department and the prosecution that my professional obligations to them came before any personal concerns for myself and my family. That sounds very strange now that I put it down on paper. But I felt it was my duty. Of course, that sense of duty was not reciprocated by the department or the prosecution. They seemed to put their individual interests first and their professional responsibilities second.

Self-promotion or self-preservation appeared to be the dominant motivation of the actors in the Simpson trial, all the way up to Judge Ito himself.

Chapter 12

THE JUDGE AND HIS WIFE

I have no recollection of the nature of any interactions between then-Officer Fuhrman and me, or any other contacts I may have had with him.

—MARGARET A. YORK SWORN DECLARATION, 11/21/94

READING ON JULY 23, 1994, that Lance Ito had been selected as judge for the Superior Court case just about made me choke on my breakfast. I was still up in Ukiah at the time of his selection, but once I returned to Los Angeles, I went down to Marcia Clark's office and told her about my history of professional conflicts with Ito's wife, police Captain Margaret York. I explained that I thought the judge had a clear conflict of interest, and would at least go after me if not derail the whole case. Marcia said that there was nothing we could do; Ito had already been accepted by both prosecution and defense. When I asked that the presiding judge be made aware of Ito's possible conflict of interest, the answer was still "no."

I can't imagine that Judge Ito didn't hear about me long before he took on the Simpson trial. His wife had known me for almost nine years, during which we had the most negative professional relationship I had experienced in my twenty years on the LAPD. I'm sure that there were some job-related problems that York didn't take home, but as a new lieutenant, she had a monumental problem with one policeman in particular: Mark Fuhrman. It's difficult to believe that she didn't complain about me to her husband.

The problems began in 1985, following the investigation of a supposed group of males at the West LA division called "Men Against Women." The group was reportedly sexist and shunned female police officers. Internal Affairs, the Police Commission, and Inspection and Control investigated the allegations, but no discrimination was found, just a few bad jokes. I was one of the subjects of the investigation, and when York came to West LA, she immediately singled me out and tried to make my life miserable.

"Men Against Women" was a tongue-in-cheek, beer-drinking joke used by officers to blow off steam, make us laugh, and try to forget the impossible job we had in front of us. Some might argue that even as a joke, "Men Against Women" is immature and sexist. Maybe in hindsight I would agree. But at the time, we were trying to relieve the pressure of a difficult situation through humor. The LAPD was in a period of transition and growing pains. Many female officers who had recently been hired were pleasant, intelligent, and competent. Unfortunately, some were not. Politics being what it is, they were trained and supervised with special rules, a hands-off policy, and blanket acceptance of all their conduct, no matter how unsafe. This created frustration among the cops who were asked to train and work with those female officers who were incompetent or inexperienced.

My problems with Margaret York might be dismissed as a disgruntled cop complaining about a strong female leader. But our problems were professional, not personal. I couldn't stand being led by someone who I thought was an inexperienced supervisor, no matter what gender. And I didn't hide it.

The confrontations between York and me were not quiet conflicts. They were loud, frequent, and impossible to ignore. York was so antagonistic toward me that virtually everyone who knew her or me was aware of the situation. York made it clear that she detested me.

When York first came to West LA patrol as a brand-new lieutenant, she appeared uneasy with her new leadership role. After all, from what I know of her career, she was originally assigned to duties other than patrol. Under Chief Ed Davis she attended a limited academy training course that taught patrol skills and allowed her to move into positions that were considered field assignments. In other words, she was field-certified. Now, although she had not worked the streets as a uniformed police officer, she could promote and lead officers who had.

York singled me out. She participated in at least one of my six-month ratings. Ironically, this rating ended in a grievance that I initiated to remove a negative comment that one sergeant told me Lieutenant York had written about me. I won the grievance, and the comment was removed. Even though she had denied writing the comment, she was still angry about this incident and more confrontations between us ensued.

Did Captain Margaret York, Commanding Officer of Internal Affairs Division and wife of Judge Ito, lie to a superior court judge?

When York was the acting captain, she did not waste any time exercising her temporary power. One afternoon, while I was checking out my radio and shotgun before my P.M. watch, York came up and asked to speak with me. I walked several feet away from my fellow police officers and listened as she told me, "Starting tomorrow you will be working day watch so I will be able to watch you."

My surprise at the statement was probably written all over my face.

"No," I responded. "I work P.M. watch. There is a change-of-watch policy, not to mention a memorandum of understanding that dictates when watch change is proper."

"Be here at seven o'clock tomorrow to start day watch," York said curtly.

"I'll be here at 3:30, my regular watch," I replied.

I immediately called the Police Protective League and spoke to Fred Tredy, a League delegate. I knew Fred from Central Division, and after I described York's order he reaffirmed my decision and told me to continue working P.M.

watch. He said he'd take care of the rest. Fred quickly set Lieutenant York straight, and I remained on P.M. watch.

But a strange reassignment soon occurred anyway. Despite the fact that I was one of the most productive patrol officers in the dangerous parts of West LA, I was reassigned to the Pacific Palisades car. Pacific Palisades is one of the wealthiest and safest neighborhoods in Los Angeles. I was used to working a very high crime, gang, and drug area. The reassignment was a rude awakening, and that was precisely York's intent. If she wanted to irritate me, she succeeded.

I also got a new partner, Tasha Ellerson, a black officer who had recently been promoted to P-3, a field training position. Tasha is a nice, quiet person who does her job and minds her own business. Sergeants loyal to me said confidentially that York had paired us because she expected that I wouldn't get along with Tasha. Tasha was subjected to weekly and sometimes daily questioning by a black male sergeant named Paul Enox, who inquired about my conduct. Whatever the motives behind the new pairing, Tasha and I got along fine. York was foiled again.

One incident between York and me became so heated that had we both been men it probably would have ended in a fist-fight. York asked to speak with me and led me into the station conference room. I listened to her description of herself and her method of leadership. She was basically laying the law down to me, and I didn't like it. Our "discussion" kept getting louder until I was at some points yelling at her. She tried to obtain some respect from me by describing her police exploits, but I quickly told her that she had not worked the streets and nothing could substitute for experience, something I thought she did not have. Not only did she lack experience, but in my view she also had no leadership qualities.

Things kept getting worse. It seemed I was spending more time in the station listening to York or one of her henchmen than I spent chasing criminals. On New Year's Eve 1986, Lieutenant York was once again the acting captain. At roll call briefing, the watch commander was emphasizing safety, as that holiday is a dangerous time for firearms. Just as the roll call got under way, York entered the room and made a statement to the watch concerning the vandalism of a poster in the report writing room. The poster, a Martin Luther King Jr. birthday flyer, was defaced with "KKK."

While York was making her statement, I was talking with another policeman in the back of the room and trying to ignore the lieutenant as much as possible. Unfortunately, I spoke loudly in response to my friend's conversation and York immediately thought I was making some sort of joke about her serious statement. York continued threatening the person who committed the vandalism and then without a pause stated: "Fuhrman, I want to see you in the captain's office after roll call."

The officers in roll call turned back toward my seat and made catcalls and snide comments. After roll call was over, I asked what the problem was. York told me that my "snicker" was insensitive and uncalled for. Then she accused me of vandalizing the poster. I was so enraged at the accusation that I almost stumbled over the words that followed. I proclaimed my innocence, but it fell on deaf ears. She handed me an entry on a comment card that described her view of the events in roll call and the insinuation that I had vandalized the poster. She simply said, "Sign it."

I could not contain my anger.

"Not only will I not sign it, I won't even acknowledge it or you," I said. "I don't go around writing on posters or walls. You're way off base."

After I said that, I walked out of the captain's office without a dismissal and went on to do my job.

There were many other conflicts with York that I cannot remember in enough detail to describe completely. But one occurred in 1994 that indicated clearly that York still remembered me and still hated me. One day, I went into the Wilshire Division station to speak with another detective about a case. As I rounded a corner into the main hall, I came face to face with Margaret York, who was the detective commanding officer of that division. From twelve inches away, she looked directly into my eyes and stared. In response, I said "Good morning." It was not a snide or sarcastic "good morning" but a genuine greeting. York continued to stare and then walked away, as if I was invisible. I sensed an animosity so great that she could not even greet me with common courtesy. I had long since stopped being angry at her, and had no desire to continue our hostility.

Although the full story has not been told until now, the Simpson defense team learned about York and me early on. Bill Pavelic wrote a memo to Cochran

and Shapiro on November 17, 1994, saying that he had been told that York had
several run-ins with me. He followed that up with at least two other memos
more than a week later. The media also learned of the connection between us,
and soon the issue was out in the open: If York and I had a history, would our
bad relationship prejudice Judge Ito against me and therefore the prosecution?
Could he be impartial? Should he step down?

After the initial media reports that York had served as my superior officer
in West LA, she was ordered to give a deposition concerning our professional
relationship. On November 21, 1994, York made a signed declaration concerning
me. In the declaration, she claimed that she could remember very little about
our professional relationship, except my name and possibly my face. As
Lawrence Schiller reported in his book, "The defense could now upset the trial
if need be. Somewhere down the line, Captain York's declaration would be a
valuable weapon."

What follows is her signed declaration, dated November 21, 1994, given
under oath and penalty of perjury in the chambers of Judge Curtis Rappe. I
reprint it in full so that it is clear that I have not used any quotations out of context.

I, Margaret A. York, hereby declare as follows:

1. I make and submit this declaration for use in the case entitled,
    "People of the State of California vs. Orenthal James Simpson,"
    Los Angeles Superior Court No. BA 097211. If called as a witness
    I could and would testify competently to the following:

2. I have been employed as a police officer by the Los Angeles Police
    Department ("LAPD") since April 2, 1968. I presently hold the
    rank of Captain II, and I am currently assigned as the command-
    ing officer of the Bunco-Forgery Division.

3. In February 1985 I was promoted to the rank of lieutenant and
    assigned to the West Los Angeles Area as a watch commander. I
    continued in that assignment until May 1986, at which time I was
    transferred to the Office of the Chief of Police.

4. West Angeles is one of the eighteen geographic divisions of
    LAPD. It, like each of the other geographic divisions, provides
    police patrol services for the residents and businesses of the area.

At the time of my tenure at West Los Angeles, the total number of sworn personnel assigned there was, to the best of my recollection, approximately 175.

5. A watch commander is defined by the Manual of the Los Angeles Police Department ("Manual") as the employee having charge of a specific watch (shift) in a division or geographic area. A watch commander is a second-level supervisor; that is, direct supervision of patrol officers is the responsibility of sergeants, who are subordinate to the watch commander. The duties of a watch commander at West Los Angeles when I was assigned there were to oversee field operations, assign duties, train personnel, review and recommend resolution of personnel matters including training deficiencies and discipline, inspect facilities and personnel, approve bookings and reports, approve evaluation of work performance, respond to emergency tactical situations, and oversee general management of watch activities.

6. When I was assigned to West Los Angeles in 1985, I do not recall being given any assignment, charge, or instructions to do anything other than perform the routine and normal duties of a watch commander with LAPD. Specifically, I do not recall being assigned, instructed, or charged to investigate the existence or behavior of a group referred to as "MAW" or "Men Against Women." Furthermore, I do not recall that at any time during my assignment at West Los Angeles was I given an assignment, instruction or charge of that nature. I believe that if I had been given such as assignment, instruction, or charge that I would recall it.

7. During my assignment at West Los Angeles, I served at different times as watch commander of each of its patrol watches, and therefore was in a position to have most of West Los Angeles patrol officers service in the watches which I commanded. I also served as Acting Commanding Office of West Los Angeles area during part of that time.

8. I recall that Mark Fuhrman was among the officers assigned to patrol at West Los Angeles during the period that I was a watch

commander there. It was my practice as a watch commander to interact with officers serving in the watches which I commanded. Such interactions could be for many purposes, including the discussion of tactical matters, personnel matters, personal matters, and other matters. The interactions could be organized and planned, incidental or spontaneous. I have no recollection of the nature of any interactions between then-Officer Fuhrman and me, or any other contacts I may have had with him.

9.   In preparing this declaration I have relied only upon my recollections and my experience as a police officer and employee of LAPD. Except for my own personnel records, which I reviewed to determine the dates of my assignment to West Los Angeles, or the Manual, I have not reviewed any documents or records of any sort in order to prepare this declaration. I do not know with any certainty what records may exist which bear on the matters discussed in this declaration, nor do I know what those records may contain.

10. Since my assignment at West Los Angeles nearly ten years ago, I have had the responsibility of command over hundreds of officers. I have promoted to Captain and have been the commanding officer of three separate Divisions in LAPD. I have written, reviewed or approved hundreds of reports, and I have interacted with hundreds of officers, sergeants and lieutenants. My present inability to recollect specific instances or circumstances from my time at West Los Angeles is due to the volume of work and the number of employees for which I have had the responsibility and to the passage of time.

I declare under penalty of perjury that all of the above is true and correct of my own personal knowledge.

Executed this 21st day of November, 1994 at Los Angeles, California

/s/ Margaret A. York

When I read this declaration, I was stunned at the position she took concerning me. It was almost as if she didn't know who I was.

York's statements to Judge Rappe are at least problematic, for the friction between her and me was no secret. Dozens of police officers knew about it. In 1992 when West LA detectives were about to get a new commanding officer, rumors circulated that York might get the position. I received calls from many officers and detectives joking that I might as well transfer if York came to West LA. In fact, the joke had a good bit of truth to it. I would have had to transfer, because York would have made working there unbearable for me.

In paragraph six of her declaration, York states that she does not recall being assigned to investigate "Men Against Women." This claim was contradicted by none other than LAPD Chief Daryl Gates himself. On national television, Gates said that Margaret York was sent to West LA to follow up on the investigation of sexist attitudes and the group "Men Against Women." On *Inside Edition*, after Chief Gates described the investigation, he said about York: "We sent her there for the very purpose of looking at the situation to make sure it no longer continued to exist." It is also worth noting that following her tenure in West LA, Margaret York was assigned to Chief Gates's office.

Jim Wakefield, my old sergeant from the Task Force unit at West LA, told a reporter that York had been sent there by Chief Gates to investigate "Men Against Women." He also said that York was privy to all the information concerning the prior investigation.

Don Evans, a senior lead officer of West LA, now retired, also went on television and described York's obsession with "Men Against Women" and her negative contacts with me. Evans worked the same watch as I, but we had only a casual friendship and worked together only a few times and never as regular partners. He didn't make these statements to stick up for me, or to stick it to Margaret York. His only motivation was the truth. In his interview, Evans made statements to the effect that he himself was "Men Against Women," that he was responsible for the joke, and he had perpetuated its fantasy existence. Evans found it difficult to believe that York lives with and sleeps with Ito, yet she never mentioned anything about me.

In paragraph eight, York states that she remembers me. *How* does she remember me? I work with divisions of officers, and I can't remember most of their names or faces. It is officers with whom I've had either good or bad relationships that I remember. That isn't the case with York. I find it difficult to believe that she doesn't remember our conflicts. But if she doesn't, then how does she remember me at all?

In paragraph ten, York provides a blanket disclaimer for her memory. Stating that she was responsible for many officers and read hundreds of reports, York claims that the volume of her work made it difficult for her to remember specific events or individuals. I'm glad that York has been so able to put our difficulties behind her that she now no longer remembers them. Perhaps the next time we meet, she'll say "Good morning."

Around the same time as her declaration, news reports quoted York as saying I was a "productive officer." While there were no statements like that in her declaration, the quotes must have come from somewhere. If she did think I was a productive officer, why did she do everything she could to curtail my effectiveness? She subjected me to intense scrutiny, both by herself and her subordinates. This attention was unwarranted and also undocumented. Perhaps that's why she finds it so difficult to remember.

York was also quoted as saying, "I possess no relevant material or personal knowledge of Officer Fuhrman, nor do I possess any information relevant to this [O.J. Simpson] case."

The same news reports also contained the defense's claims that not only was I investigated for "Men Against Women," but I was also "the subject of an internal investigation of charges that he used excessive force and that he harbored racist attitudes." Of course, if those investigations did occur, they came up empty because I never heard of them. But the defense didn't want to waste an opportunity to smear me.

In the trial, Johnnie Cochran first made a motion to call York as a witness. But then he withdrew the motion. Why would Cochran want to overcomplicate an already complicated defense strategy by calling the judge's wife as a witness to a supposedly sexist complaint? There was no relevance to sexism in the case, and no female defendant involved. There was nothing that York and I engaged in that had any bearing on this case whatsoever. It had bearing only on Judge Ito.

Cochran received an unsigned statement from Donald Evans. The statement reads, in part:

"Captain York was also directly involved in internal affairs investigations which centered on Detective Fuhrman that [concerned] alleged gender and racial bias. Captain York also personally counseled Detective Fuhrman regarding these issues while I was stationed with the two of them at West Los Angeles station, but I have read her declaration and she is factually inaccurate."

Why didn't Cochran use this statement in court? Was it because he preferred to have Ito on the bench, knowing he had material information that the judge's wife had been less than truthful?

If York remembered our professional relationship the way I did, or even came close, the inference would be that she harbored animosities that would have been conveyed to the closest person in her life, her husband Judge Ito. Had she not talked to Ito about me, then it seems to me that describing our problems to Judge Rappe would have been irrelevant, because she could truthfully say that she never mentioned me to Ito. By failing to remember me except as a name in roll call, she put more distance between the two of us than would have been necessary, unless she had something to hide.

Judge Ito might have recused himself. But he didn't. Instead, he remained on the case, putting himself in a vulnerable position that the defense could have exploited at any time.

The controversy surrounding York, Ito, and me is something that the media could have investigated further, but didn't. The evidence was there. The people were available to interview; why didn't the media pursue it? Needless to say, Marcia Clark let this slip away and we were left with Lance Ito presiding over the trial. It was the first mistake Marcia made, but not the only one.

Let's assume that York never mentioned me to Ito nine years ago. Let's assume she was unlike just about every other married professional and didn't take her work home with her. Along comes the preliminary hearing of a celebrity murder case. Would an LAPD captain and a Superior Court judge not watch any of the coverage? After my testimony in the preliminary hearing, I was on television several times, day and evening. Newspapers covered the hearings and my testimony extensively. Is it really possible that York never commented about me to her husband?

There are dozens of officers and detectives I could name who would corroborate the professional relationship Margaret York and I had in 1985 and

1986. I would gladly provide these names to county or state investigators attempting to learn the facts surrounding her statements to Judge Rappe. I would equally cooperate with the LAPD's Internal Affairs personnel, as their interest should be of a higher level; after all, York actually supervises this sensitive division.

Did Captain Margaret York, Commanding Officer of Internal Affairs Division, lie to a Superior Court judge? Did she do it in a willful attempt to deceive not only the judge, but the judicial system as well? If she did, then not only did York's conduct affect the outcome of the Simpson trial, but she could possibly have affected it more than any one person.

The defense played the race card, but Ito let them. Although armed with relevant case law concerning the racial issues in the case, which clearly dictated that race should not be an issue, Ito allowed it to become one. He allowed the defense to spin their bizarre conspiratorial fantasies throughout the trial. He had a choice: He could have controlled the courtroom and the trial, or he could let the defense get away with their race-baiting and lies. For whatever reasons, personal, legal, or political, Ito chose the road most devastating to me, the one player in the trial who had an adversarial relationship with his wife. He allowed the trial of O.J. Simpson to become the trial of Mark Fuhrman. The most tragic result was not my own difficulties which arose from the trial, but how the families of the two victims were cheated from watching O.J. Simpson sit behind bars for the rest of his life.

Chapter 13

THE EVIDENCE

T HE BUNDY MURDERS were not as complicated as they were depicted to be. Any experienced detective could tell you that the suspect would be hard pressed to leave any more evidence than the murderer did. The only way the evidence could be more incriminating to O.J. Simpson would be if he had left a videotape of himself committing the murders.

What follows is an annotated list of the major pieces of evidence found in the investigation.

PHYSICAL EVIDENCE

The suspect in the Bundy murders entered that property wearing two gloves. The left-handed glove was dropped at Bundy and the right-handed glove was discarded at Rockingham.

ON THE GLOVE FOUND AT BUNDY

1. One hair from Nicole.
2. Fibers with blood on them consistent with fibers from Ron's shirt.
3. Fibers consistent with those of Ron's jeans.
4. Dog hair from the Akita.

The glove at Bundy was not an innocently discarded item of clothing. Bloody fibers from Ron's shirt had been transferred onto the glove. That glove definitely came into contact with Ron. There were also fibers consistent with Ron's jeans on the glove, another corroborative indication that the glove came into contact with his body in at least two places. From the dog hair, we can conclude two things: that the dog's hair was prevalent throughout the entire property at Bundy, and that the dog probably investigated the bodies after they had fallen.

ON THE ROCKINGHAM GLOVE

1. Several hairs from Nicole, one with blood on it.
2. Three hairs from Ron, ripped or torn from his head.
3. Fibers consistent with those from Ron's shirt.
4. A number of hairs from the Akita.
5. One unusual type of fiber from the Bronco's carpet.
6. Blue-black cotton fibers consistent with similar fibers found on Ron's shirt.

The Rockingham glove was shown to be a match with the Bundy glove. It had many pieces of evidence that connected both crime scenes. The Rockingham glove, worn by the murderer, held the knife that committed the murders. On this glove, we have the blood of both victims and of Simpson himself. We have hairs from Nicole, one with blood on it. Three hairs from Ron, ripped or torn from his head. We have additional fibers consistent with Ron's shirt, one fiber from the Bronco carpet, and blue-black cotton fibers consistent with similar fibers found on Ron's shirt and consistent with the apparel Simpson was seen wearing earlier in the evening by Kato Kaelin.

Reviewing the evidence on both gloves, we could conclude that whoever had these gloves on was involved in the death of both Ron and Nicole. The physical evidence on these gloves connects them irrefutably as the right and left hand of the murderer. Notwithstanding any further evidence, we have connected the two murdered victims to O.J. Simpson. He can't account for his whereabouts the hour of the murders. He can't account for the cut on his finger. And how his blood could have gotten on the Rockingham glove was never addressed. Absent anything else, the Rockingham glove should have been enough to convict him.

THE SOCKS FROM THE MASTER BEDROOM

1. Blue-black cotton fibers.
2. Blood from Simpson and Nicole.

The blue-black cotton fibers are no doubt from the clothes that Simpson wore the night of the murders. Now we have the same fibers found on Ron's shirt, the Rockingham glove, and the socks found in Simpson's bedroom. This, by itself, would loosely connect the Rockingham glove and the socks found in his bedroom. But when it was discovered that Simpson's and Nicole's blood both were found on the socks, this put a bleeding Simpson at the scene after Nicole was cut.

The defense's theory that the Rockingham glove was planted and the socks were splashed with blood seems ridiculous considering that whoever supposedly committed these acts would also have had to make sure that both items had the same blue-black fibers on them.

ON RON GOLDMAN'S SHIRT

1. One hair consistent with Simpson's.
2. Twenty-five hairs from Nicole.
3. Several hairs from the Akita.
4. Four torn fibers from Nicole's dress.
5. Several fibers from the knit cap.
6. One fiber consistent with the cashmere lining of both gloves.
7. Many blue-black fibers.

Although the Rockingham glove and the black dress socks are very incriminating, Ron Goldman's shirt is an important piece of evidence. On the shirt we have one hair consistent with Simpson's, plus many blue-black fibers. We have one fiber consistent with the cashmere lining of both gloves. We have several fibers from the knit cap found at the Bundy scene, and two of the most important pieces of evidence that the shirt gives us: four torn fibers from Nicole's dress, which probably could have been transferred only if Nicole had been involved in a physical confrontation with the suspect before his contact with Goldman. The dress fibers and the twenty-five hairs from Nicole show me that Ron had contact with Nicole physically, no matter how slight, before Simpson engaged him in a battle for his life.

Of the items of evidence described thus far, we can make some absolute connections. At the time of the murders, Simpson is forever connected to both gloves, the knit cap, both victims, and the Bronco.

ON RON GOLDMAN'S PANTS

1.   Several hairs consistent with Nicole's.
2.   Several hairs from the Akita.

There were no hairs from Ron on Nicole's body or dress. This would indicate that Ron made contact with Nicole in such a way that he left no trace evidence. Considering the position of Nicole's body slumped on the steps of the Bundy residence, when Goldman would have first approached her, Nicole's hair would come in direct contact with his body. But Ron's hair would not come in contact with hers.

ON THE BLUE KNIT CAP FOUND AT BUNDY

1.   Several hairs from the Akita.
2.   Twelve hairs matching that of O.J. Simpson's. All these hairs were naturally shed, not ripped. Ten came from the inside of the cap and two from the outside.
3.   Several fibers consistent with Ron's shirt.
4.   One fiber consistent with the cashmere lining of both gloves.
5.   One unusual fiber consistent with the Bronco's carpet.

Simpson's hair was all over the knit cap. The placement of the hairs on the cap suggests they were shed naturally as he wore it. Nobody planted the cap on his head. There is no way he could argue that it wasn't his. He is connected to the cap at the murder scene. The transfer of the fibers consistent with Ron's shirt no doubt occurred during the struggle when the cap was pulled from Simpson's head.

BLOOD EVIDENCE

(All matches are based on Cellmark Diagnostics and Department of Justice DNA lab reports)

The blood evidence in this case is total and absolute incrimination of O.J. Simpson. Not one particle of blood evidence points to anyone other than Simpson and the two victims.

BLOOD EVIDENCE AT BUNDY

1. Blood drop near victims matching Simpson's.
2. Four blood drops on walkway all matching Simpson's.
3. Blood on rear gate matching Simpson's.
4. Two footprints of size twelve Bruno Magli loafers in blood matching Nicole's.
5. Blood stain from Ron's boot matched both his and Nicole's.

The blood from the footprints was tested and proved to be Nicole's blood. Further evidence at the Bundy scene still irrefutably connects Simpson to these murders. A blood drop near the victims matched Simpson's. The blood drops on the walkway to the left of the bloody shoeprints matched Simpson's. The blood on the rear gate where the suspect exited also matched Simpson's. The shoeprints matched Simpson's shoe size and were the distinct impression of a pair of expensive casual shoes that Simpson was later proved to have owned, which he denied owning until a photograph of him wearing them was produced. Then he claimed the photograph was a fraud.

Once the evidence was disseminated and analyzed, the progression of the murders could at least be generally stated, and the murderer's actions, the evidence he left at the scene, and the way he exited from the property were completely documented. Everything pointed to one and only one person—O.J. Simpson.

THE BRONCO

1. Blood drop matching Simpson's found on driver's door interior, and in two places on instrument panel.
2. Blood on the steering wheel matched a mixture of Simpson's and Nicole's.
3. Blood on center console matched Simpson's.
4. More blood on center console matched both Simpson's and Goldman's.
5. Blood on driver's side wall matched Simpson's.
6. Blood on carpet matched Nicole's.
7. Several blood samples on center console matched Simpson's, Ron's, and Nicole's together.

Although most of the evidence consisted of undocumented personal belongings, the Bronco is irrefutably tied to Simpson. What makes the Bronco crucial to the case is that Simpson admitted driving it the day before, told Vannatter and Lange that he had bled in it, and it was not at the Rockingham estate when Allan Park arrived at 10:20 P.M.

Not only does the Bronco contain blood from Simpson, it also contains blood from Nicole and Ron. How could Simpson ever explain the presence of Ron Goldman's blood inside his car?

The above is yet another piece of evidence that has the blood of all three parties. It is another unexplainable circumstance; it is another piece of evidence which Simpson or the defense team never successfully explained. One of F. Lee Bailey's theories was that I not only supposedly daubed blood on the exterior door, but then entered the Bronco and smeared blood in various places. The evidence says otherwise. Not only could I not isolate blood between Simpson and the two victims, but where the blood is and who it belongs to is consistent with how it was transferred there.

The blood on the steering wheel matched a mixture of Simpson's and Nicole's. We know his left hand was injured and ungloved, and the right hand was gloved and has blood from both victims' and himself. The blood on the center console matched Simpson's and Goldman's, more evidence that it was from the right glove. There were other blood samples that matched both victims' and Simpson's, clearly from the right-handed glove. Conversely, the one place where Simpson's blood is absent of either victim's is on the driver's door interior surfaces and on the instrument panel—he had to turn on the headlights. His left hand is bleeding. The blood on the carpet matched Nicole's, consistent with the evidence that the murderer walked in Nicole's blood and left bloody shoeprints trailing toward the alley.

BLOOD EVIDENCE AT ROCKINGHAM

1. Blood on the glove matched Ron's.
2. Four blood samples on a sock. Two matched Nicole's, and two matched Simpson's.
3. Blood drops in the foyer matched Simpson's.
4. Blood trail on the driveway matched Simpson's.

The Rockingham estate provided the Rockingham glove and an unchallenged corroborative source of the deposit of the glove by Kato Kaelin. Although the theory of the planted glove got a lot of press, nobody seemed to care who caused the thumps that Kaelin heard. It certainly wasn't me. And Kaelin had no reason to make it up. This at least was one aspect of his testimony that was irrefutable, and interestingly, he was never pressured to change it.

The reasoning was twofold. The defense wanted a reason to put me back behind Kato's bungalow, when I would have had an opportunity to plant the glove. Knowing full well that my early interrogation of Kaelin, corroborated by other detectives, could not eliminate his statement, they had to use it to their advantage. Yet, they never answered the question: Who made the thumps on the wall? In a gated residence in an upscale community at the same time a limo was in the driveway and lights were on in the house, these thumps sounded so suspicious that Kato went out to investigate, and was even scared to walk down the path.

Despite these suspicions, Simpson decided not to call the police or even his private security firm. Simpson was emphatic that he didn't want Kato to call the police or Westec. Later, calling Kato from the limo, Simpson told him to turn the alarm back on, something he had never asked Kato to do before. If anyone but Simpson himself caused the thumps, wouldn't he have wanted them investigated?

SIMPSON'S OWN EVIDENCE

Simpson's own doctor testified that the defendant had seven abrasions and three cuts on his left hand. A left-handed glove was found at the Bundy scene. Is this more than a coincidence, considering all the aforementioned evidence?

Let's review Simpson's various explanations of how these injuries occurred:

1. Rushing to get ready for his trip to Chicago, maybe cut on a coat hanger.
2. Retrieving his cellular phone from the Bronco before his departure for Chicago.
3. Chipping golf balls just before he left for Chicago.
4. Cutting himself on a broken glass in Chicago.

Looking at these possibilities, I see one stark contradiction. Most of these would be right-handed functions. After all, Simpson is right-handed. During any of these activities, he might have received a cut on his right hand. Simpson's right hand did not have any cuts or abrasions. A right-handed glove was found at Rockingham.

How do we explain three cuts and seven abrasions on his left hand, but nothing on his right? I find it hard to believe that anyone cuts himself on a coat hanger. I never considered golf a dangerous contact sport. And picking up a cellular flip phone from a car seldom results in bloodshed. The only reasonable explanation is the broken glass in Chicago. Maybe he did cut himself in Chicago—but a total of ten different injuries from one broken glass?

If the only plausible explanation for Simpson's cuts occurred in Chicago the morning after the murders, why did he admit to Vannatter and Lange that he bled in his Bronco, on his property, and in his house the night of the murders? Where did that blood come from? By Simpson's own admission, he was either attacked by a golf club, assaulted by a coat hanger, a cellular phone bit him, or a broken glass flew across the room and cut his hand. This is the most accident-prone man on earth. Is there anyone else in America who, within twelve hours, could suffer three cuts and seven abrasions to one hand, bleed in his house, car, on his property, and in a hotel room in another state, yet not remember how he cut himself?

CIRCUMSTANTIAL EVIDENCE

While the defense attorneys dismissed a lot of this evidence as circumstantial, in fact it was much, much more than what usually convicts other defendants.

Vince Bugliosi makes the point that circumstantial evidence is not a chain, but a rope. "And each fact is a strand of that rope.... If one strand does break, the rope is not broken. The strength of the rope is barely diminished" (*Outrage*, p. 215). Such is the case with the circumstantial evidence against Simpson. The level of coincidence for all these events to have different explanations other than Simpson's committing the murders is simply beyond reasonable belief.

There are only two kinds of evidence, circumstantial and eyewitness. Circumstantial includes physical and scientific evidence. With eyewitnesses, you have victim(s) or other people who viewed the crime or the suspect.

Having interviewed thousands of people who observed the commission of a crime, there's one thing that I've learned. Eyewitness testimony is sometimes weak, conflicting, or confused. The circumstantial evidence that we had in this case had no agenda, no opinion, nothing to live up to, and it did not have an ego. It was based on scientific facts that even the defense would have to admit were irrefutable. Had the defense found the same type of evidence to exonerate Simpson, their argument would have been completely reversed. But they had not one piece of eyewitness testimony or circumstantial evidence or even a believable story.

THE "ALIBI"

The most obvious alibi that Simpson could claim is that he was in Chicago or en route to Chicago at the time of the murders. This is why the defense tried to establish the time of death of both victims after 11:00 P.M. But they couldn't. And Simpson had no alibi or even a consistent story about where he was and what he was doing between 10 and 11 P.M. on the night of June 12, 1994.

The defense's attempt, through the flawed testimony of Rosa Lopez, to put the Bronco curbside on Rockingham prior to 10:00 P.M. is another example of their creating an alibi where one didn't exist.

As Allan Park testified, he drove down Rockingham, and at 10:22 the white Bronco was not there. At 10:40 P.M., Park began ringing the buzzer at the gate, which caused a phone to ring inside the house, a phone that could be heard all the way out on the street and no doubt could be heard clearly throughout the house. Park continued ringing until shortly after 10:54 P.M. Park buzzed once again, and it was finally answered by Simpson, who claimed he had overslept and just gotten out of the shower. At this time, the Bronco was now parked on Rockingham.

As previously described, Simpson's claim as to how he injured his hand is in actuality part of his alibi. After all, he was (a) playing golf, (b) getting his cellular phone from the Bronco, or (c) getting ready to leave for Chicago. I thought he had overslept. Did he cut himself sleeping, too?

Had Simpson been sleeping, does he sleep so soundly that he does not hear a phone ringing for fourteen minutes? Why did he hear the phone only after Allan Park saw the figure in the doorway?

The reason is obvious. Simpson wasn't in the house. He never went out to the Bronco to get his cellular phone, he never chipped golf balls, and he did not cut himself packing. While Park was trying to ring him, Simpson was at the murder scene.

CONCLUSION

Together, there were 488 exhibits presented by the prosecution in the trial, and every piece of their evidence pointed to O.J. Simpson. While the defense made a lot of noise about Colombian hitmen and mysterious accomplices, they didn't find one scrap of evidence indicating that anyone other than Simpson had been at the murder scene.

Confronted with all this evidence, I simply can't believe how anyone could not conclude that Simpson was guilty beyond a reasonable doubt. While there were problems with the handling and preservation of evidence, the sheer mass of incriminating evidence makes it impossible to believe that all of it was either analyzed incorrectly or planted.

The prosecution was right in saying there was a mountain of evidence. In fact, there was a Mt. Everest of evidence—and all of it pointed to O.J. Simpson. All that was necessary was that the evidence be carefully documented, collected, and analyzed—and then used effectively at the trial. But it wasn't.

Part Two

THE TRIAL

Chapter 14

THE PROSECUTION'S CASE

The prosecution just couldn't keep it sharp and simple. It was like they were never sure how to say what they needed to tell us...mostly their presentation was truly pathetic; sloppy, badly organized, and rarely eloquent even when the evidence itself was powerful.

—JUROR MICHAEL KNOX

OPENING ARGUMENTS in the trial of O.J. Simpson for the murder of Nicole Brown and Ron Goldman began on January 23, 1995. Because I was ordered not to watch the trial, I didn't. Only later did I review transcripts of the opening statements. From the onset, this was not prosecuted as a brutal double murder, because the defendant was O.J. Simpson. There should have been fire and brimstone in Marcia's voice during her opening statements. She should have pointed at Simpson and shouted his guilt, telling the jury to look into the eyes of the murderer.

Instead, she gave a testament to Simpson's status in the world, and expressed regret for prosecuting him. Reading some of Marcia's opening statement, I could have sworn she was arguing for the defense. It's tough to make a believable accusation of murder when you're busy smiling and apologizing. The jury wasn't stupid. They knew who Simpson was, and they knew Marcia was a prosecutor. She didn't have to apologize for doing her job. This was silly, unnecessary, and done just for the cameras.

Once the case was under way, this weak-willed attitude was directed not only to the defendant, but to the evidence itself. Several pieces of evidence were abandoned because they seemed too difficult to track down, prove, or explain. The prosecution had so much incriminating evidence, they were like little children on Christmas morning who just couldn't figure out which package to open first. Yet, once all the packages were opened, they played with only a few of the toys. Throughout the trial, the prosecution used evidence selectively, ignoring anything that didn't fit their neat theories or couldn't be explained without more extensive investigation.

Twenty years of policework have taught me this: You have to listen to the evidence and follow where it leads. While you might have theories about the way a crime occurred, you never want to commit your case to a single chain of events until you have strong and convincing evidence that this is the only reasonable probability.

During the investigation, the Robbery/Homicide detectives did not pursue many potential leads because they were overwhelmed by the case and wedded to a certain chain of events. They locked themselves into specific theories about how the murders occurred, and their devotion to these theories blinded them to other possibilities. Their need to figure out exactly what happened made it impossible for them to discover what really did occur.

The prosecution made similar mistakes in the trial. Clearly, they, like just about everybody else involved in the case, were intimidated by the celebrity defendant. The first witnesses in the prosecution's case were domestic violence witnesses. The prosecution didn't think they could prove Simpson's guilt unless they could show a strong motive and change the jury's image of a popular sports hero and celebrity into a man capable of killing two people with a knife. This is why they presented the case against Simpson as a domestic violence case that involved murder, rather than a murder case in which the suspect was also a wife-beater.

They did not present the far more credible theory of a love triangle murder (even if the triangle existed only in Simpson's mind), because they didn't think the jury would be sympathetic to a couple of victims who might have been sleeping together.

They did not think they could convince the jury that Simpson had opportunity unless they nailed the time of the murders down to the minute.

They did not want to use any evidence that might possibly be construed as a claim of innocence by the defendant. Therefore, they kept some of his most incriminating statements and actions out of the trial.

They did not want to use any evidence they considered tainted, and therefore lost the chance to make several important arguments. And they didn't use some very critical evidence or key witnesses, for reasons only they understand.

The fingerprint Brad and I saw on the rear gate was either lost or destroyed. The Swiss Army knife box we found in the master bathroom was never introduced, even though we were explicitly told by the Robbery/Homicide detectives to look for a knife or knife packaging. The bubble gum I found weeks after the murders was never used, or probably never even investigated. The piece of wood I found by the Bronco was never sufficiently explained in court. The gauze wrapper I found behind Kato's bungalow was never even used. These are the pieces of evidence I had personal knowledge of. How much other evidence was similarly neglected?

> **I always believed that Ron and Nicole were lovers.**

In addition to their not taking full advantage of the physical evidence available to them, the prosecution consistently refused to use Simpson's own words and actions against him. These statements and events seemed clear indications of guilt, but were not used by the prosecution because they feared that introducing them into the trial would give the defendant sympathy or an apparent claim of innocence.

Simpson's escape and the slow-speed Bronco chase were not introduced during the trial. Here he was, fleeing from arrest, armed with a gun, and either holding a hostage or aided by an accomplice. In his possession was a loaded pistol, a disguise, and nearly $9,000 in cash. If these circumstances don't indicate guilt, I don't know what does. An effective prosecutor would have argued that an innocent man does not try to escape. Simpson's "suicide note" was also never. It is a strange document and deserves consideration. I present it here exactly how it was written. [See facsimile starting next page.]

①

To WHom, I MAY CONCERN   6/15/94

FIRST EVERYONE UNDERSTAND ~~TO~~ ~~~~
NOTHING TO DO WITH NICOLE'S MURDER.
I Loved HER, ALLWAYS HAVE AND
Always Will. IF WE HAD A PROMBLEM
ITS BECAUSE I Loved Her So MUCH.
RECITLY WE CAME TO THE UNDERSTANDING
THAT FOR NOW WE WEREN'T RIGHT FOR
EACH OTHER AT ~~LEAST~~ FOR NOW. DISPITE
OUR love WE WERE DIFFERENT AND
THATS WHY WE MUATWALLY AGReed TO
GO OUR SPAERATE WAYS. IT WAS
TOUGH SPITTING FOR A SECOND Time
BUT WE BOTH KNEW IT WAS FOR THE
BEST. INSIDE I HAD NO ~~DOUBT~~ THAT
IN THE FUTURE WE WOULD BE CLOSE
AS FRIEND OR MORE.

     UNLike WHATS BEEN IN THE
PRESS, NICOLE + I HAD A GREAT RELATIONSH
FOR MOST OF OUR LiVES TOGETHER. LiKe
ALL LONG TERM RELATIONSHIPS WE HAD A
FEW DOWNS + UPS, I TOOK THE HEAT New
YEARS 1989 BECAUSE THAT WHAT I WAS
SUPPOSE TO DO I DID NOT PLEA NO CONTE
FOR ANY OTHER REASON BUT TO PROTECT OUR
PRIVIQY AND WAS ADViSE ~~IT~~ "I would" END THE
PRESS HYPE. ~~KNOCKING~~ I DON'T WANT TO
BELABOR ~~KICKING~~ THE PRESS BUT I CANT

②

BELEIVE WHAT'S BEING SAID. MOST
OF IT TOTTALLY MADE UP. I KNOW
YOU HAVE A JOB TO DO BUT AS
A LAST WISH, PLEASE, PLEASE, PLEASE
LEAVE MY CHILDREN IN PEACE THEIR
LIVES WILL BE TOUGHT ENOUGH.

         I WANT TO SEND MY LOVE AND
THANKS TO ALL MY FRIEND I'M SORRY
I CAN'T NAME EVERYONE OF YOU. ESPECILL
AC, MAN THANKS FOR BEING IN MY LIFE.
THE SUPPORT AND FRIENDSHIP I RELEIVE FROM
AAL PACKER So MANY. WAYNE HUGHES, LOUIS MARX, FRANK
THE BACK OHSON, BENDER, BOBBY KARDASHIAN I WISH
WE HAD SPEND MORE TIME TOGETHER IN
RECITO YEARS. MY GOLFING BUDDIE HASS,
ALLEN AUSTIO, MIKE, CRAIG BENDER, WYLER, SANDY, JAY
DONNIE SOFER, THANK FOR THE FUN. ALL MY
TEAMMATE OVER THE YEARS. REGGIE, YOU WERE
THE SOUL OF MY PRO CAREER. AHMAD I NEVER
STOP BEING PROUD OF YOU. MARCUS YOU GOT
A GREAT LADY IN KATHERINE DON'T MESS IT
UP. BOBBY CHANDLER THANKS FOR ALWAYS BEING THEIR
SKIP & CATHY I LOVE YOU GUYS WITHOUT YOU
I NEVER WOULD HAVE MADE IT THIS FAR.
MARQUERITE. THANKS FOR THOSE EARLY YEARS
WE HAD SOME FUN.
    PAULA. WHAT CAN I SAY YOU ARE

SPECIAL I'M SORRY WE'RE ~~NOT~~ NOT GOIN'
TO HAVE OUR CHANCE. GOD BROUGHT
YOU TO ME I NOW SEE, AS I LEAVE
YOU'LL BE IN MY THOUGHTS.

    I THINK OF MY LIFE AND
FEEL I'V DONE MOST OF THE RIGHT
THINGS SO WHY DO I END UP LIKE THIS
I CAN'T GO ON, NO MATTER WHAT THE
OUTCOME PEOPLE WILL LOOK AND POINT.
~~...~~
~~I~~ I CAN'T TAKE THAT I CAN'T SUBJECT
MY CHILDREN TO THAT. THIS WAY THEY
CAN. moveⁿ AND GO ON WITH THAIR LIVES
PLEASE IF I'V DONE ANYTHING WORTHWHIL
IN MY LIFE. LET MY KIDS LIVE IN PEACE
FROM YOU (PRESS).

    I'V HAD A GOOD LIFE. I'm
PROUD OF HOW I LIVED, MY MAMA TOUGHT
ME TO DO UN TO OTHER. I TREATED PEOPLE
THE WAY I WANTED TO BE TREATED I'V
ALWAYS TRYED TO BE UP + HELPFUL SO WHY
IS THIS HAPPENING ~~....................~~
~~..~~
~~..~~
TIm ~~............~~

I KNOW HOW MUCH IT HURTS

NICOLE AND I HAD A GOOD LIFE TOGETHER, ALL THIS PRESS TALK ABOUT A ROCKY RELATIONSHIP WAS NO MORE THAN WHAT EVER LONG TERM RELATIONSH EXPERIENCES, ALL HER FRIENDS WILL CONFIRM THAT IV BEEN TOTALLY LOVING AND UNDERSTANDIN OF WHAT SHE'S BEEN GOING THROUGHT. AT TIMES IV FELT LIKE A BATTERED HUSBAND OR BOYFRIEND BUT I LOVED HER, MADE THAT CLEAR TO EVERYON AND WOULD TAKE WHATEVER TO MAKE US WORK.

DON'T FEEL SORRY FOR ME. IV HAD A GREAT LIFE MADE GREAT FRIENDS. PLEASE THINK OF THE REAL OJ. AND NOT THIS LOST PERSON.

THANK FOR MAKING MY LIFE SPECIAL I HOPE I HELP YOURS.

PEACE + LOVE
☺. J.

Simpson is obviously racked with guilt. He is trying to confess to himself without making any incriminating statements. His claims of innocence ring hollow, and while he does show some concern for his children, it is clear that he is mostly worried about himself. He feels guilt and remorse, but not because he murdered the mother of his children. His biggest regret is that he will no longer be able to hang out with his friends. His life as a famous celebrity is over. When he says goodbye to his friends and family, is it because he is planning to kill himself, or because he knows he is going to jail for a long time? It's interesting that he says to his mentor (and possible sexual rival) Marcus Allen, "don't mess up" his current relationship.

He pretends to have adjusted to losing Nicole, and even attempts to portray himself as a "battered husband," a tactic that the defense used later in the trial. Simpson also obviously holds out hope for reconciliation with Nicole, and at the same time he says he knows that it's over.

The last paragraph is particularly interesting. "Don't feel sorry for me." Of course, he's busy feeling sorry for himself. "Please think of the real O.J. and not this lost person." In other words, think of O.J. the football player and celebrity, not the man who murdered two people. Perhaps the sign-off "Peace + Love O.J." with a happy face drawn in the first initial of his nickname is a desperate attempt to literally put a happy face on a horrible deed. In some ways, his letter seems like an awkward attempt at a positive press release for himself.

Was this letter a suicide note, or simply the incoherent rantings of an emotionally distraught man? It really doesn't matter. Either way, his guilt is obvious. Vince Bugliosi pointed out that the letter was written on June 15, not the 17th, when he took off with Al Cowlings. Before he was even charged, O.J. Simpson knew he was going to jail.

Early on in the case, I asked Cheri Lewis why the prosecution didn't try to get a court-ordered psychological profile of Simpson. Cheri asked what good that might do. I thought it might give us some idea of the personality disorders or other psychological problems the defendant might have, if any. Perhaps there was a psychological profile that would account for a popular, successful, well-liked celebrity committing a brutal double homicide. Wasn't this one of the challenges of the case?

Cheri said that it was too late, and besides she didn't think that Marcia would want to do it. From our conversation I got the feeling that Cheri agreed with me that such a profile would be helpful, but there was nothing she could do about it.

Clinical psychologist Dr. Stanton Samenow, who codirected an extensive study of criminal offenders in North America and served on a presidential task force on victims of crime, told reporters for *People* magazine the following:

"Publicly many people who commit murder are talented, accomplished. They may call themselves religious. They can be gregarious, charming, good at drawing people into their webs. In private they often have troubled personal relationships. Often it's the partner in the day-to-day relationship who eludes their control. They respond with threats, intimidation and violence."

In a comment that eerily describes the split between the cheerful persona of O.J. and the violent murderer of two people, the same person who can write "Peace + Love O.J." at the bottom of a suicide note days after he killed his ex-wife, the doctor said:

"Some people who have committed savage crimes have very sentimental minds. They wouldn't step on a bug. But they can go from tears to ice just like that.... Some people who commit a murder can shut off the violent side of their personality, almost like a light switch."

When asked whether the murderer would feel remorse, Dr. Samenow responded:

"They may feel terrible that a child is left without a parent, but more often they see themselves as the victim.... Their basic regret is for themselves, that life as they knew it is over."

Sound familiar?

Simpson has a narcissistic, possessive, and jealous personality. He was obsessed with Nicole. That obsession resulted in beatings, stalking, spying, harassment, and ultimately murder. These are documented facts, not speculation. Whatever imagined fantasy life Simpson lived, it surely involved Nicole.

I also asked Cheri why we were not using some witnesses who seemed to have important testimony. For instance, Jill Shively, a Brentwood resident, had told the prosecutors that she was driving along San Vicente Boulevard at around 10:45 on the night of the murders when she saw a large white car heading north on Bundy. The white car blew through the red light and crossed San Vicente directly in front of her. As it crossed the street, nearly plowing into Shively's vehicle, the white car ran up on the median that separated the two lanes of the boulevard. The driver of the white car yelled for Shively to get out of the way, and she recognized him as O.J. Simpson, whom she knew from the neighborhood. Shively noted down the license number of the vehicle, which later matched Simpson's Bronco.

Here was a positive eyewitness, the only one placing Simpson near the scene at the time of the murders. But Shively had already sold her story to "Hard Copy" for $5,000. That's not a lot of money by the standards of this trial, but to Shively, a single working-class woman who lived in a small apartment and spent most nights looking after her sister's child, it was probably more than she had ever seen.

I told Cheri I thought Shively's testimony would be damning.

Cheri said, "Yeah, but Marcia's upset because Jill sold her story to the tabs."

"I understand that," I said. "But why can't we use her anyway?"

I argued that the prosecution used the testimony of the owner and sales clerk from Ross Cutlery, the store where Simpson bought the Stiletto, even though they also sold their stories.

Cheri and I kicked the subject around a while, then she simply said, "Marcia didn't like her. She didn't trust her."

Much later I talked to Vince Bugliosi about the whole "cash for trash" controversy. He told me that while he would prefer that witnesses not sell their stories to the media, Jill Shively was a very strong witness. She was familiar with both the defendant and victim, and made a positive identification, including an accurate license plate report. Vince told me that if he was prosecuting the case, he would have certainly considered using her. Her testimony locks Simpson into the crime scene and contradicts his various alibis that he was either getting ready to leave town, or chipping golf balls, or sleeping, or taking a shower.

Shively's testimony would have caused problems with the prosecution's timeline for the murder. But that does not show Shively was wrong; it only shows that the prosecution's timeline was unnecessarily precise and inflexible. Besides, another witness testified that around 10:40 the night of the murders, he heard two voices in an apparent argument or struggle. Robert Heidstra, a car detailer and neighbor of Nicole's, was out walking his dogs when he heard someone shout, "Hey, hey hey." His testimony was used by the defense to call the prosecution's timeline into question. Used with Shively's, it could have been the closest thing to an eyewitness placing Simpson at the scene that this case ever had.

The prosecution didn't have any witnesses who could positively place Simpson at the scene. However, there were several witnesses who could corroborate a timeline of events at or near the Bundy residence around the time of the murders. Unfortunately, the prosecution narrowed the timeline down so tightly that they rendered some of these eyewitnesses useful only for the defense.

Marcia insisted on nailing down details she had no way of proving. When you are building a timeline for a murder, you have to remain flexible. People are often wrong or contradictory in estimating time. Their watches or clocks are set differently, and their memory can be hazy. Even a coroner cannot determine the precise time of death. Investigation of the stomach contents and body temperature can give you a rough estimate, but not an exact time.

Marcia had enough evidence and enough witnesses to place the murders at some point between 10:00 and 10:45 P.M. Instead, she claimed that the murders occurred between 10:00 and 10:15 P.M. when two of their witnesses testified hearing the Akita bark.

The dog's barking is not very strong evidence to establish the time of murders. Perhaps the dog was barking before the attack. And if the killer was Simpson, who was known to the dog, the animal might not have barked until the murders were already committed and the victims lay there dead. But the prosecution used that testimony as definitive proof for their tidy timeline.

And the defense, not surprisingly, tore it up. They called several witnesses to refute the prosecution's timeline. Francesca Harman said she drove past Nicole's house at 10:20 P.M. and neither saw nor heard anything. Danny Mandel and Ellen Aaronson were walking past the Bundy residence at 10:25 that evening; they said they saw and heard nothing. Denise Pilnak, one of Nicole's neighbors, testified that the area was completely still at 10:21 and she didn't hear the dog barking until 10:35. Robert Heidstra testified that at 10:40 P.M., he heard a male voice yelling, "Hey, hey, hey."

The prosecution attacked the defense's timeline witnesses, sometimes obnoxiously. Marcia Clark speculated that Mandel and Aaronson had been drinking heavily, and Chris Darden badgered Harman about listening to her car radio and watching the road, not the sidewalk. Treating these people as hostile witnesses only made the prosecution's case appear more tenuous, even desperate. Why didn't they use them as prosecution witnesses to establish a more workable timeline?

Another piece of evidence the prosecution refused to introduce was Vannatter and Lange's interrogation of Simpson, weak though it may have been. His contradictory statements, his lack of an alibi, and his confusion or refusal to explain his movements or actions about events the night of the murders, in particular the cut on his finger, were never introduced in the trial. The suspect's statements indicated at least confusion, if not guilt. But not only did Marcia not use the interview, she also fought hard to keep it entirely excluded from the trial. I understand the legal issues involved: You cannot cross-examine a statement, so it's not the same as putting a witness on the stand. I also understand that the prosecution did not want his statement to stand as an unanswered denial of the charges. But Marcia's often hysterical efforts to keep any mention of the interview out of the trial only made the jury suspect that the prosecution had something to hide.

Vince Bugliosi later said that with a legal pad and a hundred hours to prepare, he could have convicted Simpson on the transcript of that interview alone. Why did Marcia fight so hard to suppress it? Instead, she spent significant chunks of time arguing irrelevant and distracting details.

The defense took full advantage of Marcia's ability to focus on the unimportant. A good example of this was the heated controversy over the Ben and Jerry's ice cream cup found on the rear steps of the Bundy residence. A great deal of testimony and countless hours of investigation were spent on this insignificant piece of evidence, including a drawn-out debate on what flavor the ice cream was (while early speculation had inaccurately identified it as Chunky Monkey, the ice cream in question was eventually determined to be Rainforest Crunch).

If the ice cream cup was so important, why wasn't it even checked for fingerprints? It seems strange it was not, since you'd print something in question to eliminate it as something the suspect might have touched. Because it wasn't printed, it became an issue that the defense was able to exploit, and the prosecution spent a lot of time trying to explain. My explanation of the ice cream is simple: Nicole came home with two small children. She put the ice cream down on the stair railing to pick up one of the kids, and she never returned to pick it up.

Not only did the prosecution allow the case to get bogged down in unnecessary details, but they ignored important ones. During one of the many sessions in Cheri's office, I asked if we had a weather report for the night of the murders and the morning after. We needed ambient temperature, barometric pressure, marine layer, time of sunrise and sunset, and moon conditions. These conditions would give us a clearer picture of nighttime visibility and moisture in the air around the time of the murders and the crucial hours immediately following. If the jury, judge, defense, and prosecution were going to do a walkthrough of the crime scene, it would be helpful if we could replicate the weather and light conditions as closely as possible. This should have already been taken care of by Vannatter and Lange, as they were working an outdoor crime scene, and even if you note the weather conditions yourself—which I don't believe they did—you still have to get the weather report to corroborate your own findings.

Cheri saw my point and ordered a weather report. But what she came up with was not anything that a juror could understand. Instead, it was filled with meteorological jargon that even an experienced detective who had often worked with weather reports could not make any sense of. I told Cheri we needed something in layman's terms. There is no doubt Cheri pursued the request, but I never saw or heard any reference to weather in the trial.

Later on in the trial, the defense brought up questions about the degradation of evidence and the stickiness of the Rockingham glove. These claims, that the glove appeared moist because I planted it, could have been successfully countered by a clear and accurate weather report. In early summer, the coastal regions and west side of Los Angeles are often enveloped in a moist marine layer, known as "June gloom." But without a weather report, we didn't know the exact conditions. And the defense's questions merely caught the prosecution off guard. Once again, instead of doing things right from the beginning, the prosecution was simply waiting for holes to spring open in the dike, and then hoping they had enough spare fingers to plug them. Many of the problems the prosecution faced in this case wouldn't have happened, or would not have become disasters, if the case had been adequately prepared and organized.

In addition to evidence missed entirely, there was also evidence apparently mishandled, which the defense exploited fully. Barry Scheck's cross-examination of Dennis Fung, which began on April 4 and ended April 13, was tough, but his questions were mostly pertinent. Fung should have collected traces from all the blood drops that we found at the scene and were mentioned in my notes. He especially should have checked out the blood drops on the rear gate at Bundy. By returning two weeks later to collect evidence he should have gotten the first day, Fung undermined his own professional reputation, brought important evidence into question, and opened the entire investigation to valid questions about the gathering and storage of evidence. These were catastrophic errors that would have been avoided had Fung followed proper procedure, and Scheck quite properly subjected him to harsh questioning.

But while the defense could challenge the techniques by which certain evidence was collected and treated, they couldn't question the validity of the DNA test results. Yes, there was contamination of scenes and degradation of evidence. But no matter how amateurish the mistakes of Robbery/Homicide and SID, there is no way they would have resulted in false positives linking the blood evidence to the suspects or victims.

I'm not an expert, but I know enough about DNA to understand what it can and cannot prove. DNA testing is identity specific. You are not looking to see whether something is present, you're looking to identify what you already know is there. If the samples collected by SID were so contaminated, they would have produced inconclusive results, not false positives. The fact that they produced positive identification of Simpson from imperfect samples is only a stronger indication of his guilt.

DNA is called a "genetic fingerprint," and that is an accurate analogy. Everybody has unique fingerprints, and everyone has unique DNA. DNA testing identifies the unique genetic markers to identify a specific individual. While laypersons generally consider fingerprints to be the best form of physical evidence, DNA is even more conclusive than fingerprints. Prints are more tangible, in part because we can see them, while DNA is complex and molecular. It's difficult to comprehend what DNA is, or even imagine it. You can't take a human cell and examine it as easily as seeing the ridges and loops of your own fingerprint.

It's interesting that Barry Scheck and Peter Neufeld have made a career out of getting wrongfully convicted felons released from prison on DNA evidence. Their Innocence Project frees convicts whose convictions have been overturned based on DNA testing. It's much easier putting someone into prison than it is getting them out. Many prisoners appeal convictions, but very few ever get a retrial, much less an overturned conviction. When Scheck and Neufeld are trying to free prisoners, they believe that DNA offers positive and conclusive proof. But in the Simpson trial, they did nothing but question the collection and handling of DNA evidence, not its scientific reliability.

Before he was hired by Simpson, Scheck said: "If O.J. Simpson is not the murderer, then DNA will tell us who the real killer is." But when all the DNA evidence pointed to his client, his argument quickly shifted.

The odds of the blood found at both scenes not being O.J.'s are beyond astronomical. But some of the hair and fiber evidence was subject to challenge because of contamination. There were many human errors throughout the investigation, too many. Unfortunately, these errors were used by the defense to build a theory of racial conspiracy by an LAPD that was incompetent in gathering evidence while at the same time incredibly lucky, well-organized, and highly intelligent in planting it.

The prosecution locked itself into the theory that the Bundy murders were a case of escalating domestic abuse. This strategy was fraught with problems, not the least of which was that the jury didn't seem too concerned about a black man beating his white wife. As Marcia kept compiling evidence documenting Simpson's abuse of Nicole, it became obvious that this angle was going to be the motive for the murders of Nicole and Ron, even though the facts did not absolutely fit this theory.

I had personal knowledge of Simpson's spousal abuse from a call I answered at the Rockingham estate back in 1985. Four years after being called to Rockingham on the domestic violence call, I was asked by Mike Farrell, a West LA detective who was handling the 1989 Simpson abuse case, to write a report on what I saw:

> During the fall or winter of 1985 I responded to a 415 family dispute at 360 North Rockingham. Upon arrival I observed two persons in front of the estate, a black male pacing on the driveway and a white female sitting on a vehicle crying. I inquired if the persons I observed were the residents, at which time the black male stated,

"Yeah, I own this, I'm O.J. Simpson!" My attention turned to the female who was sobbing and asked her if she was alright but before she could speak the black male (Simpson) interrupted saying, "she's my wife, she's okay!" During my conversation with the female I noted that she was sitting in front of a shattered windshield (Mercedes-Benz, I believe) and I asked, "who broke the windshield?" with the female responding, "he did (pointing to Simpson)... He hit the windshield with a baseball bat!" Upon hearing the female's statement, Simpson exclaimed, "I broke the windshield... it's mine... there's no trouble here." I turned to the female and asked if she would like to make a report and she stated, "no."

It seems odd to remember such an event, but it is not every day that you respond to a celebrity's home for a family dispute. For this reason this incident was indelibly pressed in my memory.

In that incident I saw an agitated Simpson, a sobbing Nicole, and a vandalized Mercedes Benz. Yet I didn't think that the Bundy murder case was the result of domestic violence. In fact, this was no more a case of domestic violence escalating into murder than it was a case of vandalism escalating into murder.

The prosecution characterized the Bundy murders as a domestic-violence case involving murder, not a murder case involving domestic violence. But how do you have domestic violence when the couple no longer lives together, no longer dates, and shares nothing but the custody of two children? What we do have is stalking, obsession, harassment, control, ego, and eventually murder. By forcing the case into a domestic violence theory, the prosecution was unable to draw a credible picture of what really happened that night.

What pushed Simpson from his usual behavior into a brutal murder? I always thought, and still do, that he believed Nicole had a lover, whether she did or not, and whether it was Ron Goldman or not.

Cheri Lewis and I talked about the possibility that Ron and Nicole were lovers. Whether they were overt or covert about it, they did appear to be more than just friends.

I had pertinent information on this subject. While talking to friends of mine in Brentwood, I heard them mention Ron Goldman. One lady, who wishes to remain anonymous, seemed to know Ron fairly well as a friend, and she related the following conversation to me:

The lady asked Ron, "How are things going?"

"Great," Ron responded. "I've been seeing a thirty-five-year-old woman who has two kids. She has a white Ferrari. She's really nice."

The lady asked, "Isn't sex with an older woman great?"

Ron replied, "Yeah, it's great!"

I took this conversation down as a statement over two years ago. The statement was typed on an LAPD statement sheet and given to Lange and Vannatter. I have not seen it since. I assumed that it went into the homicide book, but I did not hear any mention of it after giving it to Robbery/Homicide. And the question of Ron and Nicole's relationship was never brought up during the trial.

Imagine my surprise when I read the following in Lawrence Schiller's book:

"An LAPD source told Pavelic that they had interviewed a beauty salon attendant who said that Ron was straight and dating an older woman with two kids, presumably Nicole."

If any other LAPD officer had talked to my source, I would have been notified. That leads me to assume that Bill Pavelic got the information straight from the homicide book, which the defense received on discovery and passed along to the former policeman to look at very closely. One thing he neglects to mention is that the LAPD source is none other than the infamous Mark Fuhrman.

I always believed that Ron and Nicole were lovers. The atmosphere of Nicole's home, the candles and soft music, seemed more than a coincidence. A love triangle was a stronger motive for murder than the ongoing domestic problems that Nicole and Simpson had for years.

The defense questioned the domestic violence motive, and with good reason. Uelmen made some pertinent arguments about domestic violence, and the one almost indisputable fact was that even domestic violence cases that lead to murder usually do not involve *multiple* victims killed with a knife. But Uelmen didn't take the argument far enough (he couldn't, because it would have implicated his client). There is one profile that often produces cases involving multiple victims: the love triangle.

We couldn't expect Uelmen to offer the prosecution a motive they hadn't explored, but when he made this argument, surely the prosecution had to see that after ten years of violent domestic disputes, something must have changed in the Simpsons' relationship that turned wife beating into murder.

I expressed these thoughts to Marcia, reminding her that I had obtained one interview that clearly indicated Ron and Nicole were at least casual lovers. Marcia was not interested in connecting the two romantically, I believe for no other reason than she felt it would have tainted the images of the two victims. I argued that there was nothing wrong with two healthy, single adults having a sexual relationship. I also pointed out that there was one person who would be outraged at the fact that Nicole chose a mere waiter to replace him in bed, and that was O.J. Simpson.

Jealousy was a better motive than domestic violence, because the situation between Simpson and Nicole had changed dramatically just before the murders. In his interrogation, Simpson described their relationship this way: "I always have problems with her, you know? Our relationship has been a problem relationship." In another part of the interview, he said, "we both knew it wasn't working, and probably three weeks ago or so we said it just wasn't working and *we went our separate ways*" (emphasis added). Simpson also told the detectives that Nicole had returned a bracelet and earrings that he had given her around the same time. Her returning those gifts seemed to indicate that she wanted to end the relationship for good. While they had broken up many times, this time seemed to be final, at least for Nicole. But did Simpson accept it? Did Nicole's final break-up, combined with what at least appeared to be a sexual relationship with a younger man, push Simpson over the edge? What about Paula Barbieri; hadn't she also just broken up with Simpson? Was he, as rumored, taking illegal drugs at the time? Did other unnoticed or undocumented personal problems cause him to snap?

Marcia didn't ask these questions. She was obsessed with the idea of Nicole as a victim of domestic violence, and refused to consider the possibility of jealous rage. Here is one possible scenario: Simpson could not deal with the fact that a twenty-five-year-old waiter had taken his place in Nicole's bed. He stalked her, and when he saw them together, flew into a jealous rage and killed them both. This would explain Ron's presence, the brutality of the murders, and the fact that the killer was so beside himself that he left damning evidence all over two crime scenes.

I made it very clear to Marcia that it didn't matter whether Ron and Nicole were lovers or just good friends, what mattered was what O.J. Simpson believed. We knew that Simpson had seen Nicole and Ron together at coffee shops and in her Ferrari. What effect did this have on an already insanely jealous man?

Marcia wanted this to be a classic case of domestic violence which resulted in murder. For all the right reasons she wanted this to be so, but I don't believe it was that clear-cut. But I think Marcia was too wedded to the spousal abuse issue because of her own personal history.

How much Marcia's personal life affected her judgment was evident one afternoon when I entered her office. As I walked in I could see that she was crying. I asked if she wanted to be alone, and she said, "No, come on in," while trying to force a smile. I asked what was wrong, and she explained that her ex-husband was trying to get custody of her children.

I felt for her, having two small children of my own and knowing that they come before anything else in my life. I could sense her desperation and tried to console her. "Don't let this case come between you and your kids; it's not worth it. Anytime you want me to stop it, let me know. I'll just go to the press about Ito and York."

Marcia smiled and replied, "No, not yet, but it's always nice to know we have a silver bullet."

Of course she never used it, but I wonder whether she wishes she had. Presented with a mountain of evidence, Marcia Clark felt she could pick and choose those pieces she felt most comfortable presenting, and throw away those she considered tainted, or did not fit her precise theories. In doing so, she started an avalanche—and the mountain quickly crumbled around her.

TEN BIGGEST MISTAKES MADE BY THE PROSECUTORS

1. They knew they had more than enough evidence to convict, and thus became self-righteous and picky about what they presented.

2. They allowed personal history and feelings to affect their prosecution of the case.

3. They felt uncomfortable prosecuting a popular celebrity. And they wanted to be celebrities themselves.

4. By trying to appear overtly racially fair, they helped select a jury that was almost entirely favorable to the defense.

5. As they tried to defuse racial issues, they actually introduced them into the trial, precluding their subsequent arguments that they shouldn't be part of the trial.

6. They locked themselves into precise hypotheses without evidence to completely corroborate them, instead of remaining flexible within the boundaries of the evidence.

7. They got bogged down in scientific details that most of the attorneys prosecuting the case did not completely understand. Could you imagine how the jury felt?

8. They did not have either Lange or Vannatter at the prosecution table during the trial to help ask questions only a detective would know to ask. Conversely, by not having a detective there, they in essence told the jury that the police had nothing to offer except their testimony.

9. They covered up for the errors of the lead detectives and left other witnesses vulnerable to the defense's allegations.

10. They forgot they represented the people of California, not themselves.

Chapter 15

THE MURDER WEAPON

---

*The prosecution and investigating detectives were obsessed
with finding a smoking gun (or a bloody knife) that would
put the case away. But they weren't willing to do the detailed
and sometimes tedious work necessary to track it down.*

—THE AUTHOR

THE DISCOVERY OF THE MURDER WEAPON would have been a substantial piece of incriminating evidence. Why wasn't the murder weapon ever found?

In the weeks immediately following Simpson's arrest, Ron Phillips, Brad Roberts, and I were often called by Robbery/Homicide to follow up on tips, leads, and to interview possible witnesses. One of our most important tasks was the search for a murder weapon. Following citizen tips, Brad and I were sent by RHD detectives to search fields, drain pipes, and alleys. At one point, I found myself scouring an empty lot with a metal detector, wearing a suit and crawling through weeds and tall grass.

Brad and I thought the piece of old fence I found by the Bronco was evidence that might lead to the murder weapon. We thought the Bronco collided with a fence or pile of wood just after the murders. In a panic, we reasoned, Simpson attempted to find some place to throw the knife from the car. He could have stopped in an alley, opened the passenger window, and thrown the knife out, leaving blood smudges on the seat and passenger door panel. When he stopped, the Bronco collided with a fence and the piece of wood got stuck in the bumper, grill, or suspension, dislodging only when Simpson quickly stopped in front of the Rockingham estate.

Brad and I searched the neighborhood, and the only place where we found similar fencing was in some alleys a block from Nicole's condominium. We informed Lange and Vannatter, but they weren't interested. My suggestion to use police academy cadets to search the alleys and yards was politely ignored.

So Brad and I searched it ourselves. The neighborhood was older, with unkempt backyards and debris in almost every alleyway. Behind many homes was old white fencing that looked just as weathered as the piece I had found by the Bronco. The knife could be anywhere, but it seemed that this was a good place to begin the search. If the murderer needed to dispose of a weapon, this was a good spot. It was the only area within miles that had old-fashioned alleys that led onto back yards and garages, and the alleys were overgrown with weeds and tall grass.

Robbery/Homicide had received a phone tip that on the night of the murders, within the proper time frame, a resident of the neighborhood had heard a car in the alley behind his house. The car was described as a sports utility vehicle, a "Bronco or Blazer." Although the witness thought it was light blue in color, a white car could have looked blue in the streetlight. The witness noticed the car because he did not recognize it as common to the neighborhood. The vehicle entered the alleyway, stopped momentarily, and then drove off. The alley had the same type of old white fencing.

This tip was not followed up on adequately, for reasons I do not know or understand. If it had been my case, instead of just relying only on Brad and me searching the whole area would have been checked out completely, with a large-scale search for the weapon. I would have sent paint samples to the FBI for comparative analysis between random fence samples in the area and the piece of wood found by the Bronco. But none of this was done, and now we will never know if Simpson stopped in that alley to dispose of the weapon.

The police investigation did not use the resources it had or needed to pursue a case of this magnitude. No one ever took tire impressions of the Bronco, or searched the alleys for tire marks, or checked for possible debris or dirt caught in the tires. Had we found tire tracks or soil samples that put the Bronco in the alleys near the Bundy residence, it would not by itself have proved Simpson's guilt, but it could have placed him in the alley, it would have been good policework, and would have helped build a solid case. A single piece of irrefutable evidence doesn't often simply fall in your lap. It takes time and effort to collect evidence that may not have obvious or dramatic value, but when taken with other evidence builds a strong case.

Why didn't Robbery/Homicide follow up on these and other clues? Was it the fear of media attention or just laziness? Did they stop looking for the murder weapon simply because they felt it was destroyed or dumped in Chicago? I don't believe he got rid of the weapon there, because that would suggest that

Not only did the prosecution not have the murder weapon; they also didn't have a credible theory of how the murders happened.

Simpson was organized and cool, a description that his behavior and the evidence does not support. Simpson was in a panic after the murders. He lost a glove and his knit cap and never retrieved them. Change fell from his pocket while he reached for his keys. A witness saw him driving fast and recklessly from the scene. He left blood everywhere he went. For some reason, he went behind Kato's bungalow, where he dropped another glove. He was still sweating and probably bleeding when the limo picked him up. This was not a cool character. I believe that Simpson got rid of the knife in a hurry. Perhaps he or someone close to him came back to dispose of it later.

The prosecution and investigating detectives were obsessed with finding a smoking gun (or a bloody knife) that would put the case away. But they weren't willing to do the detailed and sometimes tedious work necessary to track it down.

The owners and an employee of Ross Cutlery, a knife store in downtown Los Angeles, reported that Simpson bought a large German Stiletto with a 6 5/8-inch blade from their store on May 3. On this clue alone, the prosecution decided this knife had to be the murder weapon. Before testifying in the preliminary hearing, the cutlery store owners and employee sold their story to the *National Enquirer*. Cash-for-trash scandals had discouraged the prosecution from pursuing sound evidence, but in the case of the German Stiletto, they were willing to forget the tabloid taint, even though we didn't have the weapon and had no proof that he had used it.

As an initial assumption, the idea that this Stiletto was the murder weapon was not unreasonable: when a murder suspect buys a knife whose only purpose is a stabbing instrument just prior to the killings, that knife has to be considered as a possibility. However, like many of its other pet theories, the prosecution took the Stiletto hypothesis too far.

As soon as I heard about the prosecution's plans to use the Stiletto, I asked why we were locking ourselves into a murder weapon that we couldn't prove had killed the victims, and didn't even have in our possession. We could not connect the knife directly with the murder. If Simpson had purchased the knife immediately before the murders, the inference would have been stronger, but he bought it several weeks prior. If Simpson had been seen within days, or at all, with this very distinctive knife, again the connection would have been stronger. But we had no such information and, more importantly, no knife. All the prosecution did have was the knowledge that Simpson had bought a knife, and the coroner's opinion that this knife type and size *could* have caused the wounds which killed both victims. After the prosecution wed themselves to the Stiletto, any evidence that conflicted with their theory was either ignored or dismissed.

After the first search on June 13 proved fruitless (except for the Swiss Army knife box I found in the master bath), we returned to the Rockingham estate on June 28 to execute another search warrant. The second time through the house, I was once again impressed by how meticulous Simpson was. All his belongings were so neatly arranged, I wouldn't have been surprised if he alphabetized his wardrobe.

Before we went to the house, we had been briefed on certain items that Robbery/Homicide was looking for. They wanted to find a black jumpsuit or sweatsuit, a pair of shoes, and, of course, the knife, along with any packaging for a knife. I helped with the search of the master bedroom closet. We didn't find any knives, but Detective Marlow and I did discover an Uzi and a pistol on the top shelf of the bedroom closet. Simpson was rumored to have a large knife collection—where was it?

When the prosecution presented their Stiletto theory at the preliminary hearing without physically possessing the knife, they merely gave the defense a chance to head off the argument. Soon after the presentation, the defense miraculously "found" a knife in Simpson's home, precisely the sort of knife the prosecution said it was looking for.

In Jeffrey Toobin's book, *The Run of His Life,* he writes that Uelmen showed Simpson the search warrant of June 28 and asked, "Where's the knife?" Receiving instructions from Simpson, Uelmen went to the Rockingham estate and into the master bedroom, where some shelves were set behind mirrored doors. Uelmen opened the doors and found the Stiletto that Simpson had described was there. It was pristine, with no evidence of having been used in a murder.

Reading this passage, I immediately knew the place that Uelmen described and was claiming the police supposedly never looked. I had never heard exactly where they found the knife, and didn't think it was possible that we could have missed it. Brad Roberts was with me during the execution of both search warrants. He and I assisted two Robbery/Homicide detectives in searching the master bedroom during the first warrant, and Brad later told me he was certain the other detectives looked inside the glass cabinet. If they took apart the pipes beneath Simpson's bathroom sink, you can be certain they looked inside the cabinet. Even if they did not at first realize it was a cabinet, they were looking behind wall hangings and fixtures, and would have taken the mirror apart if it didn't open.

I have no doubt that Uelmen found the knife in that cabinet. But I don't understand how that knife got there—perhaps it was the work of little elves. Does the defense want us to believe that Simpson keeps a Stiletto in his medicine cabinet? Does he shave with this knife?

If another Stiletto had been discovered by the police or a citizen, the defense's knife could have been exposed as a plant. But the prosecution's search for the murder weapon lost steam once the defense came up with the mysterious envelope eventually revealed to contain a brand-new Stiletto. It was probably too late anyway. By finding this knife at Simpson's home, the defense seemed to infer that they were fairly certain the murder weapon would never be found. How could they be so confident?

Perhaps because the Stiletto was probably not the murder weapon. The testimonies of Drs. Golden, Baden, and Lakshmanan concur that the victim's wounds were caused by a single-edged knife. But the length of the knife is in question. Out of nearly thirty wounds, only one single wound went as deep as five and a half inches. All the other single wounds were four inches deep or less, with most of them in the two- to three-and-a-half inch range.

The five-and-a-half inch wound was on Ron Goldman's abdomen, forty-five inches above his left heel, which would place it somewhere below the ribcage. That wound was fatal. It was one of the few wounds that went into soft tissue instead of hitting denser tissue or bone. When you stab someone with great force, soft tissue will compress, creating a wound that is even longer than the blade itself. Picture someone hitting you in the stomach and think how far the fist pushes into your body. Now place a knife in that hand. As the blade penetrates your body, it pushes the soft tissue in. When the body recovers and the blade is withdrawn, the wound will appear longer because the tissue was compressed. In other words, a five-and-one-half-inch wound in soft tissue does not prove that the blade had to be as long as the Stiletto's. A shorter knife could have made that wound.

And a shorter knife could have made all the other wounds. Although Nicole's fatal neck wound was so deep that the blade of the murder weapon nicked her spine, this is not evidence of a large blade. As Dr. Golden described in his autopsy, the neck can be either flexed or extended, and in Nicole's case the length of the wound is greater than the depth. This type of incised wound cannot be used to determine the blade length of the weapon.

In his testimony, Michael Baden, the defense's coroner's expert, was asked about the murder weapon's blade length. He stated that the only way the blade length could be accurately estimated was if the weapon's thrust was not angled and there were no movements by the victim or the suspect to increase the cutting of the blade. In other words, he could not determine the blade length of the murder weapon. This inability was compounded by the fact that he did not view the bodies before burial.

Several of Goldman's wounds showed bruises and abrasions around the entry point of the blade, indicating that something other than just the knife blade came into contact with the skin, possibly the handle of the knife. These marks, however, were not described as being consistent with the Stiletto; it had an S-shaped hilt, which most probably would have created a distinct bruising cut on one side of the knife wound, and a dull curved impression on the other. These were not present.

During the trial, I pointed out to Rockne Harman of the district attorney's office that if the Stiletto was the murder weapon, the right-hand glove I found behind Kato's bungalow would have tears and visible impressions on it from the forceful contact with the hilt. Did the glove have any such marks? He never told me of any such findings, or the attempt to search for them.

If the Stiletto didn't kill Ron and Nicole, what did? Remember that during the first search of Rockingham, in the master bedroom where the Stiletto was eventually discovered, Brad and I found an empty Swiss Army knife box. The box was sitting on the bathtub's edge inside the master bathroom and was the size of one of the larger Swiss Army knives. The box looked out of place in the bathroom. In the bedroom closet, there were several other Swiss Army items, but all were still in their boxes. Where was the knife from the empty box?

Here we were looking for, among other things, the murder weapon, which happened to be a knife. And here was an empty knife box sitting in a visible and unexplained place in the house. Naturally I brought the box to the attention of the Robbery/Homicide detectives, but I don't believe it was ever collected as evidence, and it was never investigated. Certainly, it was never used as evidence in the criminal trial. Having read the entire evidence list for the civil trial, both plaintiff and defense, I cannot find this box listed as evidence for that trial either.

Still, a proceeding in the civil trial indicated that a Swiss Army knife might have some significance. One week before the Bundy murders, limo driver John Upson picked up Simpson after he attended a board meeting of the Forschner Group, Inc., importer of Swiss Army knives, located in Shelton, Connecticut. Simpson was a board member of the company and left the meeting with a bagful of free items, several of which were knives.

In Upson's civil trial deposition, he stated that Simpson showed him one of the Swiss Army knives. Upson stated the following:

"'You could really hurt someone with this,' Simpson said, making a stabbing motion. You could even kill someone with this.'"

During Simpson's deposition, Daniel Petrocelli, a lawyer for the Goldman family, asked: "Did you take that knife out and show it to him and make a stabbing motion?"

"Wait a minute. Don't answer that," Simpson's attorney Robert Baker interjected. "No way is he going to answer that."

Petrocelli followed up, but made a mistake that let Simpson slip out of difficulty:

Petrocelli: "Do you recall if you took a knife twelve to sixteen inches long and made a stabbing motion with it to the limo driver?"

Simpson: "I know I didn't."

It was easy for Simpson to say that, because the Forschner Group doesn't make a knife that's twelve to sixteen inches long.

"What was the longest blade of the knives that you had with you and showed to the limo driver?" Petrocelli asked.

Simpson responded: "If I took one of our utility things, I would say whatever that blade is, two inch, maybe, two and a half, maybe an inch and a half, I really don't know. You can get one and look at it."

This is a man who promotes Swiss Army knives, yet he can't come up with a name or accurate description of a knife the company makes? What Simpson is really saying is that although he didn't show the driver a twelve- to sixteen-inch knife, he did show him a Swiss Army knife.

Simpson was then asked: "When showing the limo driver the knives, did you say 'You can even kill somebody with this'?"

Of course, Simpson said no. But, in the same deposition, he admitted that he went to the Forschner Group, that he was given a bagful of knives, including one he described as "kind of a—it's a top-of-the-line thing with everything involved," that he had the bag in the car with the limo driver, and that he gave the limo driver "probably that big—whatever you call it, utility knife thing" as a gift. The only thing he won't admit was holding up a knife and making those incriminating statements. The driver had no reason to lie about it, but Simpson did. Who are you going to believe?

And for that matter, if someone were to make that statement, would they hold up a knife with a small and unthreatening blade? No, they would hold up a knife that looked like it could do damage to the human body.

As F. Lee Bailey pointed out to me several times, I was taken off the case that first night. But I can't help being a cop, so I did a little detective work. Considering the evidentiary value of the Swiss Army knife box I found two years ago, Upson's statement, the fact that the box was empty and out of place, and that the murder weapon was never found, I thought a Swiss Army knife was a more likely murder weapon than the German Stiletto. After five minutes on the Internet, I pulled up a catalog of Swiss Army knives.

One line of knives caught my eye. The Swiss Army lockback knives are single-edged, 3 1/2-inch locking blades with a contour handle and no hilt. These knives come in six models with the same blade. Could one of these be the weapon that killed Ron Goldman and Nicole Brown?

All of these weapons are capable of inflicting the wounds suffered by Nicole Brown and Ron Goldman. And a couple of them could be described as "kind of a—it's a top-of-the-line thing with everything involved." Was Simpson given one of these knives on his 1994 visit to the Forschner Group? If he was, where is the knife now?

Seeking out more information on Swiss Army knives, I reviewed catalogues from two different sporting goods stores in the Sandpoint area. The management was quick to inform me that there are two major manufacturers of Swiss Army knives in Europe. Victorinox is the original manufacturer. The Wenger version is also a true Swiss Army knife, but it is a newer manufacturer than Victorinox.

I discovered through direct contact with the Forschner Group that they import the Victorinox line of Swiss Army knives. The Swiss Army lockback knives are and have been part of their product line for years.

Maybe the murder weapon wasn't a Swiss Army knife. But why was there an empty Swiss Army knife box next to the tub in Simpson's bathroom? Why did the box happen to be there on the night of the murders? Did the glove have tears and indentations from the Stiletto hilt? Why were all but one of the wounds four inches or less? Why were there no bruises or lacerations from the knife hilt around the wounds? How could a Stiletto with a 6 5/8-inch blade be used in a violent stabbing attack on two humans and not leave one six-inch wound out of nearly thirty?

The thickness of the blade that was used to kill both victims is repeatedly described by Dr. Golden as 1/32 of an inch thick. This is an extremely thin blade. The Victorinox Swiss Army knife blade measures 2/32 of an inch. But the blade of the prosecution's Stiletto is almost 5/32 of an inch. The thickness of the wound on the bodies described as 1/32 of an inch could have, and probably did, appear slightly thinner than the blade because of the closure of the wound. Comparing the autopsy findings to the thickness of both blades in question (and standard knife-blade widths in general), one can deduce that it is much more probable that the murder weapon is the Swiss Army knife.

In addition to questions about the blade thickness of the murder weapon, the blade width is also an issue. The width of the wounds can, of course, be wider than the murder weapon blade, but I find it troubling that according to the autopsy conclusions there are wounds *narrower* than the Stiletto, especially in a wound that penetrated deeply. An example of this is the stab wounds to Ron Goldman's chest and thigh. The widths of those wounds range from 1/2 of an inch to 3/4 of an inch. Yet, the width of the Stiletto blade is 13/16 of an inch, slightly more than 3/4 of an inch. In other words, almost every wound in this region is narrower than the Stiletto blade. The Swiss Army knife is more consistent with the description of the stab wounds, as its blade is exactly 5/8 of an inch in width, which means that the few wounds which appear narrower are much closer to the dimensions of the Victorinox blade. Although I believe the Swiss Army knife might have inflicted these wounds, I'm virtually certain the Stiletto did not.

This much we know—Forschner imports lockback knives with 3 1/2-inch blades. Simpson was given several of the larger Forschner knives when he visited the company one week before the murders. He probably brought the knives home, as he did his other freebies from Forschner. On June 12, he took a Swiss Army knife out of its box and left the box on the edge of the bathtub.

What happened to the Swiss Army knife box I found in the Rockingham residence? If Robbery/Homicide booked it as evidence, you would think that Vannatter or Lange might have used it in their interrogation. Because the knife box was never mentioned in the interrogation, or in the subsequent trial, or, as far as I can tell, in the civil trial, we can assume it was never seized as evidence. Where is the box? Where is the knife that went into that box? Why did Simpson open that box on the day his ex-wife and Ron Goldman were murdered?

THE SWISS ARMY KNIFE

THE "STILETTO"

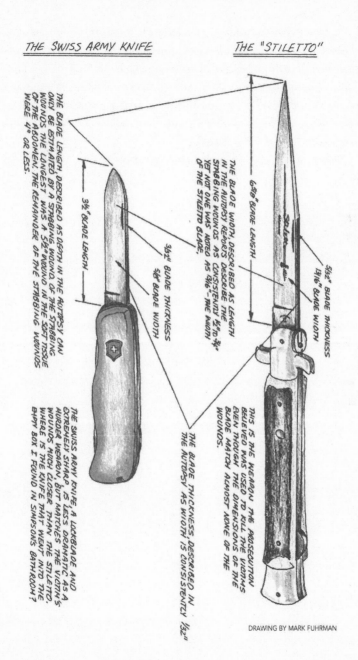

6-5/8" BLADE LENGTH

5/32" BLADE THICKNESS

13/16" BLADE WIDTH

THE BLADE WIDTH, DESCRIBED AS LENGTH IN THE AUTOPSY REPORTS DESCRIBE THE STABBING WOUNDS AS CONSISTENTLY 13/16", THE WIDTH OF THE STILETTO BLADE.

THE BLADE WIDTH, DESCRIBED AS LENGTH IN THE AUTOPSY REPORTS DESCRIBE THE STABBING WOUNDS AS CONSISTENTLY 1/2" TO 3/4", YET NOT ONE WAS NOTED AS 13/16" — THE WIDTH OF THE STILETTO BLADE.

3-1/2" BLADE LENGTH

3/32" BLADE THICKNESS

5/8" BLADE WIDTH

THIS IS THE WEAPON THE PROSECUTION BELIEVED WAS USED TO KILL THE VICTIMS EVEN THOUGH THE DIMENSIONS OF THE BLADE MATCH ALMOST NONE OF THE WOUNDS.

THE BLADE THICKNESS, DESCRIBED IN THE AUTOPSY AS WIDTH IS CONSISTENTLY 1/32".

THE BLADE LENGTH, DESCRIBED AS DEPTH IN THE AUTOPSY CAN ONLY BE ESTIMATED BY A STABBING WOUND OF THE STABBING WOUNDS THE LONGEST WAS A 5-1/2" WOUND IN THE SOFT TISSUE OF THE ABDOMEN. THE REMAINDER OF THE STABBING WOUNDS WERE 4" OR LESS.

THE SWISS ARMY KNIFE, A LOCKBLADE AND EXTREMELY SHARP, IS LESS DRAMATIC AS A MURDER WEAPON, BUT MATCHES THE VICTIM'S WOUNDS MUCH CLOSER THAN THE STILETTO. WHERE IS THE KNIFE THAT WENT INTO THE EMPTY BOX I FOUND IN SIMPSON'S BATHROOM?

DRAWING BY MARK FUHRMAN

I'm here in Northern Idaho and can't own, purchase, or even handle a lockback knife. I don't have the facilities to investigate any further. But someone else should. Or perhaps they should have back on June 13, 1994.

In a homicide case, the murder weapon can be the most crucial piece of evidence. Yes, you can still catch a murderer without one. But not only did the prosecution not have the murder weapon, they also did not have a credible theory of how the murders occurred.

What really happened at Nicole Brown's residence on the night of June 12, 1994?

Chapter 16

HYPOTHESIS OF A MURDER

I loved her, always have and always will.
If we had a problem it's because I loved her so much.

—OPENING OF O.J. SIMPSON'S SUICIDE NOTE

T HERE WERE ONLY THREE WITNESSES to the event. Two of them are
dead. The other isn't talking, or at least he's not telling the truth.
Here's what I think happened.

It's Sunday evening, sometime after 10:00. Nicole Brown Simpson is sitting in the
upstairs living room of her townhome. A telephone and two take-out menus are
nearby. Perhaps she is talking on the phone, or she could be planning to order
some food for her friend who is coming over.

The rear window overlooks the alley and driveway behind her house. She
hears a car pull into the alley and stop near her driveway. Looking out the window,
she recognizes the white Bronco. Her ex-husband steps out of the car. He's dressed

in dark clothing and a knit cap. What's he doing here?, Nicole wonders. Simpson is the last person she wants to see. He can't seem to accept the fact that their relationship is over. He acted very strangely at their daughter's recital earlier this evening. Regardless of whether she is planning to have sex with her friend or not, she does not want Simpson there when he arrives. He is violently jealous, and Nicole does not want another scene. She has got to get rid of him. Frightened and angry, Nicole leaves the living room and heads downstairs. Meanwhile, Simpson enters the back gate and goes down the walkway to the front of the house.

As Nicole passes through her kitchen, she thinks of her ex-husband's violent temper and the many times he has hit her. She pauses in the kitchen, takes a large kitchen knife out and places it on the counter, within easy reach in case Simpson gets inside. She continues toward the front door, still holding one of the take-out menus in her hand. Barefoot and wearing only a short dress, Nicole opens the door and walks onto the landing. She plans to confront Simpson and demand that he leave.

There he is, standing on the landing in a black sweat suit, knit cap, and gloves. Startled by his threatening and suspicious appearance on this summer Sunday evening, Nicole pauses.

We will never know and could forever speculate about Simpson's intentions at this point or what Nicole might have done to provoke him into a murderous rage. Perhaps she told him, again, that their relationship was over, or perhaps she ridiculed or insulted him. Perhaps she tried to calm him down and get him off her property. Perhaps she did nothing at all.

No matter what either one said to each other, at some point they both sense that Simpson's control is slipping. He tries to regain control of the confrontation by attacking Nicole with a pounding blow to the top of her head. Nicole falls limp onto the top step of the stairway, her feet wedged beneath the metal fence. The menu drops from her right hand and comes to a rest under her right leg.

If Simpson's intent is to murder Nicole, he would finish her off right now. She is unconscious and helpless. What stops him? We would like to believe that he realizes what he has done and gets control of himself. Unfortunately, I don't think that is what happened.

While Simpson stands over Nicole's body, breathing heavily, adrenaline raging through his bloodstream, his head snaps in reaction to a noise he hears from the other side of the front gate. Someone is coming.

Simpson jumps down the few steps and hides in the shrubbery of the north side of the walkway. Frightened by the noise, his heart pounding, Simpson watches Ron Goldman walk through the front gate. He knows Ron and Nicole are close; perhaps he thinks they are lovers. Ron immediately sees Nicole's crumpled body on the steps. He runs toward her and tries to help.

As Simpson sees Ron, his fear turns into rage. He becomes focused on Ron and attacks. First he wraps his left arm around Ron's neck and pulls him back into the shrubs along the walk. He has his knife out and starts stabbing. Ron fights back ferociously. Reaching up to pull away the arm that is choking him, Ron yanks a glove off his assailant's hand. The glove falls to the ground.

Ron tries again, reaching back to the head of his attacker. This time he grabs a knit cap and pulls that off. Ron flails with both hands, hitting the iron bars of the front gate repeatedly, injuring his hands. He feels punches, blows, and pain, yet inflicts little damage on his assailant, who is strong, well-positioned, and relentless.

Simpson himself is shocked at the strength of his victim and begins to panic at the thought of losing the fight. He stabs and slashes wildly. Inexperience and fear are Simpson's worst enemy; he is careless and cuts himself several times. One of the cuts is a deep gash to his left middle finger. Simpson's knife continues to puncture Ron until a final slash to the throat takes his life. Ron falls onto the dirt, bleeding to death.

It no longer matters whether Simpson planned to murder his ex-wife. He's already killed Ron. Now he has to kill Nicole.

Now whatever plans Simpson had concerning Nicole have changed. It no longer matters whether he didn't plan or didn't want to murder his ex-wife. He's already killed Ron. Now he has to kill her.

As Nicole awakens from the blow to her head, Simpson is standing above her. He begins stabbing at her head and neck. Nicole is dazed and injured; still, she fights back. As she reaches towards her attacker, her hands are sliced by repeated blows from his knife. In her final seconds of life Nicole looks into her murderer's eyes. For a long time she had been afraid he would kill her. Now it is all happening so fast—her worst nightmare comes true. In disbelief, she feels the final slash. Simpson cuts her throat so deeply that his knife nicks her spine.

Nicole bleeds profusely. Her hands clench in a death grip; she is dead in seconds.

The blood flows from Nicole's throat wound onto the tiled walkway. Simpson steps in the blood of the woman he claimed to love. Stepping over her, his own blood drips from his cut left hand on to the back of his victim, the mother of his children.

Simpson goes down the side walkway, leaving bloody shoeprints and drops of his own blood on the ground. As he approaches the rear gate, Simpson swings his left hand up to the gate knob and casts blood drops onto the gate. Opening the gate with his ungloved left hand, Simpson leaves a bloody fingerprint on the turnstile knob. His Bronco is parked in the alley next to Nicole's driveway. Simpson reaches into his pants, pulling his car keys from the pocket and dropping change onto the ground. He is in too much of a hurry and is too excited even to realize all the clues he is leaving.

Still holding the knife in his gloved right hand, Simpson opens the Bronco door, drops the murder weapon on the passenger seat, and drives away in a panic. While Simpson drives, he unconsciously transfers the victims' blood from his shoe soles onto the Bronco's carpet, and brake and gas pedals. With every movement inside the vehicle he leaves blood from his injured hand, or transfers the blood of the victims from his gloved right hand to the vehicle's interior.

His mind is now racing; he's got to get rid of this knife! Knowing the area well, he drives just a few blocks to a dirt alley and picks a location overgrown with grass and debris. Pulling over quickly, he opens the passenger window and throws the knife out. Speeding off, he strikes a fence or pile of discarded wood. The force of the collision wedges a piece of wood into the front of his car.

Out of control and remembering he has a flight to catch, Simpson drives recklessly back toward his house. Coming into the intersection of Bundy and San Vicente, he runs through the red light, nearly colliding with Jill Shively in her Volkswagen. The Bronco rides up onto the center median of San Vicente. Another car, a gray Nissan, also stops to avoid a collision. For a moment all three drivers are frozen. Simpson begins honking his horn and shouting, "Move your damn car! Move it! Move it!" Shively, a neighborhood resident, recognizes the Bronco driver as O.J. Simpson. The Nissan finally moves out of the way and Simpson drives off. Shively takes down the license plate of the Bronco.

When Simpson arrives at his home, he sees the limo waiting for him at the Ashford gate. He pulls the Bronco to an abrupt stop at the curb by the Rockingham gate. The sudden braking of the car dislodges the piece of wood that was picked up in the alley; it falls onto the parkway. The Bronco is parked haphazardly, but Simpson either does not notice or does not have time to correct it.

Simpson walks toward the front door, blood dripping from his left hand. He sees limo driver Allan Park ringing the buzzer at the Ashford gate. If it is possible, Simpson becomes even more panicked. Even in the dim light, Simpson thinks the driver recognizes him. After all, he is O.J. Here in the doorway, there is at least enough light for Simpson to see the cut on his left hand. This may be the first time he realizes he is cut. He puts the hand into his pocket to keep from dripping more blood.

After seeing the limo driver and his own injury, Simpson does not know what to do. But he realizes that if he walks into the front door, the limo driver will think he is returning from being out. This will ruin whatever alibi he might come up with. Simpson turns toward the garage and runs down the narrow path which goes behind the bungalows. He knows the path will ultimately lead him around to the pool area where he can enter his home through the patio door. Running down the dark path, he collides with an air conditioner braced at about chest height. Simpson hits the air conditioner with force and spins clockwise, striking the wall.

It is approximately 10:40 P.M. On the other side of the wall Kato Kaelin is talking on the phone with his friend Rachel Ferrara when he hears loud thumps. Kato sees a picture on his wall shake, and tells Rachel he thinks it might be an earthquake. When no further noises or movements occur, Kato continues talking with his friend. They stay on the phone for another ten minutes.

Frantic and stunned by his collision, Simpson remembers that his single house key opens all the outside doors to the main house, including the maid's service entrance just off of the walkway where he now is standing. Perhaps Simpson pulls the glove from his right hand and reaches for his keys. In any event, he drops the glove on the ground.

Running back to the service entrance, Simpson fumbles with the key before he finally enters the house. The first thing he does is reach for the light switch in the bathroom, leaving a bloodstain. Once the light comes on, he is momentarily blinded. Then Simpson sees himself in the mirror. He is looking into the face of a murderer.

Remembering the cut on his left hand, Simpson grabs a small gauze bandage to stop the bleeding. Tearing open the bandage wrapper, he remembers the glove he dropped back along the pathway. As he goes back outside, Simpson takes the bandage from its wrapper and covers the cut on his finger. Then he discards the wrapper across the cyclone fence.

Simpson's eyes are not yet accustomed to the darkness and panic gnaws at his mind. Inside the house, the phone is ringing. No doubt the limo driver saw him. He's got to get cleaned up and catch his flight. There's no time to get the glove now. Simpson runs back toward the driveway and walks into his front door, trying to take control of a situation that has already gone sideways countless times and in countless ways. Allan Park sees him enter the house. It is approximately 10:55 P.M.

After stopping to take his shoes off in the foyer, Simpson rushes up the stairs and finally answers the phone. Allan Park says he is downstairs waiting to take him to the airport. Simpson explains that he overslept and just got out of the shower. It is now 10:56 P.M.

Simpson finishes stripping his clothes off as he approaches his bath. First he takes off his socks, leaving them at the foot of his bed. Then he removes the rest of his clothing. The cool water of a shower can't stop his body from sweating. He is not in control.

After he hangs up the phone, Kato walks outside to investigate the noises he heard against his wall. He goes to the entrance of the path, but it is dark and the flashlight he has taken is dim. He is afraid to go any farther. Instead, he comes around to the front of the residence, where he sees the limo and Allan Park. He opens the front gate for the limo to enter the estate grounds.

As Kato comes back to the house, he sees Simpson just inside the front door, sweating and agitated. Kato tries to tell Simpson about the noises he heard, but Simpson rudely silences his permanent houseguest, instructing him not to call the police or Westec. Unknown to Simpson, the gauze bandage on his sliced finger is saturated and he is dripping blood on the foyer of his house.

Luggage in hand and still sweating uncontrollably, Simpson goes out of his front door, leaving yet another blood drop on his brick walkway. It is now 11:02

P.M. He allows the limo driver to pack his luggage in the car, except for one small black bag, which only he handles. Then he gets in the back seat of the car. There he opens the windows and complains of the heat. Yet it is a cool evening—the temperature is 60 degrees.

As Allan Park drives him to the airport, Simpson's mind is racing. Will he be caught? What will happen to his career and reputation? What will his fans think of him?

One thing that does not enter his mind is remorse over the fact that he just killed two people, one of them the mother of his children.

This is one possible scenario of the events on June 13, 1994. My hypothesis is not definitive or absolute. However, from the evidence at both the Bundy and Rockingham scenes, we can deduce certain points that seem almost irrefutable.

The case will remain open in the mind of the public, and there will always be speculation. But the speculation will not address who committed the crime, because any honest reading of the evidence points to only one man. Instead, there will be questions of how he did it and why. Some of the questions we will never be able to answer. Others we can at least try.

From the first moments at the Bundy scene, I felt that at least one of the victims was not the target of the suspect. The victims did not match and were obviously not walking together. Early in the investigation the cause of death was not known, but the eventual conclusion that both victims were killed with a knife seemed to confirm my theory. One victim was a surprise to Simpson.

I don't think Simpson planned to murder Ron Goldman. If he wanted to kill Ron, he wouldn't have done it at his ex-wife's house. Also, Simpson had no idea that Ron was about to arrive at Nicole's to return eyeglasses her mother had left at the restaurant where he worked. Ron was just at the wrong place at the wrong time.

In fact, I'm not sure Simpson planned to kill Nicole either. Would he plan to murder Nicole at her home, leaving the body for their children to find? Even Simpson could not be that coldblooded. And even if he were, I could not imagine a worse place for him to kill his ex-wife than her home. The neighbors knew Simpson and knew that he drove a white Bronco. Why would Simpson plan a murder and then park his vehicle behind the house? For that matter, why use the Bronco at all?

The other problem is the location of Nicole's body. It would seem that the victim dictated the location, not the reverse. Having walked onto the front landing several feet and leaving the door open, it seemed that Nicole was not just responding to a knock at the door or the ring of a doorbell. She saw or heard something or someone outside. This conclusion is bolstered by the fact that she probably held a takeout menu in her right hand when she opened the door. If she had calmly gone to answer the door, she probably would have put the menu down first.

Perhaps Simpson went to Nicole's home to threaten or scare her, not to kill her. But the fact is, we will probably never know what was going on in Simpson's mind the night of the murders. Only one thing appears absolutely certain—he killed Ron and Nicole.

❦

Chapter 17

MARCIA'S CASE

You may not like me for bringing this case.
I'm not winning any popularity contests for doing so.

—MARCIA CLARK TO THE JURY

F OR MONTHS I KEPT EXPECTING to hear whose fingerprint was
on the rear gate at Bundy. Even if I did not read about it in the news,
I figured that at least Ron, Brad, and I would hear about it, as Lange
or Vannatter told us about almost every other scientific discovery relating to the
evidence. The arrest of Simpson, the preliminary hearing, and the second search
warrant came and went. Still, no news about the print.

In January 1995, as the prosecution was well into preparation for the trial,
I was discussing the case with Marcia Clark and asked her about the print. She
looked somewhat taken aback and acted as if she didn't know what fingerprint
I was talking about. I didn't know why she reacted that way, since we had gone
over my notes in detail during the preliminary hearing. I reminded her about

my notes and the observation of the bloody fingerprint. I saw the hesitation in her face as she told me: The print was never photographed or lifted.

"How could they fuck up a crucial piece of evidence like that?" I exclaimed. "It was right there in my notes."

Marcia looked at me with sympathy and said, "Mark, they didn't read your notes."

Shocked would be a mild way of describing my feelings. I ranted and raved for a few minutes. When I calmed down, Marcia consoled me, "I wish you and Ron had kept the case, [the crime scenes] would have come out completely different."

I left her office disgusted. The words, "They didn't read your notes," echo in my mind every time I think about the Simpson case.

I hope everyone reading this can understand the professional frustration I have felt for two years over this one issue. I have not spoken about it except to Ron Phillips and Brad Roberts, with whom I've discussed it at length.

I saw Phillips give my notes to Vannatter when he arrived early in the morning of June 13, 1994, and watched Vannatter place them in his notebook without reading a word. Had either Vannatter or Lange, upon taking over the Bundy crime scene, read my notes, they would have checked out the fingerprint and ordered SID personnel to recover it. Had the print been properly photographed and tested, this case could have been a wrap. The print was no doubt Simpson's, and it would have irrefutably connected him to the scene with his own blood, and possibly that of the two victims. The mention of this print in my notes and its implications were easily seen by the prosecution. But at every point in the trial, they glossed over my notes and any reference to the print. True, if the print was gone, there was not much point in dwelling on it. But the way the prosecution avoided the issue was typical of the way the case was handled and how it was lost.

In the beginning, I had confidence we were all working together. It was only gradually that I realized the prosecutors were compounding the mistakes made at the crime scenes, either by trying to cover them up or ignoring them instead of addressing them directly. This was characteristic of the way the case was handled. Intimidated by the celebrity client and his celebrity defense team, acutely self-conscious because of media scrutiny, and eager to propel their own careers, the lead prosecutors, particularly Marcia Clark and Chris Darden, blew the case.

The one thing I kept noticing about the "O.J. room," the prosecution team's headquarters, was the lack of organization and leadership. Marcia Clark had an office elsewhere on the opposite side of the Criminal Courts building, away from the other attorneys. When somebody needed to see her it was like asking for an audience instead of just working together.

I spent many hours in Marcia's office, watching her smoke cigarettes, a five-foot poster of Jim Morrison looming behind her desk. Marcia was very surprised to discover that I knew who Jim Morrison was, and that I was a big Doors fan myself. She laughed when I told her that the only rock concert I had ever been to was the Doors in 1969. We told each other what our favorite songs were, but, thank God, neither one of us started singing.

I probably spoke to Marcia on every important issue relating to the case and my personal struggles. Marcia had a quick laugh and seemed optimistic most of the time. I believed she regarded me with respect and confidence, two things that would have gone a long way in the Simpson trial if she had maintained her courage. But she didn't.

"They didn't read your notes" echoes in my mind every time I think about the Simpson case.

Marcia was outgoing with everyone, and she liked the power this case offered her, as I'm sure many prosecutors would have. In retrospect, I can see that she thought the mountain of evidence would bury any doubt of Simpson's guilt. In fact, she was counting on it.

Every time testimony suggested careless, preventable mistakes were made by Vannatter, Lange, or the criminalists at the crime scene, Marcia always said the same thing to me: "I wish you and Ron would have kept this case."

At the beginning of March 1995, just days before I took the stand, Marcia asked how I was going to answer the question concerning the fingerprint on the gate at the Bundy scene.

This seemed rather silly to me, but I answered her anyway:

"I saw a bloody fingerprint, several points in quality, on the gate turnstile knob."

Marcia seemed uneasy about my response and said, "Since you are not a fingerprint expert, you can't say that it was a fingerprint for sure, can you?"

"Well, I've got ten, I've seen hundreds, and I've lifted quite a few," I replied.

Marcia nodded. Then she said, "But not being an expert you would not be changing your testimony by saying, 'possible fingerprint,' would you?"

"No, I wouldn't," I replied. "But why don't we have Roberts testify? He saw it, too."

"I don't think we need Roberts," Marcia said curtly.

Later on, when the defense was hammering Dennis Fung for not collecting the extra blood drops from Bundy until nearly three weeks after the murders, I explained to Marcia that Brad Roberts and I had seen those drops of blood on the gate and I had written those observations in my notes. Why not have Brad and me testify to the drops being there on June 13? I thought this would go far to dispel the planted blood theory at Bundy. Again, her answer was: "No, we don't need Brad to testify."

Now I began to wonder why Marcia seemed intent on keeping Brad Roberts off the stand. Why were we throwing away the testimony of one of the first detectives on the scene, and someone who could corroborate most of the evidence we found? I hoped Marcia had a damned good reason to keep Brad out of the trial, but I couldn't think of one.

Another incident made me even more curious. While Cheri, Marcia, and I were speaking of other case matters, Marcia answered her phone and started talking about the black socks in Simpson's bedroom. I knew that the defense had tried to claim that the socks had been planted. Their argument stemmed from a video made at Simpson's Rockingham estate on June 13; the socks were not visible on the tape. Yet, because they had both Simpson's and Nicole's blood on them, these socks were another piece of extremely incriminating evidence.

When Marcia hung up the phone, I commented, "Brad and I saw those socks early on the morning of June 13 when we evacuated the house."

"You can just forget those socks," Marcia said, smiling.

I smiled back, at first thinking she was just joking. But she was not.

Walking out of her office it dawned on me: On every point of evidence for which Brad could provide critical corroboration, Marcia was choosing to let the evidence suffer rather than call Brad to testify. For some reason, she did not want Brad Roberts to testify, no matter what he knew. Conversely, he could corroborate everything I had observed at Bundy and many items at Rockingham. He could give convincing testimonial evidence against any conspiracy theory or charges of planting or tampering with evidence. I began to wonder: Why didn't he testify? Who didn't want him on the stand? What knowledge did Brad possess that would damage the prosecution?

It hit me that if Brad testified to my observations at Bundy, then he would corroborate my notes, our observation of the other drops of blood, and the bloody fingerprint. If he did that, the obvious question would be why Lange and Vannatter hadn't followed up on these clues. The obvious answer, just as Marcia had admitted, was "They didn't read your notes."

By not calling Brad to corroborate my notes, Marcia seemed to be protecting Vannatter and the entire prosecution from embarrassment. If Brad had been called, Vannatter would have had to admit on the stand that he broke one of the cardinal rules of a homicide detective by not reading my notes. And the prosecution would have had the reputation of their lead detective seriously compromised.

If Marcia was protecting Vannatter, she wasn't alone. When Darden handled Vannatter's testimony, he too failed to ask him basic questions concerning my notes. Here is an excerpt from the transcript of March 16, 1995, with Darden examining Vannatter.

> **DARDEN:** Now, after your arrival at the Bundy crime scene, were you ever given any documents at all?
> **VANNATTER:** Yes.
> **DARDEN:** What documents?
> **VANNATTER:** I was given Mark Fuhrman's notes that he had completed before my arrival.
> **DARDEN:** And who gave you those notes?
> **VANNATTER:** Detective Phillips.
> **DARDEN:** Okay. And you've seen Detective Fuhrman's notes, on the Elmo [overhead projector] here in court, have you?
> **VANNATTER:** Yes, I have.
> **DARDEN:** Are those the same notes Detective Phillips gave you?
> **VANNATTER:** Yes.
> **DARDEN:** And did you maintain possession of those notes?
> **VANNATTER:** That's correct.
> **DARDEN:** And do you recall what time it was that Detective Phillips gave you those notes?
> **VANNATTER:** Would have been shortly after 4:05, my arrival. We stood and talked for approximately five minutes and during that period of time, he gave them to me.

DARDEN: Now, as you walked down the walkway at Bundy and exited the rear gate, did you notice anything on the rear gate at all?

VANNATTER: Yes, I did.

DARDEN: What did you notice?

VANNATTER: I noticed what appeared to be blood wipings along the upper rail of the gate and what appeared to be blood drops on the bottom rail of the gate.

DARDEN: And were these blood wipings and blood drops pointed out to you by Detective Phillips?

VANNATTER: They were.

DARDEN: You've told us that you have visited approximately 500 homicide scenes; is that right?

VANNATTER: Approximately yes.

While he asked Vannatter whether he received my notes, he never asked whether he had read them. Of course, Vanatter hadn't read my notes. Marcia knew it. And so did Darden, or he would have asked Vannatter if he had.

While Darden was examining Vannatter, my notes were displayed on the Elmo, an overhead projector which made them visible to everybody in the courtroom. There, in letters the size of my own hand, was the following:

13) AT REAR GATE ON N/S OF RESID - TWO BLOOD SPOTS AT BOTTOM INSIDE OF GATE. THIS AREA MIGHT HAVE BEEN WHERE THE DOG WAS KEPT. SUSP RAN THROUGH THIS AREA. SUSP POSSIBLY BITEN BY DOG?

14) REAR GATE, POSS BLOOD SMUDGE ON UPPER RAIL OF GATE.

15) REAR GATE, INSIDE DEAD BOLT (TURN KNOB TYPE) POSS BLOOD SMUDGE AND VISIBLE FINGERPRINT.

16) BLOODY PAW PRINTS OF LARGE DOG LEADING FROM RESID, S/B ON SIDEWALK

Despite the fact that the fingerprint notation was clearly projected on the wall, nobody mentioned it. Vannatter was not alone in failing to read my notes. None of the journalists sitting in the courtroom that day read them either. Here was a front page story staring them right in the face, but the press corps was too distracted to notice.

Had Marcia's decision not to call Brad as a witness affected only the Bundy scene, specifically the fingerprint, I could maybe understand that, as the fingerprint was already lost. But it also hurt the rest of the case. By refusing to call Brad as a witness, the prosecution lost the opportunity to answer many other claims made by the defense. What follows are important incidents that would have been cleared up by Brad Roberts's testimony:

1. Brad was with me at the Bundy scene, where he saw one glove and a knit cap.
2. Brad saw the additional drops of blood on the walkway gate at Bundy.
3. Brad saw a bloody fingerprint on the turnstile knob of the Bundy walkway gate. Brad believed it to be identifiable.
4. Brad had a discussion with me on the street outside the Bundy crime scene as we waited for Robbery/Homicide. We made plans to go to breakfast. No conspiracy here.
5. Brad joined me at the Rockingham estate and observed the blood inside the Bronco. Brad and I called Vannatter over to the Bronco to see it. Considering his excitement, I'd say this was the first time Vannatter saw the evidence. Brad thought so, too.
6. Brad observed drops of blood on the driveway leading from Rockingham and began numbering them for evidence collection. Vannatter might have also seen these drops, but Brad certainly did.
7. Brad saw the large drop of blood outside the front door of the Rockingham estate and the three drops inside the foyer. Again, Vannatter might have made these observations, but Brad could have corroborated them.
8. Brad helped me evacuate the house of whomever arrived there before the Rockingham estate became an official crime scene,

and in doing so we both observed the two dress socks in Simpson's master bedroom.

9. Brad was the detective to take Simpson from the officer who had handcuffed him around noon on June 13. Simpson made statements to Brad that appeared very incriminating, accompanied by bodily reactions that were definitely incriminating. I had Brad put these statements to paper within hours. These statements were never told to the jury, yet appeared in the homicide book, a total history of the investigation.

10. During the period of the first search warrant, Brad found dark clothes in the washing machine and blood on the bathroom light switch in the service area.

When Marcia refused to have Brad testify, she seriously compromised the case.

An interesting coincidence: The only two people not already teamed up who knew each other from the beginning of this case were Phil Vannatter and Marcia Clark. Remember that Vannatter called Marcia into this case in the first place. They recently had worked together in another case, and they no doubt had a professional friendship. Marcia probably had more loyalty to Vannatter than any of the other detectives involved, and she probably took his advice. Did Vannatter's advice include keeping Roberts out of this case, so his own mistakes didn't become public knowledge?

Marcia Clark didn't set out to blow this case. She became a victim of celebrity, both O.J. Simpson's and her own. The pressure and attention were so much, and Marcia was so afraid that either she or her detectives would look bad, that she ignored important evidence and witnesses.

Once the trial made her famous, Marcia became a different person. Hearing of the troubles she had after the trial, I felt sorry for her. When Vannatter first called Marcia to the scene, she had not even heard of O.J. Simpson. Perhaps she might have been better off never knowing anything more about him.

Chapter 18

DARDEN FOR THE DEFENSE

---

*Still, I was torn. My responsibilities as a prosecutor clearly
told me to take the case. But I had other responsibilities as a
black man, and they were difficult to sort out.*

—CHRISTOPHER DARDEN

THE PROSECUTION LOST the Simpson case for two reasons. As we have already seen, the prosecution team did not argue all the evidence they had. The other reason they lost is that they didn't have an effective strategy for countering the defense's race card. In fact, not only did they not counter these bogus tactics, but in some cases the prosecutors joined in, creating racial controversy themselves.

By the time Marcia Clark, Chris Darden, Cheri Lewis, and I began working together in earnest, the preliminary hearing was over, many racial issues had arisen about me, the defense had spun the planted glove theory, and we all knew that I would be the defense's primary target. Still, I thought that the prosecution would fight to keep the trial focused on the evidence instead of the sideshow.

As it turned out, the prosecution never had a clear strategy from the beginning. They should have appealed Judge Ito's decision to allow racial issues and the use of the "N" word into the case. And throughout the trial they should have fought hard to convict O.J. Simpson instead of caving in on racial issues.

Personally, I got along with everyone on the team, and they treated me with friendship and respect. Chris Darden is the only member of the prosecution team who has admitted that he harbored anything other than a professional attitude toward me during this time. Chris let his personal emotions enter this case in too many places and times. It wasn't professional. He wasn't a team player.

As he wrote in his book *In Contempt* about our initial meeting:

"I didn't like him from the first time I saw him. I looked at him sitting in Scott Gordon's office, waiting for me, and I had the urge to run."

Chris was an hour and a half late for our meeting, but that didn't bother him. As he said in his book: "I didn't give a shit."

Chris Darden is a brooding, confused man. He is hotheaded, immature, and not in the least bit organized. He didn't seem concerned with the case, or, if he was, he did a good job of hiding it. He pouted constantly, and when things didn't go well, he seemed to feel persecuted. He is obsessed with race, and throughout the trial he appeared more concerned about his image in the black community than his effectiveness as a prosecutor.

Chris was acutely sensitive to any criticism, especially when it came from other blacks. "Where the hell were these people when the LAPD was vilifying me, calling me 'too black' and 'too militant?' " he said to *People* magazine. "Am I supposed to have surrendered my skin color just because I'm doing my job? I'll tell you, when this case is over, the families of black victims will be asking for me."

Darden often saw himself as a black man first and a prosecutor second. In the following quote from his book, he discusses his ambivalence about accepting the district attorney's offer to join the prosecution team. "Still, I was torn. My responsibilities as a prosecutor clearly told me to take this case. But I had other responsibilities as a black man, and they were difficult to sort out."

This statement illustrates the problems that Chris brought to the case—racial hypersensitivity, callowness, an inability to make up his mind, and amnesia about his oath as a prosecutor.

What if I arrived at a homicide scene—which appeared to be the murder of a black man by a white man—and said that I was not sure I wanted to investigate this case, since I was torn between my responsibilities as a homicide detective and my responsibilities as a white man? I would be justifiably criticized, if not run off the force. But Darden's public anguish was either passed over without criticism, or seen as an example of his thoughtfulness and racial pride.

I don't understand why Chris was brought into the case. His obsession with race and police misconduct was not a secret. Chris claims that during his tenure in the Special Investigations Division, he prosecuted a lot of cops. In fact, he may have investigated a lot of cops, but he took only a couple to trial. One was a good friend of mine, who had allegedly mistreated a suspect, an undercover cop, and supposedly used a racial slur. This officer was forced into early retirement because of the incident, even though the suspect's charges were completely unjustified. My friend was branded as a racist, despite the fact that he is married to a black woman. It doesn't make any sense, but racial politics rarely do. And Chris Darden used racial politics to advance his career. Turning the Simpson case into a racial issue would position him as the only black person on the side of justice. It would also make him rich.

Darden often saw himself as a black man first and a prosecutor second.

If a racist is someone obsessed with race, whose perception is clouded by the color of a person's skin, and who sees himself as a member of a racial group first and a human being second, then Chris Darden could be called a racist. But I won't.

Despite all this, Darden was initially given the responsibility of handling my testimony. In fact, he was awarded the job precisely because of racial considerations.

In his book, Chris describes the meeting when it was officially decided that he would examine me. Marcia had just said she would examine the timeline and police officer witnesses:

> That left me. I looked around the room and realized how white they all looked. All these white people and me. How would that look to the homies in South Central: one brother surrounded by all this whiteness, sticking out like a scratch on a new Mercedes? Damn, I thought, I really am going to pay hell for this.

'Chris, you have Fuhrman and Vannatter.'

Damn. We had talked about this, but to hear it was like getting kicked. Those two were the most controversial witnesses in the case, the two who could turn the case, lose it for us. This wasn't putting witnesses on the stand, it was taking cattle to the butcher. Vannatter was going to be drilled by the defense for statements he made applying for a search warrant, and—worse—there were reports Fuhrman had gone through some psychological tests that uncovered deep racist sentiments.

The other lawyers seemed to freeze, maybe expecting me to throw up or let loose with a wild string of expletives. They waited. Only Marcia didn't look up at me. She continued to stare at the pages in front of her.

'Yeah,' I said. 'No problem.'

On the way out the door, I passed Dana Escobar, one of the brand-new baby-cake deputy D.A.'s [sic] we had on the case.

'So?' I asked him. 'What do you think of the way the witnesses were split?'

'I think it's fucked up,' he said. 'I feel sorry for you.'

In this scene, Escobar is not the only person feeling sorry for Chris Darden. Chris wasn't happy about having to cross-examine me. Tough. It was his job. I wasn't very happy when people were shooting at me, punching, biting, and kicking me—but that was my job. I didn't whine about it.

Before my appearance in court, Chris and I were supposed to prepare for my testimony. Since the grand jury was not in session, the prosecution took over the grand jury room and used it for a practice trial session. This practice session shocked me. There were too many non-essential people in attendance. The district attorney's office already knew there were leaks to the media, yet they allowed people inside the room who I didn't even recognize.

I didn't like this situation, and I didn't cooperate the way I know they wanted me to. Consciously, I changed my demeanor; I felt uncomfortable and showed my irritability. At one point I became so detached from participating in the session that I began eating a submarine sandwich while the attorneys were talking among themselves. The practice session was totally unproductive.

Almost immediately there were media leaks from the practice session, and these leaks became a big problem for the prosecution. Soon after stories about the session were published, Gil Garcetti held a meeting with the Simpson prosecutors to remind everybody that such information was supposed to be confidential and that leaks often result in erroneous news reports, such as the ones that had just come out. During this meeting, Darden went on a tirade, screaming about the leaks and promising an Internal Affairs investigation. Why did Chris unleash such an outburst—was he simply protesting too much? In hindsight, he was the only person who had anything to gain from leaking information to the press. Was he the leak? Did he do it in order to keep from having to cross-examine me, or even to keep me from appearing?

The defense, the media, and others were concerned that what had happened during the practice session was improper. But later in the trial, when those involved in the session were deposed by Judge Ito, no inconsistencies with my testimony were found. Ito could have saved himself the trouble and just asked me. I would have told him the practice session was short and useless.

Chris and I got nowhere on my testimony preparation. He asked me questions like, who were my favorite sports stars? (My answer: George Foreman, Michael Jordan, and Larry Bird.) Whenever possible during our sessions together, Chris avoided discussing the continuing racial controversy surrounding me. My testimony drew closer, and still we got nowhere.

One day I was sitting in Chris's office, and he was doing what he usually did, reading something intently and glancing up at me only for an occasional question. While he was trying his best to forget that I was sitting right across from him, I looked around his office. On a hat rack in the corner was a black baseball cap with green lettering. I leaned forward to read what the cap said, and was surprised to see "Black Law."

Maybe it was some kind of fraternity gift, or it had sentimental value. Still I thought it was inappropriate to display in the office. It's not a big deal, just a baseball cap with a little slogan on it. But as a white man, I couldn't even ask him what it meant.

After weeks of putting up with Chris's attitude and intransigence, I finally confronted Marcia with the problem. I told her that Chris wouldn't work with me and I would prefer that she did my direct examination. Marcia told me that she couldn't just take this important job away from Chris. My response was,

"If something doesn't happen quickly, we are going to screw up what doesn't need to be screwed up."

This went on for two weeks. Marcia didn't want to make the decision, and Chris and I still weren't getting anywhere on my preparation. The defense was taking its time deciding whether Cochran or Bailey would cross-examine me, hoping that the apparent indecision would affect the prosecution's strategy. *Newsweek* characterized Cochran as a "good cop" and Bailey as a "bad cop," although to compare either one of them to policemen is an insult even to bad cops. Meanwhile, the prosecution was having problems of its own figuring out what to do. Finally, Marcia informed me that she would do my direct examination, and I was very pleased with the decision.

In his book, Chris states that he was the one who asked Marcia to do my direct examination. If that's what Chris wants to say to make himself look better, fine. But Cheri Lewis saw what happened and she also sat in Marcia's office at least once when I pleaded with Marcia to do my direct.

And Chris portrayed a different attitude in the media. During an interview with *People* magazine, the following exchange was recorded:

Marcia Clark: "When Bailey starts in on Fuhrman, maybe Chris and I should create our own diversionary tactics for the jury. Chris will come over and begin to strangle me, and then I'll fall to the floor, and then ... "

"Why can't I take some testimony from Fuhrman?" Darden interrupts in a mock whine. "I don't get anything."

Darden said that if he had examined me, he would have gone after me, treating me like a hostile witness. He calls his book *In Contempt*, and I agree, he is in contempt—in contempt of the people he is supposed to represent. The only difference between Chris Darden and Johnnie Cochran is that Chris worked for the city and made less money. After the trial, someone said about Darden: "I don't know, he's just an unhappy person." The person making this observation was none other than Simpson himself, in a call to CNN. Even someone as self-absorbed as O.J. couldn't help but notice Darden's brooding, troubled character.

While he has made many harsh statements about me, I don't think Chris really meant all of them. In fact, Chris was not all that unfriendly toward me. The day after Bailey's cross-examination of me, Chris, Vannatter, and I had plans to play basketball. Vannatter dropped out at the last minute, so we never played. Now that it's all over, I imagine Chris is glad the game was canceled. Shooting hoops with Mark Fuhrman is not something Chris Darden would want to have to look back on.

Despite all the conflicts and mini-dramas in the district attorney's office, in the media, and in the courtroom, I thought that my testimony could clear up some of these problems. I should have known better. With my appearance at the trial just a few days away, I sat in Marcia's office discussing my upcoming testimony. Chris Darden opened her door without knocking, looked in, and spoke to Marcia. Before leaving, Chris looked at me and said, "Remember, you didn't use the 'N' word in the last ten years…right?"

Chris smiled and shut the door.

I was shocked that he would make that kind of a comment. He never joked with me very much before, especially about race. I wrote the comment off as sarcasm, but I have to admit that since Chris had never asked me the question in preparation, his words buzzed around in my head.

Chapter 19

TAKING THE STAND

Is he a racist? Yes. Is he the worst LAPD has to offer? Yes. Do we wish the LAPD had never hired him? Yes. In fact, do we wish there were no such person on the planet?

—MARCIA CLARK, FROM HER SUMMATION

O N THE MORNING OF MARCH 9, 1995, I entered Judge Ito's courtroom. Walking past the rows of the audience, I saw heads turn and I recognized many faces from the media. I was sworn in, took my seat in the witness chair and stared directly into the eyes of a murderer. Simpson tried to stare back at me but I locked my eyes on him. Eventually Simpson blinked and turned away.

Marcia began my direct testimony with a line of questioning that would appear out of place in any trial other than *People vs. Orenthal James Simpson*.

CLARK: Detective Fuhrman, can you tell us how you feel about testifying today?
FUHRMAN: Nervous.

CLARK: Okay.

FUHRMAN: Reluctant.

CLARK: Can you tell us why?

FUHRMAN: Throughout—since June 13, it seems that I have seen a lot of the evidence ignored and a lot of personal issues come to the forefront. I think that is too bad.

CLARK: Okay. Heard a lot about yourself in the press, have you?

FUHRMAN: Daily.

CLARK: In light of that fact, sir, you have indicated that you feel nervous about testifying. Have you gone over your testimony in the presence of several district attorneys in order to prepare yourself for court and the allegations that you may hear from the defense?

FUHRMAN: Yes.

CLARK: And in the course of that particular examination, sir, was the topic of your testimony concerning the work you did in this case, the actual visitation to Bundy and Rockingham, was that discussed?

FUHRMAN: No.

CLARK: It dealt with side issues, sir?

FUHRMAN: Yes, it was.

By being the first to bring up the subject of racial allegations, Marcia was gambling. She knew that the defense would bring it up, and she thought by mentioning it herself, she might be able to defuse the issue. Well, there was no way a few questions and comments were going to get the issue of race out of the Simpson case as it was now being conducted. And her mentioning racial issues first made it difficult for her to object or even argue when the defense brought them up on cross-examination. Whether or not race was relevant to the murder of Nicole Brown and Ron Goldman, once Marcia Clark introduced it in her initial line of questioning, race became an established issue in the trial.

We continued as I testified about my first encounter with O.J. Simpson in 1985. I described how I had responded to the Rockingham estate for a family dispute involving Nicole Brown and the defendant. One statement Marcia refused to include in my testimony about my first and only encounter with Nicole was my last comment to her before I left. Sensing Nicole's fear and anguish, I asked if she wanted to make a crime report against her husband.

She said no.

I wanted to make her realize her desperate situation, so I said, "It's your life."

Marcia felt the comment was cold and insensitive; and I agreed. I wanted it to be cold and insensitive, perhaps it would wake Nicole up. Marcia still disagreed, arguing that it was not relevant. Of course, because she decided which questions were asked, once she made her decision it was a dead issue. Since Marcia would not ask me about it, my statement to Nicole was never brought up in court. The statement would have shown that far from having an obsession with either O.J. or Nicole, I treated the visit to Rockingham professionally. While I was willing to give Nicole any help she required, she had to ask for it. She had to help herself.

F. Lee Bailey successfully argued that I had been opened up for cross-examination on several issues, including race. Marcia's preemptive strike had backfired.

The direct testimony continued, with Marcia again bringing up racial issues with questions about Kathleen Bell and Andrea Terry, two of the defense's witnesses against me. Once the racial allegations were explored and refuted by Marcia's line of questioning, my testimony got back on track. Now she asked about my participation in the murder investigation, and I laid out everything in detail. There were no surprises, no revelations, no conspiracy, no planting of evidence, just my recollections and observations concerning a brutal double homicide.

As the direct testimony progressed, Marcia came to the observations I made concerning the rear walkway gate at the Bundy crime scene. Her questioning definitely addressed the amount of blood drops on the gate:

> **CLARK:** When you got to the rear gate area, did you make any observations there?
>
> **FUHRMAN:** Officer Riske pointed out some blood on the gate, some smudging on the upper rail of the gate. I noticed some blood dropping on the center of the gate, the mesh part of the gate.

BAILEY: Excuse me, your honor. The print [courtroom visual] is gone.

COURT: You don't have to have it there to point it out.

FUHRMAN: There appeared to be evidence of blood on the bottom rung of the gate. I noticed a blood smudge around the doorknob lock on the interior or east side of the gate.

Just by this exchange of questions and answers, the prosecution established evidence of blood on the gate's upper rail, drops on the center of the gate in the steel mesh, blood on the lower rail of the gate, and a blood smudge around the gate's doorknob lock area. The defense's attack on Dennis Fung centered around these very issues, that the extra drops were not present early the morning of June 13, but planted by Vannatter after obtaining blood from Simpson. My testimony should have been enough to contradict the defense's preposterous theory that Vannatter tried to plant evidence. But later on in the trial Fung proved to be such an ineffective witness that Barry Scheck was able to insinuate suspicion of conspiracy, instead of mere incompetence. All the more reason Brad should have been called to corroborate my testimony.

Instead, Marcia continued her examination without asking if anyone else had seen these additional drops of blood. Eliciting more facts about the gate, Marcia asked the following:

CLARK: Okay, and is that the rear gate where you just described seeing the blood dropping on the lower rear— lower rung and the middle and then the smudge on the latch?

FUHRMAN: Yes.

CLARK: And what else were you able to see on that gate, sir?

FUHRMAN: Not at that time, but later, I saw a partial possible fingerprint that was on that knob area.

CLARK: Did you then walk through the rear gate, sir, with officer Riske and Detective Phillips?

I'm not an attorney, but I have been questioned in hundreds of criminal trials. To me the obvious next question should have been, "Did anyone see this possible fingerprint other than you?" But Marcia didn't ask this.

Instead of following up on a seemingly obvious line of questioning, Marcia continued with the slow and methodical depiction of my movements, observations, and conduct at the Bundy scene. As Marcia led me through the facts, there came a point when the importance of my notes came to light.

> **CLARK:** Okay, and when you say the first round of notes, sir, can you explain a little bit more what you mean by that?
>
> **FUHRMAN:** Most of these notes were what Officer Riske was pointing out to Detective Phillips and myself, and what I observed.
>
> **CLARK:** What did you intend to do—were these rough notes?
>
> **FUHRMAN:** Yes.
>
> **CLARK:** What did you intend to do with these notes later on?
>
> **FUHRMAN:** Use them to go back to these areas and use them as a guide in what to go back to and prioritize them.

In her direct questions concerning my notes, Marcia actually had me describe what Vannatter should have done after receiving them. He should have analyzed the various evidence and put priority on fragile items such as the fingerprint, a piece of evidence that should have been isolated and recovered.

Marcia continued, asking questions about each item listed in my notes. When she arrived at item #15, the blood smudge and fingerprint, she asked what I saw, but once again did not ask what I thought about those items or who else observed them.

The trial progressed rather slowly, breaking down every thought, movement, and discovery into testimony. The trip to Rockingham was covered, as were the observations that first brought the Bronco into questionable light—the blood on the driver's door.

As the questioning reached the end of my second day of testimony on Friday, March 10, Clark had me introduce the shovel and plastic sheeting found in Simpson's Bronco. Clark also had me introduce the piece of wood found near the Bronco on the parkway. The shovel was just as I remembered it, as was the piece of wood, but as I opened the package containing the plastic and unfolded it I realized that it was in fact a large bag. I had never been told anything about this item of evidence since I saw it on June 13, 1994. As I described to the court my actions of unwrapping and unfolding the plastic, you had to hear the surprise in my voice. I wondered why nobody had told me it was just a plastic bag.

Over the weekend, the prosecution learned that some Broncos, including Simpson's, were equipped with these factory bags in which to place a flat tire to keep the dirt from soiling the interior if the tire needed to be transported. It was kind of embarrassing to introduce evidence the detectives, or SID, never even looked at, much less determined what it actually was.

On Monday, March 13, court was once again in session and I was on the stand.

Marcia had attempted to end Friday with the introduction of the Bronco evidence and the speculation of what it meant. By Monday she had to clear up an obvious mistake, and I was the witness she had to use.

> **CLARK:** Okay, now that plastic, do you happen to know whether it belongs in a Bronco or anything about it?
>
> **FUHRMAN:** Well, now I do.
>
> **CLARK:** And what's that?
>
> **FUHRMAN:** It is the spare tire bag.
>
> **CLARK:** Okay.
>
> **FUHRMAN:** In other words, when a tire is taken off the vehicle and it is dirty, you place it in the bag so you can place it in the cargo area.
>
> **CLARK:** And that is standard equipment for a Ford Bronco, is it?
>
> **FUHRMAN:** I was told it was, yes.

We should have known this information before trial. As it happened, we looked a little foolish that day.

The description of my movements, thoughts, and conclusions were reduced to testimony. From the scaling of the wall to the discovery of the Rockingham glove, Clark walked me through the case, step by step, as if she were clearing a minefield.

Judge Ito called a fifteen-minute break. When the court resumed, I once again took my place in the witness chair. Before the judge ordered the bailiff to summon the jurors, it was decided that Bailey would be heard on a motion. In his motion, citing the "Anthony P." case, Bailey successfully argued that the people had opened me up for cross-examination on several issues, including race. Marcia's preemptive strike had backfired.

Chapter 20

CROSSING THE LINE

Bailey's continual use of the "n" word...did nothing but heighten racial tensions both inside and outside the courtroom, and it was completely unnecessary.

—ROBERT SHAPIRO

T HE MEDIA HYPE before I took the stand to face the great F. Lee Bailey was more like the cheap theatrics before a heavyweight fight. The famous trial lawyer said that "any lawyer in his right mind who would not look forward to cross-examining Mark Fuhrman is an idiot." Then he compared me to Hitler. He promised that he would perform the most "annihilating, character-assassinating" cross-examination ever.

Of course all this hype was created, planned, and exploited by the defense. We listened, not in fear, but in amusement to Bailey's claims that he would prove the Rockingham glove was planted. I knew that was impossible. But to say that I wasn't nervous would be untrue. A lot of people were counting on me, and I certainly put a lot of pressure on myself. And despite everything she said later,

Marcia Clark had confidence in me. I felt that if I took the stand, told the truth, and didn't let Bailey shake me, everything would be all right.

During a statement to the court just prior to his cross-examination of me, Bailey made an assertion that he could never prove, and he knew it. He said I was "...definitely a suspect for having carried that glove from Bundy where he found it to Rockingham where he deposited it, and that's what we intend to show by circumstantial evidence far stronger than the people will offer against O.J. Simpson on the murders." Bailey had a better chance of being abducted by aliens at lunch than proving I had planted any evidence.

After Bailey guaranteed the court that he would produce evidence that I planted the Rockingham glove, he began his cross-examination of me. Bailey likes to think of himself as a tough guy. He struts around the courtroom like a thug, wearing elevator shoes to make himself look taller. Even when Bailey tries to appear civil, every smile seems planned and ingenuous. Meanwhile, he's plotting his attack on some undeserving witness. Although he had a coffee cup and water glass at the defense table, he kept drinking from a short stainless steel thermos that he brought into the courtroom. I have no idea what was in that thermos, but it appeared to stimulate him.

He came out with questions regarding the shovel and the plastic, but did not ask about the piece of wood found lying on the parkway in front of the Rockingham estate. In review of the transcript, that seems odd—perhaps he wanted to play down its importance.

Then Bailey asked me about the taped interrogation of Simpson by Lange and Vannatter. Bailey became agitated that he couldn't get me to admit that I had talked to Lange and Vannatter about the interview. But I hadn't. I knew the important point of the interview without asking anyone its content, that Simpson hadn't confessed.

Bailey shifted gears and began routine background questions to lay the foundation of his next line of questioning. Moving on to the Bundy crime scene, he questioned my abilities as a homicide detective in subtle ways. He made snide insinuations that I would take Riske's word about evidence at the scene, or that I neglected to notice the word "Daddy" on the telephone speed dialer.

The cross-examination was not without its moments of humor. Bailey asked me about the grand jury room practice session, and I told him that I was asked only a total of maybe ten questions by three different lawyers. Bailey was flabbergasted.

BAILEY: Do you know of any lawyer on this earth who is capable of asking only three questions?
FUHRMAN: Not currently.

As the courtroom audience laughed, Bailey said, "Touché."

At another point in the cross, Bailey went over my interview with Kato Kaelin. I described my technique of questioning, often changing topics to keep the subject off-guard, and sometimes interrupting his answers to ask new questions.

BAILEY: Do you normally ask somebody a question and then before they have a chance to answer, cut them off and ask another one?

The great trial lawyer had done this so often to me already that the audience simply broke out in laughter at Bailey. I answered his question, and for once Bailey did not cut me off.

Bailey slowly walked me through my observations, notations, and conclusions about the Bundy scene without any startling revelations. I continued to make eye contact with Bailey. Whenever he looked up to pose another question, I was staring him right in the eye. He did not intimidate me.

The cross-examination suddenly changed from the Bundy scene to the Kathleen Bell letter. Bailey dissected this issue six ways to Sunday, but I honestly could not remember Kathleen Bell or her friend Andrea Terry.

During this area of questioning, Bailey tried to compare the finding of the Rockingham glove with my memory of Kathleen Bell, by asking, "Now, Detective Fuhrman, are you as satisfied with the quality of the truth of your denial of knowing Kathleen Bell as you are of your claim that you found the right-handed glove on Mr. Simpson's property? Is the quality of the truth of those two statements the same, or is one stronger than the other, if you know?"

If I know? Hell, I couldn't figure out what he said. It didn't make much sense, and if it did, what a whopper of a compound question! Luckily Clark objected that the question was vague, and Ito sustained the objection.

When the court recessed for lunch, I returned to the "O.J. room." As I passed case coordinator Patty Jo Fairbanks's desk, she stopped me and told me I was doing great and handed me a fist full of florist cards. People were sending lots of flowers. Patty Jo and I talked briefly, and we decided that the flowers should be sent to the Children's Hospital, and so she sent twenty-five or thirty arrangements there. I kept the cards.

I think everyone should know that this case could not even have gotten off the ground had it not been for Patty Jo. She was beyond indispensable, and probably the best source for accurate information. Patty Jo is a genuine "great person," and I'm glad I know her and consider her a friend. She has called me several times since the verdict and reassured me that the failure of this case was not my fault. With some friends, this would not have the same impact because it is an emotional response, but Patty Jo knew the truth in this case.

Some of my friends were in the district attorney's office watching my testimony, and at every break they offered support and praise. Retired Lieutenant Chuck Higbey, a legend in the LAPD who led the Officer Involved Shooting Team, sat with me and gave me confidence, laughed with me, and made me stand tall. I was honored and still am that this man gave me the time of day, let alone his friendship. My attorney Bob Tourtelot sat in the "O.J. room" throughout my testimony, especially important to me during Bailey's questioning.

Back in court, Bailey continued his cross, still on the Bundy scene. While he asked a series of questions regarding the viewing of a wound on Ron Goldman's body from the vantage point of the north fence, Bailey tried to establish that I took some evidence from the scene.

> **BAILEY:** There is a problem that has been brought to your attention, isn't there?
>
> **FUHRMAN:** No.
>
> **BAILEY:** When discussing this event in the preliminary hearing and talking about the glove, your tongue slipped and you said "them" didn't you?
>
> **FUHRMAN:** Yes.
>
> **BAILEY:** And you have examined that in the transcript, haven't you?
>
> **FUHRMAN:** Yes.
>
> **BAILEY:** And you know it has been played on video to the jury? The word "them" is clear?
>
> **FUHRMAN:** Yes.
>
> **BAILEY:** That is a slip of the tongue?

FUHRMAN: No.

BAILEY: It was not, okay. Now when Vannatter came, you were off the case?

Bailey infuriated me with his inference, trying to establish that I took a glove from Bundy. The word "them" referred to the one glove and a knit cap at the Bundy scene, not another glove. I thought there should have been an objection right there, as Bailey misstated the preliminary hearing testimony simply by not reading the testimony before and after my statement about "them."

Moving on to the Rockingham estate, Bailey went through the various items of evidence, Kato's statements about the thumps on his wall, and my investigation of those noises which led to the discovery of the bloody glove behind Kato's room. While appearing to focus on the pathway, reciting distances and estimates of a man's walk in a minute, he asked:

BAILEY: All right. Did you know there was blood in the Bronco?
FUHRMAN: No.
BAILEY: Have you ever testified that there was blood in the Bronco?
FUHRMAN: I'm not sure if we testified to that in the prelim or not.
BAILEY: Did you wipe a glove in the Bronco, Detective Fuhrman?

Bailey is using classic interrogation-type questioning, going down one path, and then without warning, switching gears to launch a new line of inquiry. I hope most people can see the fallacy of Bailey's accusation here. He accuses me of wiping the bloody glove found at Rockingham in the Bronco to account for the blood inside.

Did Bailey even realize that what he claimed was impossible? The bloody glove contained blood from both victims and Simpson, so how could I wipe the glove on the driver's side carpet in the Bronco and leave evidence of only Ron and Nicole's blood? The driver of the vehicle had these two blood mixes on his shoe soles when he entered and drove the Bronco, transferring the blood to the carpet. Wiping the glove on anything would have left traces of all three. But Bailey conveniently forgot these crucial details in his attempt to paint his conspiracy scenario. Also, Bailey seemed to forget that Simpson admitted to Vannatter and Lange that he had bled in his home, on the driveway, and in the Bronco.

When Bailey said that he would soon call Max Cordoba to testify that I had addressed him with a racial slur, Marcia rose to object.

"We have interviewed Max Cordoba a long time ago," Marcia said. "He never made such a statement, and he never alleged that Mark Fuhrman made such a statement."

Bailey puffed up like a gamecock and addressed the court:

"Your honor, I have spoken with him on the phone personally, Marine to Marine. I haven't the slightest doubt that he will march up to that witness stand and tell the world what Fuhrman called him on no provocation whatsoever."

That evening on the television show *Dateline*, Cordoba said that he had never spoken to Bailey—Marine to Marine or otherwise. He also claimed that I called to him using the slur. The next day, after Marcia aired Cordoba's interview in court, Bailey admitted that he hadn't actually spoken to Cordoba about the case, but that he had talked to him the night before and Cordoba said he misspoke on the television show.

Did Bailey even realize that what he claimed was impossible?

The next day, March 14, Bailey attempted once more to get Max Cordoba on the witness list. The issue at hand was a statement Bailey had made to the court that Cordoba had personally spoken to him, "Marine to Marine," and that Cordoba would testify, describing an incident where I supposedly called him a racial slur. Of course, months prior, Cordoba had been on television and described me as a "nice guy he always got along with." Since that time he had a dream that made him remember the slur.

That night Cordoba was again on television and again stated that he had never spoken to Bailey "Marine to Marine," as Bailey had told the court.

The next morning I told Clark that she had to get in his face about this. Bailey had already gotten away with enough. Cordoba was lying about me, but I was sure he'd been truthful about the conversation between him and Bailey. Why else would he say it on national television? Clark agreed, and I told her, "Bailey will lose it if you challenge him that he lied to the court."

The morning of the March 15, the fireworks started in earnest. Marcia Clark said that Bailey misled the court on this issue. Bailey jumped up, looking like he was going to burst, and interrupted Clark's statement. Bailey's response was less than believable, but Clark made the statement precisely to watch Bailey lose his temper. It worked.

Although I was not in the court, I believe this was when Bailey attempted to have the court allow him to do a glove demonstration. Bailey wanted to demonstrate how a glove could be put into a plastic bag and then carried in someone's sock. This was how I supposedly transported a second glove from Bundy to the Rockingham scene. Of course the judge wouldn't allow it, because the glove Bailey wanted to use was not the same size as the gloves in evidence.

"Size small—must be Mr. Bailey's," Marcia said, examining the glove, a comment that was obviously sexual.

Bailey's blood pressure went up, and the demonstration was shot down.

After he eventually composed himself, Bailey resumed cross-examination and continued drawing more testimony of facts and observations from me, with racial issues intermingled throughout. Using the "grand jury" practice sessions as a springboard, Bailey asked, "Did you tell the lawyers in that room that you never used the word 'nigger'?" I answered, "It was never asked." Then Bailey launched into the race issue head on:

> **BAILEY:** I'm asking, do you?
> **COURT:** Rephrase the question.
> **BAILEY:** Do you use the word "nigger" in describing people?

Bailey had yet to establish a time frame for his question, which from my understanding of the court's ruling was use of the word in the past ten years.

> **FUHRMAN:** No, sir.

My answer here was in response to Bailey's blanket statement concerning the use of the word. The question in my understanding then and now referred to habitual use in the course of a lifetime.

> **BAILEY:** Have you used that word in the last ten years?
> **FUHRMAN:** Not that I recall, no.

At this point of the cross-examination, Bailey directly asked if I "ever" use the word, and my answer was, "Not that I recall."

> **BAILEY:** You mean if you called someone a nigger you have forgotten it, sir.
> **FUHRMAN:** I'm not sure I can answer the question the way you phrased it.

I didn't answer the question because he never restated it.

> **BAILEY:** You have difficulty understanding the question?
> **FUHRMAN:** Yes.
> **BAILEY:** I will rephrase it. I want you to assume that perhaps at some time, since '85 or '86, have you addressed a member of the African American race as a nigger. Is it possible that you have forgotten that act on your part?
> **FUHRMAN:** No, it is not possible.

Bailey quite clearly asked, since '85 or '86 have you "addressed" which means, "directly called," an African American with that word. I previously answered no to that. So I answered no again.

> **BAILEY:** Are you therefore saying that you have not used that word in the past ten years, Detective Fuhrman?

By stating, "are you therefore saying…" Bailey is referring to the previously asked question and answer, which clearly described addressing African Americans, not referring to them.

> **FUHRMAN:** Yes, that's what I'm saying.
> **BAILEY:** And you say under oath that you have not addressed any black persons as a nigger or spoken about black people as niggers in the past ten years, Detective Fuhrman.

This question is compound at the least, and when I answered this question I continued to answer the portion that was connected to the rest of the cross concerning this issue, "Have I addressed or called any black person a nigger."

For this statement to be perjury, of course, it has to be relevant and material, which it clearly is not. But perjury must also be willful, and I can guarantee that at no point was I willfully lying to the court.

The screenplay tapes only could prove the "use" of the word, not the direct addressing of an individual. The attorney general could come up with only one person who claimed that I addressed him with that word in the past ten years. This person was Roderic Hodge, a suspect whose statements could easily have been impeached. The crime of perjury is supposed to require more corroboration than one person.

As we all know, the attorney general did eventually file charges of perjury against me. My plea had nothing to do with what I have described here; it had to do with the ability to finance a defense and the realization that I could not receive a fair trial.

My detective work in this case was never successfully challenged. Bailey never laid a glove on me. The only problems with my testimony were areas in which I defeated myself.

I could have answered "yes" to the accusations that Bailey leveled against me, but I truly do not address people with that word. Perhaps I was a little stubborn, a little embarrassed, and felt like I was carrying the reputation of too many people on my back. All these factors resulted in my blanket answer of "no." As I sat in the witness chair, there seemed to be no right or wrong answer. I did the best I could.

Marcia's redirect was short and to the point, focusing exclusively on how it was impossible for me to have planted the glove and ludicrous to think I did.

> **CLARK:** The first time you walked out on the south pathway at 2360 South [sic] Rockingham, did you know the time of death for Ron Goldman and Nicole Brown?
>
> **FUHRMAN:** No.
>
> **CLARK:** Did you know whether Mr. Simpson had an alibi for the time of their murders?

FUHRMAN: No.

CLARK: Did you know whether there were any eyewitnesses to their murders?

FUHRMAN: No.

CLARK: Did you know whether anyone had heard voices or any sounds or any words spoken at the crime scene at the time of their murders?

FUHRMAN: No.

CLARK: Did you know whether Kato had already gone up the south walkway before you got there?

FUHRMAN: No.

CLARK: Did you know whether any fibers from the Bronco would be found on that glove that you ultimately found at Rockingham?

FUHRMAN: No.

CLARK: And did you know the cause of death?

FUHRMAN: No.

That's the redirect in its entirety. After just those seven questions, anyone who still thought I planted the glove must have been drinking from F. Lee Bailey's thermos.

Chapter 21

CENTER STAGE

---

*Mark is a very fine officer. He may not be a choirboy, may
not be a perfect individual. But he's an aggressive officer.
He's exactly the kind of individual you want.*

—FORMER LAPD CHIEF DARYL GATES

O NCE AGAIN, AFTER MY TESTIMONY, Marcia came up and said, "You are
one of the best police witnesses I've ever seen."

In the following days and weeks, I remained the prosecution's
star witness. Despite all the charges and innuendos, despite the fact that the
defense still claimed, without even a wisp of evidence, that I framed O.J.
Simpson, I was congratulated everywhere I went. The media continued to
hound me for interviews, but they were continually disappointed.

One night I went to my attorney Bob Tourtelot's house, and Gerry Spence
happened to drop by. I was glad to meet the cowboy lawyer, despite the fact
that he was regularly commenting on the trial and had close ties to the defense.
I don't know whether he knew I was at Tourtelot's or not, but at least he

respected my request to keep the evening off the record, even though he was accompanied by John Gibson, a local news anchor who was covering the Simpson trial. John had a lot of class, and I never heard a hint that he knew me, spoke to me, or was ever even in the same room as me. I hope that someday I can return the favor.

Gerry is a great guy, unorthodox, friendly, and intelligent. At Tourtelot's house we briefly discussed my testimony, and he said he thought I had exhibited a Zen quality. I got a laugh out of his description, but admitted to having studied martial arts many years ago, and joked about having positive *Chi*. He got a kick out of that.

While Gerry tried to keep the conversation centered on the Simpson trial, I wanted to talk about anything else. I was especially interested in the Ruby Ridge case, and asked him all about it. For the remainder of the evening, through coffee and dessert, I had him go over all the details in this very interesting and tragic case. We never got back to the Simpson trial.

What I found most striking about Gerry Spence was his honesty. Whatever he said seemed to be carefully thought out and spoken with conviction. And Gerry never asked me two obvious questions: Did I plant the glove? Did I think Simpson was guilty? I figure Gerry had answered those questions long before he ever met me.

The next evening, the Protective League arranged to take me to dinner and then to a private club called The Magic Castle. Accompanying us for the evening would be former LAPD Chief Daryl Gates. When we all met at the Hollywood police station, I realized that most of the League's directors and their wives were all coming along.

Our party of twenty or so first had dinner in the private dining room of an elegant restaurant. Chief Gates sat to my left, and we talked all through dinner. I kept calling him Chief, and he tried to get me to call him Daryl, but I couldn't. I think he loved being called Chief anyway.

We talked a lot about the trial and my role in it. I had a great time talking with the Chief, asking him a lot of things that had been on my mind for years. We laughed about most of them. At one point I proposed a toast. Holding up my glass, I said: "To Daryl Gates, who in my mind is still the real chief of the LAPD."

Everyone cheered and drank to the toast. I sincerely meant what I said. Gates was a street cop's chief, and we all loved him.

After dinner, we went on to the Magic Castle, and saw a first-rate magic show. I really enjoyed the evening, but it got late and was soon time to go. As I said goodbye and thanked everybody, Chief Gates congratulated me for a job well done. I was proud to have his respect. Although I knew the trial wasn't over, and I could still be recalled, I thought my participation in it was just about finished. I felt I had done a good job, and had made Chief Gates proud.

When I was getting hammered in the media and by the defense, it was rumored we did have a chief of police, but most of the time we didn't know where he was. Had Daryl Gates been the chief, he would have been on every television show defending his officers against the defense attorneys' making of outrageous claims against us. Even without having an official position, Daryl Gates still spoke out more forcefully and more frequently than our missing-in-action chief, Willie Williams.

Shapiro wore a blue ribbon on his lapel, signifying support of the LAPD; he knew that the defense had already gone too far, and he wasn't comfortable with it.

When Bob Shapiro cross-examined Vannatter the week after my testimony, he wore a blue ribbon on his lapel signifying support of the LAPD. Since the controversy had started about the LAPD, and specifically the allegations that I had planted the glove, a movement sprang up within the Protective League to demonstrate support for the detectives in the case. The League had made a blue ribbon lapel pin for friends of the LAPD who wanted to make their support visible.

When Bob put on this pin, he knew that the defense had already gone too far, and he wasn't comfortable with it. For Bob I'm sure it only got worse from this point forward. Following my last day of testimony, he told the press:

"My preference was that race was not an issue in this case and should not be an issue in this case, and I'm sorry from a personal point of view that it has become an issue in this case."

Bob Shapiro began to have difficulties with the case almost as soon as Cochran came on board. Although he was a major leak to Jeffrey Toobin and probably others about the defense's racial strategy and attempts to discredit me, Shapiro quickly made it clear that he did not approve of Cochran's racial obsessions, his overblown rhetoric, and his willingness to do almost anything in order to win. After the trial he was quick to distance himself from the race strategy and said that he would no longer talk to his former friend, F. Lee Bailey, or work with his former colleague Johnnie Cochran. He made these remarks just after the verdict, a time when you'd think the team would be enjoying the glow of victory. But the acquittal, or at least the way it was won, left a bad taste in Bob Shapiro's mouth, and he didn't waste any time telling the public how he felt.

Although we know of some of the conflicts between Shapiro and other members of the team, I have often wondered what made Bob sever ties with his two prominent colleagues, one of them the godfather of his son. What did Bailey and Cochran say or do that would make an experienced defense attorney so angry and disgusted?

I know he'd be crushed if I didn't at least mention him, so I suppose I should talk about Alan Dershowitz. From his ivory tower in Cambridge, Massachusetts, Dershowitz spun his theories and fantasies, regardless of what relevance they had to the case or what connection they had to reality. I don't know how many times I've seen Dershowitz on television, but he always has something to say, and it's often a complaint about the police. He was one of the biggest promoters of the planted glove theory. Of course, Dershowitz frames his argument so that all he can actually claim is "doubt," which means he never actually has any proof, just wishful thinking and innuendo.

The only piece of supposedly hard evidence Dershowitz had against me was an experiment he performed at home with a pair of gloves, a plastic bag, and a bottle of wine. After spilling wine on both gloves, he put one inside the plastic bag, and the other he left out. Miraculously, the one in the bag stayed damp, while the other soon dried. Of course, the conditions in no way matched the physical evidence at Bundy and Rockingham. And Dershowitz's experiment would hold up only in the court of his own fevered mind, where evidentiary standards are non-existent. But I'm glad he had fun performing his experiment.

Dershowitz is a real piece of work. Here's a guy who, to my knowledge, has never participated in gathering evidence at a crime scene or analyzing evidence in a crime lab, yet he uses such evidence to spin his weird theories. He spends his time in a university, a courtroom or a television studio, not on the front lines where the real policework is conducted and the real facts are uncovered. But people were intimidated by him because whoever challenged Dershowitz or the other Simpson defense attorneys could be branded a racist.

Simpson either is a murderer or he isn't. But Dershowitz couldn't face such a clear choice. He preferred to obscure rather simple issues in academic cow puddles. For him, a trial is not a search for truth, but a game played by advocates.

Just days after Simpson's arrest, Dershowitz appeared on his favorite legal forum—television. On the June 20, 1994, *Charlie Rose* show, Dershowitz said, "The case may end up not with a bang but a whimper. I mean, this may end up something like a hung jury. It may end up in a plea bargain."

The day after Dershowitz made that statement, Robert Shapiro hired him for the defense team. Was that the only way Bob could get Dershowitz to shut up? Now he seems to acknowledge that his client was guilty, or at least that reasonable people would think so. Of course, he doesn't want to alienate significant portions of his television audience or future client base, most of whom realize that Simpson killed two people. But Dershowitz also doesn't want to admit that he knows his client is guilty. So he makes the distinction between "legal truth" and "factual truth." According to Dershowitz, a factual truth actually happened, and a legal truth is what can be established in court. In his convoluted reasoning, legal truth has nothing to do with morality or the facts. Legal truth is whatever lawyers can get away with.

Dershowitz says that cops supposedly lie all the time, in search warrants, in police reports, and on the stand. Does this mean that defense attorneys always tell the truth and we should always trust defense attorneys? I have a question for Alan Dershowitz and everybody else who says they don't trust cops. Who are you going to call if your house is broken into? The fire department? The PTA? Ghostbusters? No, you're going to call the police. Why do you call the police? Could it be that you trust them to protect you? So, you *do* trust them when it is in your best interests. But you *don't* trust them when it is not in your best interests. Like, when you're a defense attorney and you have no other defense for your client.

Alan Dershowitz is not just a defense attorney. He's an appellate defense attorney, which means he usually deals only with convicted criminals. Most of his clients are in prison or out on bail. But can he trust them? Are they all telling the truth? I forgot, they're only legally guilty.

Criminals often come from a life of poverty, broken homes, or lack educational or economic opportunity. While I can't condone what they do, at least I understand how their deprived backgrounds led them to crime. But what excuse does a defense attorney like Alan Dershowitz have? I have so much more respect for criminals whenever I stand next to a defense attorney like him in court.

Bailey got a lot of media mileage out of his cross-examination, even though it was a failure. He told *Time* magazine the cross-examination gave him "very good vibes" and claimed that Norman Mailer, famous writer, pugilist, and friend of Lawrence Schiller, said his work was flawless.

"We met the objectives that we set out to meet," Bailey said on the *Today* show, which at times seemed like a special access program for the defense. "But we dug him in the hole that we wanted to dig and he jumped into it."

Bailey bragged that he would prove I planted the bloody glove at Rockingham. But he failed to offer one scintilla of evidence to prove that I did, or even could have done it. This famous trial lawyer's complete, abject, and pathetic failure concerning the planting of evidence should have ended all speculation about the Rockingham glove.

Chapter 22

DEFENDING THE INDEFENSIBLE

Now, every trial attorney has his or her particular quirks
when it comes to picking juries. I, for example, excuse any
man who shows up wearing either white socks or a string tie.

—JOHNNIE COCHRAN

U NABLE TO SUCCESSFULLY CHALLENGE the evidence I found at both crime scenes, the defense attacked me. Johnnie Cochran knew that a racial defense would immediately put the prosecution on the defensive, and switch the focus away from his obviously guilty client. Tactically, he was right. Morally, he was indefensible.

Johnnie Cochran has been playing the race card for much of his professional life. He made a virtual career out of suing the LAPD for civil rights violations and use of excessive force. Over a period of about ten years, Cochran's clients were estimated to have won more than $40 million, of which Johnnie himself probably pocketed around $15 million. Was Johnnie Cochran really concerned with racism, or just money?

One of Cochran's more infamous cases was the suit of Reginald Denny, a white truck driver who was beaten during the Rodney King riots in 1992. Of course, Cochran didn't sue the black thugs who beat Denny half to death, but claimed the incident was the LAPD's fault for not providing enough protection in the dangerous neighborhood of South Central Los Angeles. As this book went to press, there was still no verdict in the case, but the sheer audacity of Cochran to sue the police instead of the perpetrators shows his perverse sense of justice.

Before the Simpson trial, I had no personal or professional contact with any of the defense attorneys who handled his case. I had heard about Bob Shapiro's work on the Christian Brando murder case because it occurred in the West LA division, but I had never worked a case that he was involved in. Neither had I been involved in a trial where Johnnie Cochran represented the defendant, and I was never the defendant in any of his numerous lawsuits against the LAPD and its officers.

Since I had never faced them before, I didn't know how the members of the defense team would conduct themselves. I expected them to be tough, but I also expected them to be fair. I had no idea that they would go after me in such a personal and inflammatory manner. I expected them to hammer me on the facts, but not try to brand me as a racist.

How ironic that out of the whole team, the defense attorney with the lowest profile and the least experience conducted himself in the most professional manner. I'm talking, of course, about Carl Douglas. He worked hard, knew the law, and stuck to the law. Throughout the trial, Douglas avoided all personal attacks against anyone, even me. In the court and to the media, he remained a responsible and honest professional. If every member of the team had been like Carl Douglas, the trial of O.J. Simpson would not have become a travesty.

In reading Lawrence Schiller's *American Tragedy*, I came across one comment Carl Douglas made concerning race that was eye-opening, to say the least. The remark made it appear that Douglas seemed to think that because Simpson was a black man, he must have been innocent. Yet even with this public comment, I feel the same way about Douglas that I did during the trial. His personal thoughts are his own, and his professional conduct was always of the highest level. This is all we asked of any member of the defense.

The other defense attorneys used a tactic that sometimes is used as a diversion in robberies. You start a fire or set off an explosion nearby, and while the police are preoccupied with the crisis, you complete the crime unnoticed. They used the planted glove theory, the blood in the Bronco theory, the planted blood at Bundy theory, the bloody socks theory, the LAPD is incompetent theory, the LAPD knows everything theory, the unreasonable search and seizure theory, the cross-contaminated blood evidence theory, the Colombian hit men theory, the disappearing-reappearing Stiletto, the wandering alibis, and countless other explanations or speculations that had only one thing in common—an utter lack of plausibility. The defense had an answer for everything, but none made any sense. The defense had no defense except for smoke and mirrors.

To anyone who gave it a moment of honest thought, the planted glove theory was ridiculous, but the obvious absurdity of this theory didn't stop Johnnie Cochran from spinning it. He was behind the entire race defense and was responsible for turning the trial from an examination of O.J. Simpson's guilt or innocence into a campaign of slander against me.

Cochran had a very narrow and clear agenda. He was going to get his client off no matter what it took, no matter who he hurt or even ruined, no matter how far he had to twist or even disregard the truth. In doing so he played a lot of people for fools.

> **Johnnie Cochran was going to get his client off no matter what it took, no matter who he hurt or even ruined.**

He misstated evidence throughout the trial. In his opening argument, he referred to the testimony of fourteen different witnesses whose identities and statements he hadn't made available to the prosecution during the discovery process. Even though some of these witnesses were never used, he gave synopses of their testimony as if it were gospel. One of the witnesses, Mary Anne Gerchas, said she saw four men in knit caps fleeing the murder scene. She proved to be completely unreliable, and the defense never used her testimony. But Cochran's reference to it remained part of the record.

Cochran told the jury that Simpson's arthritis was so bad he couldn't deal a deck of cards the day of the murders. Then he said that Simpson was chipping golf balls at the time of the murders. Meanwhile, Simpson had already told limo driver Allan Park that he had been sleeping. And he told Lange and Vannatter that he was running around trying to get ready. Simpson's alibis flowed in different directions with each and every new discovery of evidence or new prosecution witness. But since these alibis came not from the client himself, but from his mouthpiece attorney, he was never nailed down to a single, consistent story. To this day, we don't really know how Simpson accounted for his movements on the night of the murders. And as his lawyer, Cochran could say just about anything, claiming that he was merely stating what he thought to be correct at the time. The story sometimes changed from one day to the next, but no matter. The spin was fixed, and the defense would set off on another tangent.

Throughout the trial, Cochran pushed Judge Ito to see how much he could get away with, and to see how far Ito would allow him to go when it counted. Knowing about my past friction with Margaret York, and making it clear to Ito that he knew about it, gave Cochran leverage over the judge.

Cochran aligned himself with all the right people and always said the right things. But his professional conduct was abominable. He constantly relied on underhanded tactics, including every possible technique of character assassination he could think of. Taking advantage of racial sensitivities, he made everyone in the courtroom and the press afraid of being branded a racist. That's precisely how he got away with his absurd and inflammatory tactics.

He used religion the same way he used race, in order to gain sympathy with the jury. I have no personal knowledge of Cochran's religious beliefs, but I have seen him play up his own religion in the courtroom, the media, and particularly his own book, which is phony and self-serving even by the standards of O.J. books. I find his use of religion especially distasteful, because he played on the sincere beliefs of the jury and the black community. Having worked much of my career in black neighborhoods, I know how religious most working-class black people are, particularly women. Black churches are a powerful force in the community. Cochran worked this fact to his own advantage, peppering his courtroom speeches and media pronouncements with quotations from the scriptures. But there is one passage from the Bible that he seemed to have forgotten: "Thou shalt not kill."

Now that the trial is over, Cochran won't let go. He's had his moment in the spotlight and he can't bear to leave it. Most defense attorneys can move on to other cases, but Cochran has decided to make a career out of the Simpson trial. He steadfastly argues that his client was innocent. If he truly believes that, he's not very intelligent, and if he doesn't believe it, he's not very honest. Either way, he should never have used a defense that ruined other people's lives in the process.

The irony of the Simpson defense strategy is that if they had stuck to the material issues and evidence, they would have had some strong arguments. Whether or not those arguments would have resulted in an acquittal is another question. The Robbery/Homicide detectives, SID criminalists, and prosecution made significant mistakes throughout the investigation and trial. And the lawyers and experts who critiqued these mistakes often had very good points, which were unfortunately taken too far. The detectives had made mistakes that the prosecution would later compound. But the defense team assembled around their celebrity client, uniquely situated to take advantage of these blunders.

Mistakes by the investigating team and prosecution were the only case the defense had. At the beginning of the trial, the defense investigators were supposed to find out who really killed Ron and Nicole. But aside from a few crackpot witnesses and some vague theories about Colombian "neckties," they never came up with one piece of evidence pointing to anyone other than their client. You'd think that with all that manpower they could at least have produced something, but instead, the investigators focused solely on attacking the prosecution's witnesses. And since I had done nothing wrong during the investigation, and had discovered a great deal of incriminating evidence, the defense played the race card against me.

This country has become so hypersensitive to race that we ignore the facts: antisocial behavior, crime, and immoral acts are not color coded. To either judge or disregard people's behavior because of their race is the biggest crime our society can commit.

That's exactly what the defense did. They took advantage of racial sensitivities and exploited this country's horrible legacy of injustice toward black people. They had no defense other than their client's skin color. If that isn't racism, I don't know what is.

Chapter 23

THE TAPES

They're important, and we know you're going to get them.
We just want the opportunity to try and sell them first.

—LAURA HART MCKINNEY'S ATTORNEY,
MATTHEW SCHWARTZ, IN A CONVERSATION WITH
JOHNNIE COCHRAN AND ROBERT SHAPIRO

I MET LAURA HART at an outdoor cafe in Westwood in 1985. She was sitting at a table drinking coffee and working on what appeared to be a small typewriter. Looking closer, I could see that it was a computer. I had heard about laptop computers but had never seen one, so I walked over and asked her about it. She told me a little about the machine and that she was a writer.

Her interest was obvious when I told her I was a police officer. Somewhat jokingly, I told her that she should write something really good about policework, not like all the phony stuff you see on television. She said that she had always wanted to do a screenplay based on a police story. Naturally, I was interested; I told her that I had some ideas for a really good screenplay. Laura seemed intrigued, and we exchanged phone numbers.

We met a couple of times to discuss ideas for a screenplay. I mentioned how the department had taken a tongue-in-cheek joke about a group called "Men Against Women" and turned it into a serious investigation. She was interested in the concept, and I started fleshing out ideas based on a fictional group that made females' lives in the department a living hell. I envisioned the film with a female role-model hero, several subplots, and lots of down and dirty action. Laura was interested in the story I began to spin.

Meeting at her apartment in Santa Monica, we began laying out the goals of the screenplay. During these sessions we also socialized, and ultimately we became involved in a casual sexual relationship. We were both single, but neither one of us wanted to carry the relationship further, or so it seemed.

Laura sometimes sent me letters, which I guess could be described as love letters. She bought me gifts once in a while, but I never reciprocated. I just didn't feel the same way.

Early into the screenplay project, I discovered that Laura was clueless when it came to policework, or the realities of violence and life on the street. She was extremely naive and slightly eccentric.

Agreeing that we needed hard-hitting action and tough characters, we began a series of interviews where I laid out police procedures, stories, characters, and situations. These were all on tape. I let my imagination run wild. Throughout the interviews, I was creating fictional situations, sometimes based loosely on true incidents. Characters were developed from composites of many people, from police management down to the lowest criminals. Dialogue in the screenplay was a mix of conversations I remembered, and others that were imaginary.

When I was making up dialogue, I spoke in the first person. But these weren't my own words, my own experiences, or my own sentiments. They were the words of fictional characters I had created based on my imagination and experience. I knew I had to exaggerate things to make the screenplay dramatic and commercially appealing. I knew enough about Hollywood to understand that producers didn't want a nice, warm and fuzzy movie about good cops, but something dark and hard-edged. And since Laura and I sometimes drank wine while we had our recorded conversations, occasionally I got a little carried away.

As I mentioned, Laura was extremely innocent, and I got a charge out of shocking her with some of the things that I said and making her laugh with others.

The bulk of these tapes were made during a period of three to four months. The purpose of the tapes was twofold: to educate Laura about the sinister side of the world, about which she knew nothing, and to create characters and action she might use in a screenplay. Laura used the tapes and transcripts as a library she could refer to while writing the script.

Laura always emphasized that unless you are a sought-after writer, there isn't much money in screenplays. Although I would be paid if the screenplay sold, Laura told me that the way for me to make real money would be as a technical adviser. I tried to make myself unique and indispensable as a source of police street smarts.

F. Lee Bailey asked me if I had ever used the "N" word in addressing a person. I could truthfully answer that I had not.

Writing these memories down on paper, I can see the misguided, get-rich-quick mentality I had then. In hindsight, I can see how these attitudes, combined with my sexual relationship with the writer, led me to try to impress or shock her.

Laura and I enjoyed each other's company, but after several months we both realized that we didn't have much in common outside of the project. So, without arguments or guilt, we simply ended the romance, but remained friends and continued to work on the project.

As Laura wrote the screenplay, she would send manuscripts to me in the mail or I would pick them up, then review them, make corrections or suggestions, and return the manuscripts to her. It was obvious that we were working on a fictional screenplay, and not an autobiography or the true story of my police career.

As months turned into years, my interest in the screenplay diminished. Laura moved to North Carolina, married, took a new job, and had children. I was glad she had found someone who made her happy.

My life ran the same path. I married, bought a house, started a family, and worked extra jobs to pay the bills. I always thought Laura was naive about the street, but I guess I was equally naive about Hollywood. Maybe the screenplay wasn't good enough or perhaps the timing wasn't right. For whatever reason, I eventually accepted that it probably would never sell.

Still, Laura and I never really gave up on the project. Periodically, she flew to Los Angeles to have lunch with a producer. Laura always wanted me to attend these meetings because she felt I could help sell it. In others words, I was on stage. Whether it was necessary or not, I gave them the Dirty Harry meets Attila the Hun routine. If the screenplay ever sold, I wanted to be technical adviser on the project. I needed to impress these people as someone they could not do without.

After the Simpson arrest and preliminary hearing, Laura and I met once at my house. She brought her two children and met my wife and kids. We talked about a last-ditch effort to sell the screenplay now that I was, temporarily at least, a minor celebrity. Even at this late date, I never thought about the tapes having an impact on the trial or any negative reflection on me. We were doing background for a fictional screenplay. I didn't think we had done anything wrong.

At one point during the trial, we had a meeting in Westwood with Laura and someone else whom I believe was connected in some way to actor Fred Dryer. Laura's agent had previously contacted Fred Dryer's people and given them the screenplay to read. They seemed interested in it, and wanted me to meet with Fred Dryer. I didn't think this was a good idea, but said I'd talk with one of his representatives.

The lunch meeting took place at Alice's Restaurant in Westwood Village. We discussed the screenplay, and Laura taped the conversation, as she always did, with her mini tape recorder in plain view. Nothing came of the meeting, and the screenplay wasn't sold.

Or was it?

When I testified in the Superior Court trial, I did not think about the tapes. Bailey asked me if I had ever used the "N" word in addressing a person. I could truthfully answer that I had not. I never thought that screenplay notes and character dialogue could be misrepresented as my own words. I hadn't told Marcia about the tapes simply because I didn't remember them at first, and when I did, I didn't think they were at all relevant to the case.

But when the tapes became public, I worried. I had seen how the defense and the media had already twisted previous statements of mine. While I couldn't remember exactly what I had said on those dozens of hours of tapes, I was sure that the defense would find a way to make the tapes an issue as part of their strategy to turn the trial of O.J. Simpson into a trial about race and about me.

While I was still in Los Angeles and about to retire from the department, the custody of the tapes was being fought over in a North Carolina court. During this hearing, Johnnie Cochran argued his case in the court of public opinion as well as the court of law. Still, he was defeated. On Friday, July 28, Judge William Z. Wood ruled that I had been a technical adviser on a work of fiction and therefore the tapes were not material to the Simpson case. The defense team quickly appealed, and Cochran's strategy eventually paid off. The North Carolina Court of Appeals, bowing to public pressure and curiosity about the tapes, overturned Judge Wood's ruling.

While the tapes were still in court action in North Carolina, I called Laura from my attorney's home, and pleaded with her to destroy the tapes. "Nobody will believe what we were trying to do," I said. "These will destroy me. This has nothing to do with this trial about a murderer."

Laura wouldn't destroy the tapes. I asked her as a friend, but she said that her attorney, Matthew Schwartz, told her that the tapes were about to become evidence and she couldn't legally do anything to them.

In his book, Lawrence Schiller reports the rumor that Laura feared I'd kill her over the tapes. I sincerely doubt that Laura felt that way. Even when I knew she was giving the tapes up, we never had a cross word, and we still haven't. But the rumors helped the defense highlight the supposed importance of the tapes.

At first I thought any use of the tapes would be seen as just one more desperate measure by a defense team that was quickly running out of options. As mistake-ridden as the investigation and prosecution had been, the evidence against Simpson remained irrefutable. Unfortunately, the irrefutable evidence was about to be overshadowed by the completely irrelevant tapes.

Anthony Pellicano, my private investigator, called me in Sandpoint to tell me that Laura's attorney had been trying to sell the tapes to the tabloids for two months, asking a six-figure fee. I knew Pellicano had accurate information, but I didn't want to believe a trusted friend like Laura would sell me out for money.

Pellicano's discovery reminded me that Laura's attorney had requested that we turn our verbal agreement about the screenplay into a written contract, because after the trial there might be renewed interest in the script, and we should have our agreement in writing. We went back and forth several times on the wording of the contract and eventually both signed a document. This occurred while Simpson's attorneys were appealing the lower court ruling in North Carolina. I can see now that Laura and her attorney wanted a written agreement because they were preparing to sell the tapes.

Whether the tapes were sold or not, they were soon in the hands of the defense team, who leaked the most shocking and offensive segments almost immediately. Of course the excerpts were never put into context. The news reports mentioned that these were interviews with an aspiring screenwriter, but they also treated my tall tales as if they were personal memoirs, conveniently forgetting that we were trying to write a screenplay, not an autobiography. Hearing my ugly words and not knowing the context, the public was understandably outraged.

It's easy to think that if people get to know the real you, they'd understand and sympathize. No doubt everyone feels that way. But I was a lead witness in a high-profile murder trial that just about everyone in the country was following on a daily basis. Ever since they realized that I had found the most crucial piece of evidence and had not made any mistakes in my investigation, the defense team tried to impeach me by making my personal character an issue. If they hadn't found the tapes or my disability claim, they would have made an issue out of something—anything—else. Unfortunately, I had inadvertently provided the bullets.

The legal wrangle over the tapes was far from over, since Ito still had to rule on their admissibility. And now my problems with Margaret York would once again become an issue, because Laura had been interested in females in the department, and I therefore said a few things about York. Since I thought the conversation would be confidential, and only used for the screenplay, I not only spoke my mind, but vented. The result was not pretty.

Now the tapes were in front of York's husband. Since the beginning, both the prosecution and the defense could have derailed the trial by challenging York's declaration to Judge Rappe, which could have been contradicted by numerous witnesses who had already made public statements contradicting her statements. But the prosecution didn't want to risk a retrial. And the defense figured that it was more useful not to press the issue, but rather simply to remind Ito of the power they held.

Before Ito heard the tapes or read any excerpts, he called an in-camera hearing to discuss the possibility of his wife's becoming a material witness.

In Ito's chambers, Cochran told the judge, "This is a very delicate issue.... It is going to have to do with credibility, because you know, her declaration—this guy, unless he is absolutely lying—and Marcia will back me up on this—the contacts he has with Lieutenant York are the kind that are very hard to forget."

All of a sudden I was Johnnie Cochran's best witness, and the defense had a new strategy. After reminding Ito of his wife's position, Johnnie Cochran promised they would never call York as a witness. To the defense team, getting the tapes into the trial was more important than holding the York issue over Ito's head.

And the prosecution changed course as well. While Marcia knew from the start that she could derail the trial at any time, she had not wanted to question York's declaration or call her as a witness. Now, during the in-camera hearing, she said that the prosecution might call her after all.

The argument shifted to the courtroom, where Ito held an open hearing without the jury present. Here, Cochran played to the cameras, using the forum to publicize the tapes and play racial politics. His argument in open court was theatrical and long-winded, even for Johnnie Cochran. Among other things, he said, "This is a blockbuster! This is a bombshell! This is perhaps the biggest thing that's happened in any case in this country in this decade." Cochran continually downplayed York's role in the tapes, and the issue of her testimony was obscured by a blizzard of inflammatory rhetoric and carnival barking that could only heighten the public's interest.

Still, a decision had to be made. If York were called as a witness, either another judge would have to hear her testimony, or Ito would have to step down and declare a mistrial. At this stage of the trial, nobody wanted to start all over again. Ito recused himself from the issue of deciding whether or not his wife was a material witness. The conflict of interest dispute was eventually settled by Judge John H. Reid, who ruled that York could offer no relevant testimony to the Simpson trial. Reid's ruling established that Ito would stay on the case. The York issue was finally laid to rest.

Judge Reid found that York could testify to no relevant issue in this case, despite the fact that she was married to the judge, and had made a sworn declaration that was problematic at best. Meanwhile, my use of an epithet in notes for a fictional screenplay is supposed to be relevant and material? Is there something wrong here?

Now Ito had to decide whether the tapes should be admitted as evidence. But before he did so, Lawrence Schiller created an edited tape version for use in the courtroom. Schiller's job was to enhance the sound quality and select vignettes for the court. What he did was to wrench my statements out of context and make them seem even more hateful.

While Ito considered the issue, the defense leaked selected portions of the tapes to the media. Not only had the public heard these excerpts, but no doubt members of the jury, who had a conjugal visit over the weekend the tapes were leaked, did also.

On August 29, Ito had been reviewing the material for nearly a week and still hadn't come to a decision. He called for oral arguments from both the prosecution and defense, without the jury present. Laura was called in to testify, and Schiller's excerpts from the tapes were presented. After a fifteen-minute recess, Ito said from the bench: "I think that there is an overriding public interest in the nature of the offer. I don't want this court ever to be in a position where there is any indication that the court would participate in suppressing information that is of vital public interest."

In other words, politics and publicity had once again overwhelmed the law. The tapes could be admitted as material evidence in O.J. Simpson's trial for murder.

Sitting in Sandpoint watching this mess unfold, I received a phone call from Laura's husband, Dan McKinny. Dan called to tell me that Laura was subpoenaed to appear at the Simpson trial. I knew this already, but Dan added that Laura didn't want to speak to me in case they asked if she had been in contact with me since being served with a subpoena. Dan went on:

"Laura wants you to know that if she's asked on the stand about your relationship with her, she is going to admit that you and she had a sexual relationship in the beginning."

Dan also added that he knew that Laura and I had had this type of relationship when we first started the project. I thanked Dan for the heads up.

My wife could tell that something was wrong. I turned to her and, although it wasn't easy, told her what Dan had said. I had never admitted to her that Laura and I had been sexually involved because I still had to meet Laura periodically and I didn't want my wife to think anything was going on. I shouldn't have worried about it.

Caroline simply said, "I've known that for years, even if you didn't want to admit it. I once found a letter she wrote you. It was a letter only a lover writes."

At that moment I saw the profound strength in this woman I thought I already knew so well.

I was in Los Angeles, waiting to be called back to the stand, when Laura testified. I avoided following the trial during her testimony, but my wife watched carefully. When Laura was asked if she and I had had a sexual relationship, she testified, "No, it was a business relationship."

My wife was furious. The moment she heard Laura's statement, she called Patty Jo Fairbanks in the "O.J. room" and told her about the love letter and the phonecall from Laura's husband. Patty Jo was plugged into the prosecution table by computer, so she immediately typed the information and sent it on to Clark and Darden. This message to the prosecutors caused Darden to ask Laura about the letter, but she denied writing it.

Darden asked Laura one question that should have been the pivotal issue in putting the whole tape controversy into its proper context. Darden asked Laura, "Did Mark Fuhrman talk this way when you were not taping for the screenplay?"

"No."

The prosecution should have followed up on that question and later used it to argue that I was not expressing my own thoughts or feelings, but those of fictional characters. Unfortunately, the inflammatory nature of the excerpts and the media and public reaction to them made the prosecution run scared. Not only would they not defend me, but they ran away from me as fast as they could. And sometimes they even spent more time and energy attacking me than the defense did.

I don't want to sound as if I'm trying to justify what I said on those tapes. I am ashamed of my words. Taken out of context, they are worse than horrible. And even in context, they are ugly. There is no excuse, not even literary license, that can justify or condone the pain I caused people of all colors. I had no idea that the tapes would ever be made public, but I should have thought about how my friends, black and white, would feel if they heard them. Notwithstanding my shame about what I said on those tapes, there are issues and comparisons that reasonable people should at least consider.

Johnnie Cochran deems the "N" word as a term of affection. Here is a description of life in his law firm according to Lawrence Schiller:

"In Cochran's office, there were few whites. A distinct minority, they came and went. There was a camaraderie among the entire staff that transcended racial politics. For the most part, the white world stayed outside. Inside the firm, you were family. Words that shocked and offended white society were coin of the realm. 'Nigger' and 'motherfucker' were terms of affection."

It appears Johnnie Cochran is offended by certain hateful words only when it suits his own self-interest.

Joseph Wambaugh is America's premier cop novelist. I am a big fan of Joe's and have read every book he has written, one of which is *The Choirboys*.

The Choirboys is a fast-paced book about street police with all the action, sex, racism, and controversy Hollywood likes, but that would take any normal cop six lifetimes to experience. I read the book long before I worked with Laura on the screenplay, and I'm sure it influenced how I viewed a good cop story.

Recently, I pulled out my copy of *The Choirboys*. Here's what's written on the back jacket: "*The Choirboys* is fiction, but every major scene in it happened; the most bizarre events depicted are all real. Joseph Wambaugh gives us action scenes reminiscent of *In Cold Blood* and surrounds them with humor scenes equally strong. For this is the story of a group of men endangered ultimately not by the violence of their jobs but by their choice of off-duty entertainment. The result is a novel as boisterous and freewheeling as a Rabelaisian romp and as chillingly authentic as only a veteran police officer can make it."

Wambaugh himself said about *The Choirboys*, "This is the truest novel I have ever written."

Rereading *The Choirboys*, I discovered countless examples of characters describing African Americans and others in extremely crude and racist terms. Taken out of context—by someone like Johnnie Cochran perhaps—they are the words of Joseph Wambaugh, *racist*. But within the structure of the novel, they are the words of Joseph Wambaugh, author, and are necessary for the tone, theme, and character development of the book.

The Choirboys was the first novel Joseph Wambaugh wrote after leaving the department. Joe was drawing on his own experiences, no doubt embellishing them; but he also did research, including interviews, and most probably tapes of several policemen, past, present, and retired, who have different personalities, different imaginations, and different abilities to expound on humorous and dangerous situations. In some ways, I think Joe Wambaugh was an unconscious mentor of my novice attempt at writing a work of fiction. In writing *The Choirboys*, Wambaugh no doubt sifted through countless notes and tapes, and one can only imagine what he left out. In the research material Laura and I worked on, there are forty-one references to the "N" word. In the published edition of *The Choirboys*, there are fourteen references to the "N" word. Does that mean Joseph Wambaugh is a racist?

The similarities are not mere coincidence. Joe and I are both widely experienced former police officers and detectives of the Los Angeles Police Department. Joe's novels are best-sellers, while my screenplay was never produced, but both of us, in our own ways, have taken our experiences on the street and tried to transform them into gritty, dramatic works of imagination.

Joe wrote *The Choirboys* at a time when we weren't so thin-skinned, when we had a better sense of humor and a greater appetite for realism. Even a movie as sweet and innocent as *Forrest Gump* uses the "N" word several times, as of course do other works of fiction like *Huckleberry Finn*. When is the word evil, when is it ironic, and when is it legitimately used by an author to capture the realities of life on the street?

I believe the "N" word is evil if it is meant to pierce someone's feelings, to demean and dehumanize them. Used in a story like Joe Wambaugh's, the word either reflects the hatred of a character, or shows how that character is attempting, however insensitively, to make light of racial pressures and troubling situations. When some fictional cops use the word to refer to criminals, they mean it to be insulting. It's difficult to work the streets every day, to see innocent people robbed and beat up and sometimes killed, and not have strong feelings about criminals. But just because Joe used harsh dialogue doesn't mean many of today's cops actually talk that way. Any one of the epithets in Joe's book would result in a suspension or possible civil rights lawsuit. Either way, when the word is used in a story, it's not an attack on anybody, just artistic license.

Joe wrote *The Choirboys* in an attempt to give the public what it seemed to want, and, judging by its success, he must have done just that. Drama is always exaggerated, with larger-than-life heroes and villains. *The Choirboys* was a best-seller that was made into a movie and eventually earned its author millions of dollars. Wambaugh went on to write several other best-selling novels and nonfiction books, many of which also became films or television specials. He's a talented writer and a smart guy who actually has real experience out on the street. There are a lot of other people out there writing cop books, but Wambaugh's struck a responsive chord.

People want realism in novels, movies, or television shows about cops, though our ideas of realism change. In the 1950s people responded to *Dragnet* and Joe Friday, ramrod straight and stone cold sober, decked out in a suit and a flattop, wanting nothing but the facts, ma'am. In the 1990s, people respond to *NYPD Blue* and *Homicide* and characters like Andy Sipowicz, a tough, troubled man who makes mistakes but has a good heart, who's trying to do an almost impossible job and somehow keep his life together. People still want cops who are dedicated to the job, and they also want to know what makes these people tick. They want to know about the problems cops have with their families, with alcohol, with stress and the pressures of their job. People want to see the toll the job takes. They want to feel like they're experiencing policework at the gut level.

If *NYPD Blue* and *Homicide* were on cable instead of the networks, the racist, sexist, and violent language on those programs would probably be much like the screenplay I tried to write. Go to any theater or video store and check out the current selection of cop movies. I guarantee you'll find racism, sexism, vile language, and despicable actions by cops and criminals alike. In real life, people need cops to perform some of the most distasteful tasks that civilized society requires. In entertainment, people need cop stories for catharsis, to work out some of their own frustrations and moral confusion, to pursue criminals who all too often go unpunished, and to express the difficulties of living in a fallen world.

That's all I was trying to do in writing a screenplay with Laura Hart McKinny. She wanted gritty realism about life on the streets, so I told her some stories and did some play-acting. These stories were, in part, based on my own experiences and the experiences of others. But they were also stories that had gone through the meat grinder of my own imagination. They were embellished, exaggerated, even entirely made up.

The issue of truth versus fiction aside, we have to recognize that there is a difference between words and deeds. O.J. Simpson murdered two people. I said some horrible things. Somehow the defense, aided by the media and a public eager to let a popular celebrity off the hook, was able to turn the trial around. Of course, Judge Ito and the prosecution helped out. Ito could have ruled that my use of the "N" word was irrelevant to the murder trial. The prosecution could have fought harder to exclude the tapes or, once they were introduced, put them in their proper perspective. But in the end, since I made the tapes, I bear the responsibility.

Even accepting my own responsibility for what occurred, it was incredibly frustrating to have the world pass judgment without knowing the real me. Soon after the tapes came out, several of my colleagues in the LAPD were interviewed by the press. Here's what they said:

Bob Tapia, my former supervisor at West LA, said, "Mark's not prejudiced against blacks. He's only prejudiced against criminals, whatever their color."

"If he were back on the job he would risk his life for anyone on the job or anyone in the city, just like he always had," Sergeant Paul Partridge told the *Los Angeles Times*. "And he wouldn't care who they were."

"The person that the world knows…on the tape…is a racist, who made terrible remarks, who probably represents all the filth the world has to offer," said Roberto Alaniz, a former partner of mine who's a Latino and a police sergeant. "The Mark Fuhrman I know…is not that. He's not a racist."

Ed Palmer, a black police sergeant, said, "There have been times I have worked with people [and] you wonder about them. I never wondered with him. I knew he was aggressive. I knew he was a little arrogant. But I never got racism at all. If he were that way, and as much a racist as the tapes indicated, then it would have come out somewhere, and somebody would have spoken up."

The cops who knew me understood. They worked with me on the street and saw how I dealt with people of all colors. They knew I was not a racist. They were shocked and offended by what they heard on the tapes. But they knew that I didn't talk that way, I didn't feel that way, and I certainly didn't act that way. I wish everyone else who doesn't know me could understand this. If I must be judged, I wish it were on the basis of my record as a police officer, and not on my play-acting, intentionally shocking comments to an aspiring screenwriter.

Chapter 24

TAKING THE FIFTH

---

*Throughout the trial, the sad irony was that the defense
attorneys seemed to be fighting harder for injustice than the
prosecutors were fighting for justice.*

—VINCENT BUGLIOSI

I N LATE AUGUST, I was called back to Los Angeles to take the stand again,
although I didn't know when I would be asked to appear. I flew into LAX,
but for security reasons, instead of exiting through the gate, I walked down
a stairway and onto the tarmac, where Ron Phillips was waiting with an
unmarked police car flanked by two black and whites.

"You're on the radio, want to listen?" Ron asked me.

They were playing excerpts of the tapes in court. I didn't want to hear it, so
Ron turned the radio off.

"I bet there are a lot of people pissed off at me."

"Pissed off? They want to tar and feather you, and then they want to hang you."

The district attorney's office put me up in an apartment in downtown LA and assigned a team of investigators to run a security detail. For the next week, I had at least two district attorney investigators as round-the-clock bodyguards.

For days, I waited, and waited, and waited for the prosecution to talk to me before I was called to the stand.

I spoke to Ron Phillips regularly. Each time we spoke, I asked him, "Have Marcia or Chris call me, I've got to talk to them."

I waited for their call. Nothing.

It was time to hire a criminal defense attorney. I had known Darryl Mounger for ten years. He was a friend, and I knew his wife—quite well—as she'd worked as a detective in West LA. Darryl is a great criminal defense attorney and was experienced in high-profile cases, having represented Stacey Koon in the Rodney King case. I hired Darryl, knowing I would need his counsel.

At the same time, my civil defense attorney Bob Tourtelot called me.

"I have to work in this city. I can't be your attorney any more."

"Yeah, Bob, I know," I responded. "I've already seen it on TV."

Before calling me, Tourtelot told reporters that he would no longer represent me, saying he was "shocked and sickened" after hearing the tapes. I understood Bob's decision. It was a knee-jerk reaction, the same kind of response that many people had after hearing the tape excerpts. Bob had been defending me in court and in the media for over a year. But when he was confronted with the tapes, he quickly distanced himself from me. As much as I wish he hadn't done it, or had done it differently, I can't say that I blame him.

Because of these out-of-court statements concerning a client, Tourtelot was investigated by the state bar. When an investigator called me in Sandpoint, I told him I didn't think Bob had acted with malice. He just dumped me, the same as almost everyone else.

In LA, I had nobody to talk to but my bodyguards and a few loyal friends. And while I was beaten up daily in the press, the prosecutors continued to ignore me.

"Have Marcia call me," I said every time I talked to Ron. "I'll fall on my sword. I'll go back on the stand for as long as it takes. I'm willing to do whatever they want. But I need to talk to them first. I need to know what to do."

Ron relayed the message, but I never heard from Marcia, Chris, or anyone from the district attorney's office. I would have done anything the district attorney's office asked me to. But they wouldn't talk to me. Their star witness was tarnished.

Finally, I got the word. Get dressed, we're moving you down to the Criminal Courts building. They're probably going to call you in the morning.

On September 5, I was brought to the Criminal Courts building and made to wait in the snitch room, where witnesses and cooperative suspects wait before they appear in court. I stood beside the empty desks and barren bookshelves waiting and talking to my attorney.

"What do you want to do?" Darryl asked me.

I needed to be examined by the prosecution. Otherwise the defense would ask set-up questions that would elicit only the answers that they wanted to hear.

Once the tapes came out, I might have been beyond rehabilitation for the prosecution. But other witnesses could corroborate my investigation and evidence. In this case, that was essential. As a rebuttal witness, Brad Roberts would have been indispensable in disputing the defense's theories about planted evidence. After all, Brad saw the single glove at Bundy. He saw the fingerprint on the back gate, the extra drops of blood, the blood inside the Bronco, the blood in the foyer, the black socks at the foot of Simpson's bed, all at the same time I did. And he also saw the empty Swiss Army knife box at the edge of Simpson's tub. Brad was ready and eager to testify, but the prosecution still refused to use him.

I took the Fifth because I had no choice. The prosecution had abandoned me, and I was left twisting in the wind.

The defense was claiming that I committed a crime, specifically that I allegedly planted evidence to incriminate O.J. Simpson, with racism as my supposed motive. Now, abandoned by the prosecution, with no chance to defend myself against the defense lawyers' deviously phrased yes-or-no questions about my use of the "N" word, and no opportunity to provide narrative or explanatory answers, I would be vulnerable to the defense's attempts to maneuver me into self-incrimination. Without the prosecution's support, I had no ability to refute the defense's charges. I was innocent, but the prosecution wouldn't help me prove it, no matter how much their failure would harm their case.

I had to make the toughest decision of my life.

"As much as it kills me," I told Darryl, "as much as it goes against everything I believe in, as much as I wish I could fight it, as much as I know how bad it will look, I don't have any choice. I have to take the Fifth."

"Okay," Darryl said. He understood there was nothing else I could do.

It was tough walking into that courtroom. But I tried to carry myself professionally. I stood tall and looked straight ahead.

As soon as I entered the room, Judge Ito stopped talking. Everyone turned their heads. I saw the lawyers and the cops and the reporters. Art Harris of CNN, who had always been decent to me, was seated by the aisle. He looked at me, his arm swung over the bench behind him. As I passed by, I put my hand on Art's shoulder.

I walked to the stand and took the oath.

Gerald Uelmen handled my questioning without the presence of the jury. The defense had never officially completed their previous cross-examination, hoping they would find a witness to impeach me. Now they thought I would impeach myself. Ito wanted to see how I would respond to questioning before he brought the jury in.

> **UELMEN:** "Detective Fuhrman, is the testimony that you gave at the preliminary hearing in this case completely truthful?"
> **FUHRMAN:** "I wish to assert my Fifth Amendment privilege."
> **UELMEN:** "Have you ever falsified a police report?"
> **FUHRMAN:** "I wish to assert my Fifth Amendment privilege."
> **UELMEN:** "Is it your intention to assert your Fifth Amendment privilege with respect to all questions that I ask you?"
> **FUHRMAN:** "Yes."
> **UELMEN:** "I only have one other question, Your Honor."
> **COURT:** "What was that, Mr. Uelmen?"
> **UELMEN:** "Detective Fuhrman, did you plant or manufacture any evidence in this case?"
> **FUHRMAN:** "I assert my Fifth Amendment privilege."

What many people don't realize is that you cannot pick and choose the questions you will answer when you invoke your Fifth Amendment right. If you answer one question, you open the door to other questions. So if you take the Fifth, you must take it on all questions.

Gerry Uelmen is a smart lawyer, so he played the game and asked me patently absurd questions about planting evidence. I had no other choice but to plead the Fifth and refuse to answer. Even Uelman knew the answer to all of his questions was *no*, but he also knew that asking the questions made for good drama.

I took the Fifth because I had no choice. The prosecution had abandoned me, and I was left twisting in the wind. When I took the Fifth, I was seen as a demon. When Simpson took the Fifth and refused to testify about his whereabouts the night of the murder, his relationship with Nicole, and the many pieces of damning evidence, he was constitutionally protected and issued a self-serving statement that allowed him to profess his innocence without subjecting himself to examination by the prosecution.

After my court appearance, I was transferred to a hotel in the San Fernando Valley where, by chance, the Hispanic officers of the LAPD were having a conference. When Ron came to visit me at the hotel, an officer from West LA recognized him. Everybody working in the West LA Division knew that Ron and I were best friends, and it didn't take long for the word to get out where I was. The media was camped out in the lobby, and I was stuck in my room.

My bodyguards discussed ways of getting me out of the hotel and out of Southern California. I listened and then came up with my own plan.

"Very early in the morning we sneak out the back through a fire exit. Have a car waiting for me. Then we go to Ukiah to my friend Kevin's house. From there, Kevin and I will rent a car and drive up to Sandpoint."

Being the most obvious method of escape, the media wouldn't expect it.

That night in the hotel, I had four district attorney investigators with me. I was in a lost mood, sick and tired of everything, disgusted with myself and the fact that I had let down so many people. I had to get my mind off things.

"Hey," I told my bodyguards. "You know this television has pay-per-view. Want to watch a movie?"

"Sure, why not?" they answered.

We got chicken take-out and some beer, Ron and Brad came by, and we watched *Braveheart*, starring Mel Gibson. At the end of the movie, when William Wallace is strapped down, disemboweled, and finally beheaded, it was as if he were being sacrificed for the sins of others. Boy, did I feel a lot like William Wallace. People wanted a sacrificial lamb so they wouldn't have to deal with the fact that a popular celebrity brutally murdered two people. The jury wanted an excuse to vote not guilty. The defense wanted to cast guilt on others. The prosecution and investigating detectives wanted someone to take the blame for their mistakes.

So I was drawn and quartered in the forum of public opinion. At least William Wallace could feel proud that he was a hero of his people. But I had nothing to fall back on, except my family, a few good friends, and the sincere belief that I hadn't done anything wrong.

We woke up early the next morning, well before dawn. After scouting the area and finding no media, my bodyguards loaded the car, got me out of the hotel, and drove out of town. We kept looking behind us, but nobody was on our tail. We were on our way to Ukiah, and from there I would be going home.

On the ride up, my bodyguards tried to make me feel better.

"You got the shaft."

"Don't worry, you didn't do anything wrong."

Because they worked for the district attorney's office, they were up on the law. They knew that I didn't commit perjury and assured me that Garcetti wouldn't file charges. I wish the state attorney general's office had listened to them.

When we arrived at Kevin's house in Ukiah, I was tired but also relieved to be out of LA and among friends. Kevin, his wife Cindy, and I drank beer and ate dinner. My bodyguards spent the night at a motel, and took off for LA the next morning.

My bodyguards were really great guys. I'm sorry I hadn't met them earlier in my career. While working for the prosecution, they had investigated the witnesses who made statements against me, and literally found stacks of evidence to impeach them, including Roderic Hodge, the only man who ever claimed that I had addressed him with a racial epithet. Despite the fact that these investigators had uncovered so much evidence, the prosecution never used it against the people who were attacking me. If they had introduced even some of the evidence, and argued that the tapes were only the record of a fictional screenplay, we could have fought back and I would not have taken the Fifth. If you want to win, you've got to play the game. But the prosecution only played dead.

Kevin and I drove to Sandpoint, and I was finally reunited with my family. My wife and kids were at the next-door neighbor's house, and I had to sneak in the back door to avoid the media, who were already waiting for me.

I kissed my wife, hugged my kids, and thanked my neighbor Sherry for helping out. Sherry is a truly remarkable woman; she's seventy years old, but that doesn't stop her from parasailing and swimming in the lake every day in the summer.

"Welcome home," she said. "We're glad to have you here."

Sherry was incredibly supportive. She gave the media enough heartache for two lifetimes. When journalists tried to interview Sherry, she'd say, "You're just slimy bastards. Leave him alone. Get out of here."

After tirades like this, the media changed their tactics. They tried giving Sherry flowers. Still, she gave them nothing but holy hell.

Sherry and the others in Sandpoint understood that I was used as a scapegoat. I wasn't rich. I wasn't famous. I wasn't powerful or well-connected. I could be used and thrown away when I was no longer needed. I'm not treated that way in Sandpoint. And I don't treat anyone else that way.

Now, I was officially retired from the force. I hadn't started working as an apprentice electrician yet, so I fixed up our house. I laid down tiles, put in new doors, repainted the interior. The media was camped outside, which only made it easier for me to stay inside working.

One day, the carpet installers came. After putting in a full day's work, they went back out to their truck to go home. On the way, the media people tried to ask them questions, which of course they didn't answer. Driving off in their truck, one of the carpet installers dropped his drawers and shot the media a full moon. I often wished I could have done that myself.

My life was irrevocably, irreversibly, and irresponsibly changed. Even if I were guilty of everything that people said or thought that I did, that didn't change the fact that O.J. Simpson had murdered two people. But the death of Nicole Brown and Ron Goldman was old news. For all intents and purposes, the trial of O.J. Simpson was over. It was now the trial of Mark Fuhrman.

Chapter 25

CLOSING ARGUMENTS

Nobody wants to do anything to this man. We don't.

—CHRISTOPHER DARDEN IN REFERENCE
TO THE DEFENDANT O.J. SIMPSON

ON SEPTEMBER 26, 1995, closing arguments began, exactly a year to the first day of jury selection and more than fifteen months since the murders. The case had veered so far off course that what had begun as a murder trial had become a discourse on race and alleged (though never proven) police misconduct. This is exactly what the defense attorneys intended, and the extent to which they succeeded is clear from the summations of both sides.

The prosecution felt forced to play the race card because of the defense team's focus on racial issues. Much of the prosecution's time and energy was taken up either attacking me or making excuses for prosecuting Simpson, when there was no reason to do either. Moreover, there was no reason for Marcia and

Chris to spend so much time presenting their close. The jury had heard all the evidence; every detail about DNA test results didn't need to be repeated. What the jury did need to hear again was that not one shred of evidence pointed to a murderer other than O.J. Simpson.

Vince Bugliosi points out that a summation can't be effective if the advocate does not believe absolutely what he's saying.

He says, "Throughout the trial, the sad irony was that the defense attorneys seemed to be fighting harder for injustice than the prosecutors were fighting for justice." He goes on to say that although the soft sell might work in selling insurance, it doesn't win murder cases. Throughout the trial, from opening statements to closing arguments, the prosecuting attorneys apologized for doing their jobs, when they should have been forcefully—even angrily—stating what they believed and what the evidence proved: Simpson was guilty of murder.

Not only was Marcia Clark unconvincing; she also seemed to know it. Instead of using fire and brimstone, instead of dramatically pointing out the obvious guilt of O.J. Simpson in no uncertain terms, Marcia was dull and obviously fatigued, so she tried to make a virtue out of her weakness:

> In the course of this trial you have heard some testimony of a very emotional nature. I expect that during the course of argument you are going to be hearing some very impassioned speeches. Fiery speeches that may stir up feelings of anger or pity. Although your feelings may he aroused, as may be natural and understandable for all of us, as the instruction tells you as the trier of fact, you, the judges, are to remain neutral and impartial and not be influenced by such passion or sentiment, no matter how sorely tempted you may be to do so.

Marcia showed almost no emotion except when she started talking about one of her most important witnesses:

"On the other hand, although it would be completely understandable if you were to feel angry and disgusted with Mark Fuhrman, as we all are, still it would be wrong to find the defendant guilty [or] not guilty just because of that anger and disgust."

In her closing, Marcia Clark not only indicted me, but she also tried, convicted, and figuratively sentenced me to death. And she did so without appeal to reason or evidence, but with emotional responses to inflammatory issues: precisely what she asked the jury not to do.

I'm sure the prosecutors felt fairly confident that in the weeks or months ahead I would be indicted for misconduct in the course of my policework. But instead of waiting for the facts, Marcia took a stand of moral superiority and condemnation, knowing full well that her case failed not because of anything I had said or done, but because of her own mistakes and those of her lead detectives.

"Did he lie when he testified here in this courtroom saying that he did not use racial epithets in the last ten years? Yes. Is he a racist? Yes. Is he the worst LAPD has to offer? Yes. Do we wish the LAPD had never hired him? Yes. In fact, do we wish there were no such person on the planet? Yes."

No such person on the planet? A little melodramatic, isn't it, Marcia?

"But the fact that Mark Fuhrman is a racist and lied about it on the witness stand does not mean that we haven't proven the defendant guilty beyond a reasonable doubt, and it would be a tragedy if, with such overwhelming evidence, ladies and gentlemen, as we have presented to you, you found the defendant not guilty in spite of all that, because of the racist attitudes of one police officer."

Chris Darden admitted he didn't have the moral depth to sit on a jury in a case where race could possibly be an issue.

In other words, I'm guilty, but so is O.J. The only difference is that Simpson had a trial, and I was convicted without one.

Marcia went on to say that I was not that crucial to the prosecution's case, and they didn't even need to call me as a witness. Well, if this had been true, I sure wish she had told me then, because I would have gladly walked away from the Simpson circus in July 1994. But the prosecution wouldn't let me.

This is what Marcia should have said about the tapes:

The only evidence against Mark Fuhrman are notes and tapes for a fictional screenplay and witnesses who are easily impeached.

Regardless of what Mark Fuhrman said, did, or thought—these are the facts. Mark Fuhrman did an outstanding job investigating and testifying in this case. No, he didn't admit to something he said a long time ago. Perhaps he forgot or was embarrassed or felt too much pressure, some of which I may have been responsible for. But your decision should be based on his professional approach to this case, the job he did, and the evidence he found, and not the soap opera this trial has become.

Chris Darden's summation was often indistinguishable from that of the defense. Not that he made the same arguments that they did, but he seemed to agree with them on certain issues, even if he did think they took things too far.

"And there are some people that think because Fuhrman is a racist, that we ought to chuck the law out the window, throw it out the window, perhaps it shouldn't be applied in this case."

But that's exactly what happened, and Chris himself deserved much of the blame for allowing it.

"You heard from the defense in this case and they presented testimony about slurs, epithets as they call them, a bunch of nasty, hateful, low-down language used by Mark Fuhrman."

Chris doesn't mention that the slurs and epithets were testified to by only a couple of witnesses who were easily impeached, and the other language was used in a fictional screenplay.

Then Chris went on to say: "This is the case of O.J. Simpson, not Mark Fuhrman. The case of Mark Fuhrman, if there's to be a case, that's a case for another forum, not necessarily a case for another day, because today may be the day. But it is a case for another forum, another jury perhaps." In other words, he was expecting another trial with me as the defendant. Perhaps he was hoping to prosecute it.

His advice to the jury was even worse than Judge Ito's comments about my taking the Fifth.

"I am going to ask you to consider the fact of his misstatements or lies or untruths, however you want to term it, because you have to consider that. That's the law. You have to consider everything Fuhrman said on the witness stand because that's evidence in this case. And I want you to consider it. I want you to consider all the evidence. So don't think that I'm saying, hey, just overlook it, just overlook what he said, just overlook the fact that he lied about having used that slur in the past ten years. But I'm asking you to put it in proper perspective. You decide what it's worth. You decide what it means. If it helps you in assessing his credibility—and it should, or his lack of credibility, I don't know—then you use it."

Chris assumed that because I took the Fifth I must have been lying. Then he tells the jury to use that in assessing my credibility (which Chris himself doesn't have much confidence in) despite the fact that it had no bearing on the rest of my testimony or any of the other evidence.

Chris apologized repeatedly for prosecuting Simpson, and constantly offered the jury an excuse for voting to acquit. "Nobody wants to do anything to this man," he said.

We don't want to do anything to this man? Sure we do; he's a murderer. We want to put him away for the rest of his life. Is Darden saying that even though he is supposed to be prosecuting Simpson for murder, he doesn't want to do anything to him? Is Darden speaking for himself, or for the prosecution team? What about the victims' families, who were sitting right behind him—didn't they want to do something to Simpson? What about the people of California? If Chris didn't want to put Simpson in prison for the rest of his life, what was he doing prosecuting him? It was almost as if Chris knew what the verdict would be, so he was making a disclaimer.

The jury could have made the right decision had they been led by strong advocates for the prosecution. But Chris Darden kept giving them reasons to vote for acquittal. At one point, he said to the jury, "Whatever you do, the decision is yours, and I'm glad it's not mine." If Chris felt that way, why didn't he just sit down and shut up? He had no business asking the jury to make a decision that he himself admitted he didn't have the courage to make.

With a different set of prosecutors, perhaps the jury would have voted for a conviction. They might have been able to see behind the smokescreen of race. But Chris Darden admitted he didn't have the moral depth to sit on a jury in a case where race could possibly be an issue. And his obsession with race surfaced many times during his summation. Consider his reference to black police photographer Willie Ford: "You heard that brother testify. Did he look like a co-conspirator to you?" Ford was also referred to by Johnnie Cochran, who said that the photographer was the only law enforcement professional not involved in the conspiracy.

Chris and Marcia both told the jury that Simpson is innocent until proven guilty. But Mark Fuhrman is guilty without a trial or even a formal charge against him. We're going to strip him of his LAPD title, the respect he got from this case, and his twenty-year career. Then we're going dig a deep hole and throw him into it. If he isn't guilty, so what? We're finished with him. He got us here. Now we're trying to use him to get us out.

As they did throughout the trial, Marcia and Chris tried to do too much, but in the end, they didn't do nearly enough. Marcia kept getting bogged down in details of evidence that the jury had already seen. She tried to convince the jury that she knew what was going on inside Simpson's head the night of the murders.

In a murder trial where you don't have an eyewitness and the suspect does not confess, the only thing you have to prove is that he is the only person who did or could have committed the crime. The prosecution in this case tried too hard to establish Simpson's every movement, action, and thought—an impossible task. Instead, all they had to prove was that he was there and committed the crimes. There was no reason to lock themselves into inflexible theories that the defense could later tear apart.

Of course, the defense took advantage of every opportunity the prosecution handed them. In the opening arguments of both Clark's and Darden's summations, the defense objected only three times, which is about normal for this stage of a trial. But when the prosecutors returned to make their rebuttals, the defense repeatedly objected in an attempt to rattle the speakers. In Darden's rebuttal, the defense objected twenty-one times. In Marcia Clark's final address, they objected fifty times. Yet out of a total of seventy-one objections, Judge Ito sustained only two.

The defense's closing argument, presented by Johnnie Cochran, deserves little if any attention. Like the rest of the defense case, his argument never said who did commit the murders. He didn't cite any evidence that pointed to anyone other than his client. And his close was almost devoid of reason.

I don't enjoy revisiting what Cochran had to say about me, but it's even more difficult to read Clark's and Darden's summations. Whether these two prosecutors ever liked me, whether they ever felt that I was evil or corrupt, these were simply their opinions about someone they didn't know. But there are hundreds, maybe thousands, of people who do know me. Marcia's and Chris's words hurt me, but they also hurt my family, friends, and colleagues, who had no forum and therefore no way to prove that I was not a racist or a rogue cop.

Marcia and Chris wanted to think that they were all right and I was all wrong. But deep down they must have known that this was crap. They knew who screwed up this case. They knew who bungled evidence. They knew who failed to collect evidence. They knew who lost evidence. They knew who ignored evidence. They knew who wrote bad search warrants. They knew who failed to follow up on clues. They knew who blew the interrogation. And it wasn't Mark Fuhrman.

Because of this trial, and throughout the writing of this book, I have talked at length with Vince Bugliosi. Vince is a classic example of a dedicated man, a man who, after the trial of mass murderer Charles Manson, could have embraced fame and fortune and left behind the ideals that made him what he is. But he didn't do that. He maintained his professionalism, his honor, and his integrity. Unlike Clark and Darden, Vince is a famous prosecutor, but he's also an exceptional prosecutor, who won convictions in twenty-one consecutive murder cases and won 105 out of 106 felony jury trials. As Vince describes my situation in the Simpson case, he told me he would have confronted the problem head on, worked with me, and had me explain my story in court.

That's exactly what I wanted to do. Unfortunately for this case, and for justice, these prosecutors acted more like spoiled children instead of adults charged with a professional responsibility.

How would it have hurt them to sit down with me and talk about the tapes? They could have hated me. They could have even told me they hated me. But then at least we could have resolved that issue and gone back to doing our jobs—prosecuting a murderer.

Chapter 26

VERDICT

About three hours into it, one of the jurors said "ladies and gentlemen, what do we have here?" And it came up, well, what we really have here is reasonable doubt.

—ARMANDA COOLEY, JURY FOREMAN

I WAS AT HOME in Sandpoint standing in the kitchen when my wife told me the jury was in and they were going to announce the verdict in the Simpson trial. Since the jury had only deliberated a few hours, I figured they would return a guilty verdict.

I was too nervous to sit down and watch, so I stood and just listened. As I heard the clerk read the verdict of not guilty, I went numb; I couldn't believe that the jury could be so wrong. My wife said, "They're going to blame this all on you."

She was right. As you might imagine, the day of the verdict was not a fun one for us. The media was already outside our house, and although we had been the subject of media frenzies before, this was the worst we had ever experienced. The sharks were everywhere.

Cameras lit up the whole neighborhood like a football stadium. Outside our windows, we could see antennas climbing into the sky. Power cords were stretched across the road. Cars and vans were parked hundreds of feet down the block. Journalists, camera crews, technicians, and gofers crowded on the sidewalk and spilled into the street. Reporters tried interviewing the locals, but they weren't getting the sound bites they wanted. Instead of offering commentary on the trial, or about me, my neighbors told the media to leave us all alone.

Night came, but the street remained blindingly bright. Inside our house we had the curtains drawn and the lights out, yet still it was brighter than daylight. Ron Chaney, my good friend and the mayor of Sandpoint, saw the disruption the media was causing and called in the police to tell the camera crews to turn out the lights and shut down the generators. This is a residential neighborhood, the police said, people are trying to sleep. So ended the first day after the verdict.

When we woke up, the media was still outside waiting in shifts to make sure they didn't miss a movement. Still, I was able to smuggle my wife and kids in and out of the house, as our neighbors created diversions. But I had to stay in the house.

After a couple of days, I got stir crazy and decided to play with the media. It was October and already growing cool. The reporters were spending more and more time near their cars. I opened a window in one of my kid's bedrooms and jumped down onto the backyard. Then I made my way across a street, down an alley, and back around three hundred feet away from the shivering journalists. I dropped in on a couple of good friends of mine, Vicki and Gale Dolesby, without anybody seeing me. They greeted me warmly and asked me inside, where we sat and drank a beer and laughed at the whole pathetic spectacle.

But it wasn't really that funny. I knew as well, or even better than anyone, that O.J. Simpson was guilty. I knew I hadn't done anything wrong in handling the case. And I knew that I never would have become a target of the defense if I wasn't a good detective.

Meanwhile, the media was beating the hell out of the story. They interviewed the jurors, and while some mentioned me, others said that it wasn't racial issues but "doubt" that made them vote for acquittal. I don't know how a juror presented with that evidence could have had any doubt about Simpson's guilt.

I thought the jury would be able to make a decision based on the facts of the case. But it seems they just didn't want to convict O.J., no matter what evidence was presented. They didn't want to believe that a popular celebrity could have murdered two people. So when the defense came up with their ridiculous theories and the prosecution made countless errors the jury latched onto whatever slim speculation would justify a verdict of not guilty.

It wasn't only the jury's fault; their verdict was a reflection of the attitudes that many brought to the case. The people who lined the freeway, shouting "Go, O.J., go!" The defense groupies who tried to peddle bogus evidence. The trial junkies who watched it like a soap opera. The media, long bored with the day-one story that Simpson obviously did it, who wanted the trial to be as long and as controversial as possible. The talking heads who had to say something different about the trial every night or they wouldn't have any reason to appear on television. The prosecutors, more worried about politics and looking good on television than doing their jobs. The defense, willing to say or do anything that might divert attention from their client's guilt. And the judge, star-struck by the cameras and intimidated by the defense.

Somebody had to take the heat. To the world, I was the racist cop who may or may not have planted evidence, but either way I was definitely the reason that Simpson got off. I could live with false accusations and personal attacks; the media didn't know me personally, and I wasn't about to give them a chance to learn any more than they already knew. I've been shot at before, so someone sticking a camera in my face is no big deal. But the difference is, when someone shoots at you, you can shoot back. When someone points a camera at you, you're defenseless.

> **"Is [Fuhrman] the worst LAPD has to offer? Yes. Do we wish the LAPD had never hired him? Yes. In fact, do we wish there were no such person on the planet? Yes."**
> —from Marcia Clark's closing statement

After the verdict I was portrayed in a worse light than at any point during the trial, because now, even the people who thought Simpson was guilty turned on me, since I apparently had lost the case. A lot of people in the media and in Los Angeles blamed me for the verdict. But the people who knew me, the people who knew the case and were honest about it, and my friends in Sandpoint didn't blame me.

Several days after the verdict, I went on a long-planned hunting trip to southeastern Idaho with a good friend of mine from Sandpoint named Jeff Free. Jeff was acting as guide on a mule deer hunt, and asked me to help out on the trip.

I managed to sneak out of the house and make my way out of town, bound for the wild country. Pulling into camp I met for the first time with Larry Heathington, the outfitter, a retired cop, and former head of his department's SWAT team. He told me, "Listen, you got screwed. But here in camp, you're just guiding a few hunters. That's all. Don't expect anything different, and don't worry about a thing. You're among friends."

One of the hunters on the trip was an actor named Marshall Teague, who recently played one of the bad guys in *The Rock*. Jeff and I buddied around with Marshall and his girlfriend Lindy and became friends with both of them. Marshall still calls to check up on me, and last year I put ivory handles on a knife that was very special to him.

I spent the next few days in the wilderness, perhaps the one place the media couldn't find me and wouldn't be able to catch up to me even if they did. It was great being out in the woods with Jeff and our hunter, Chuck Davis. But eventually I had to go back.

Returning to Sandpoint, I had to sneak into my own house. The media were staked out all over town, waiting for me to return. Their presence was so obvious my friends were able to get me through undetected.

The next morning I was supposed to go elk hunting with Scott Clawson, my boss. I woke up at 4:30 in the morning, put on my hunting jacket, picked up my rifle, and walked out of my house. I heard footsteps, and then lights shined in my eyes. Somebody shouted at me:

"Mr. Fuhrman, could we ask you a few questions?"

I went back inside cursing and shouting. No elk hunting for me that season.

A while later, too angry to go back to sleep, I answered the phone and heard the same voice that had already ruined my morning: "We'd really like to talk to you. Let you tell your side of the story."

Yeah, I'm sure they would have.

"Listen," I told them. "First, it's October in Idaho. It's going to start getting pretty cold out there. In here by the fire, I'm going to stay nice and warm. Another thing: If you're hungry, call Second Avenue Pizza. Just tell them you're across the street from Fuhrman's house."

That's all the information the media was going to get from me. I suppose that other people in my situation would have held press conferences and submitted to interviews. But I didn't see how it would do any good. The trial was over, the verdict was in. Whatever I said wasn't going to bring the killer of Ron and Nicole to justice. While I certainly didn't enjoy constant criticism by people who didn't know me from Adam, I knew that giving them anything would only prolong the whole sordid drama. So I kept my silence and waited for them to go away.

It was almost enjoyable to embarrass the media whenever I got the chance. When they tried surveillance, locals reported them. Even though the media was set up with tag teams for a round-the-clock stakeout of our house, we virtually came and went at will. The neighbors would create a diversion, and when the media people fell for it, my family and I could make our moves.

I always wondered what the media would ask if they ever caught up to me. Would they ask if I thought Simpson was guilty?

I don't think the verdict was America's verdict. There are a bunch of people in Los Angeles, black and white, who are either star-struck or have a chip on their shoulders. They want to think that a likeable football star isn't capable of brutally murdering his wife and her friend. Or they want to repay the city and police of Los Angeles for Rodney King. Either way, they're wrong and the rest of the country knows it, even if they refuse to admit it, and the media will never tell the true story.

O.J. Simpson is not a symbol for racial prejudice or a victim of police misconduct or an example of the absurd argument that a black man cannot get a fair trial in America unless he's a millionaire. And I'm not a rogue cop or a poster boy for police racism or an indictment of the LAPD. I was just a detective whose phone happened to ring at 1:00 in the morning. If it had been my choice, I would have stayed in bed. But I didn't have a choice; I had a job. And I did my best.

Race is the original sin of American society. But we're not going to get rid of it unless we start dealing with it honestly. The vast majority of black people in America are honest, decent, law-abiding people. I know that because I've worked in their neighborhoods, protecting them from criminals. But within those neighborhoods, the criminals are predominantly black.

Most black criminals prey on black victims. They rob and kill people, they sell drugs, they make the inner cities uninhabitable. Of course, there are white criminals, too. But the black community is more threatened by people of their own race in their own neighborhoods. And the black community is more threatened by black criminals than by white cops. Sure, police officers aren't perfect. Sometimes we make mistakes or give in to the immense pressure of an impossible job. But we're trying to do good. If we didn't think we could make a difference in people's lives, make their streets safer, and protect them from people they can't protect themselves against, then we wouldn't have become cops in the first place.

It should be so obvious that I don't have to say it, but when you take an oath to become a policeman, you vow to protect and serve all people, no matter what color, religion, national heritage, or whatever. I took that oath very seriously, and so do most other cops.

Racism is stupid, especially for a cop. A police officer has to work in communities where there are often people of many races, and it's his job to protect them. And the last thing he wants to do is walk into a case with prejudices or preconceptions. You can't be a racist and a good policeman.

Life on the street is too complex for ideology. That's why lawyers, academics, and other intellectuals are so obsessed with race. They can afford to be; they don't live in the real world. Chris Darden said that he had obligations as a prosecutor and as a black man. I'm not sure exactly what he means, but it sounds as if he thought he had to make a choice between doing his job and remaining loyal to his race. If he was a cop and worried about such things, I wouldn't want Chris Darden as a partner.

Cops don't have the luxury of believing what they want to believe. They have to look at things honestly. They have to listen to the evidence and follow where it leads them. Any preconceptions about who did or did not do the crime, or about how the crime was committed, are distractions that will keep them from doing their job.

There is no more racism in the LAPD than any other large organization. But almost everywhere else, the racism is silent and less vocal. A cop's world is full of racism, hatred, anger, and violence. A cop has to deal with racism every day, often from the people he's trying to arrest or even trying to help. It doesn't make sense, but then much of what a cop sees doesn't make any sense. I remember my first autopsy back in 1977. On the table next to it was the body of a beautiful three-year-old girl who had been beaten to death by her parents. Why does this happen? I don't know. But if you're a policeman, you can't ask why. It's the wrong question. And it will make you crazy.

Most jobs you can walk away from. If you don't want to do an assignment, you can hand it off to someone else. But cops don't have that luxury. We've got to deal with things that nobody else wants to deal with. It's called doing our job. My job as a homicide detective was to investigate murders, no matter where those investigations led.

If I had found evidence at Bundy that it was my own brother who had committed the double murder, I would have implicated and indicted him. If the murder suspect had been my friend, someone I knew, or anybody other than O.J. Simpson, I would have done exactly what I did.

Let's turn the tables on race. Say I was a black detective, a vocal activist for radical black causes, active member of the Muslim Party, and supporter of the Black Panthers. Would Simpson be guilty now? What if all that applied, and O.J. was white—would race become an issue in his trial?

Because I'm white and Simpson is black, I'm seen as a racist and he's voted not guilty. It has no basis in fact, but people believe what they want to believe. And it was a lot easier for many people to believe that an LAPD detective was a suspect-framing racist than it was for them to believe that O.J. Simpson murdered two people.

Race is a murkier issue than many people like to think. Since we have become more aware of the power and persistence of racial animosity, a cruel double standard has emerged that has done little to advance racial equality and much to widen the racial divide in our society. Anyone charged with being a racist is immediately presumed guilty. The charge itself is a term of guilt, and can be made without regard to the person's life and character. A few insensitive or unthinking words, a human mistake, and that person is branded for life.

Because it is impossible to prove a negative, people charged with racism can never completely silence their critics. Every defense is seen as an excuse or a cliché. When the defense lawyers started claiming I was a racist, I immediately thought of all my black friends. But that would have sounded like the familiar refrain, "Some of my best friends are …."

Those who make charges of racism always take the moral high ground, and others are quick to scramble for position. Meanwhile, all this fingerpointing and blame casting merely divides the two races farther. Throughout the trial, there were millions of words written and spoken about racism. But the result has only been an increase in racial tension. Race was and still is a problem in Los Angeles because no one wants to talk about it rationally or candidly.

In order to have a story, you must have conflict, and conflict always plays better in the starkest terms, like black and white. Race was used in the trial as a diversion and excuse. Even Chris Darden tried to get out of handling my testimony, a job that might have tarnished his image as a down brother. He should have just done his duty as a prosecutor and nailed O.J. Simpson, whether he was black, white, or pink polka-dotted.

The prosecution knew that the defense's race strategy and conspiracy theories were garbage, but they wouldn't fight back because they were afraid of being branded racists. So they never stood up and defended their star witness, the one person who found almost every important piece of evidence, and had not made any mistakes.

The media is equally to blame. As Jeffrey Toobin wrote in *The New Yorker* shortly after the verdict:

> Fear of being called racist transcended everything in that newsroom. This extended, I think, even to discussions of the evidence. The safe course for those of us covering the case was to nitpick along with the defense attorneys…. Our caution and fear, however, misled. The case against Simpson was simply overwhelming. When we said otherwise, we lied to the audience that trusted us.

But by the time Toobin wrote this, it was already too late. Simpson was acquitted, and most of the media was off being cautious and fearful, misleading their audience about other stories.

The entire Simpson trial was not a search for the truth or a journey to justice or any other courtroom cliché. It was theater, or more accurately, television. If O.J. Simpson wasn't a millionaire celebrity and the trial hadn't been televised, then nobody would have thought twice about Mark Fuhrman, LAPD detective. I would have been able to retire in peace and live the rest of my life without having to apologize to people because they think I'm someone I'm not. I wouldn't have to explain to my children why they can't lead a normal life. My wife wouldn't have to share the pain of my own small failures and monumental bad luck.

Throughout the media frenzy, I was angry. But I tried not to feel sorry for myself. There were innocent victims involved here who had suffered much more than I had. And they had often been forgotten in much of the hysteria and hype over the verdict. First of all, there were Ron and Nicole and their families, who had suffered not only the tragedy of murder but the avoidable travesty of watching the killer go free. Then there was my family.

My family did nothing wrong and had nothing to do with the Simpson case, except for the fact that they were related to me. I made some mistakes and said some awful things. Even if it's a stretch, and irrelevant to the case, you can't say I was an entirely innocent victim. But my wife and kids should never have been brought into it. My wife suffered pain, embarrassment, and hassles that still haven't ended. We had to cover our children in their coats to sneak them in and out of the house. My daughter would look through the blinds and ask, "Are the bad people still out there?" That's something she will always remember, something I will have to explain. A five-year-old girl should never have to go through this. But at least I have my kids, and I didn't murder their mother. O.J. Simpson also has a young daughter. On her birthday, the Juice played golf.

After the verdict, Simpson revealed himself to be either utterly without remorse or completely uncaring about the fact that the mother of his children had been brutally murdered and her killer was apparently walking free. When he went golfing, he made jokes about his gloves for the television cameras. He told a journalist that since the verdict he learned that "fame and wealth are illusions. The only thing that endures is character."

I always thought that a person's character is reflected in the people around him, his friends and colleagues. But after the verdict, Simpson was dumped by his girlfriend Paula Barbieri, who complained that when they were first reunited, he seemed more concerned with getting photos for the tabloid he had sold an exclusive story to than rebuilding their relationship. His talent agency dumped him, as did all the companies he used to shill for. He was booted from his beloved country clubs. Most of his friends couldn't run away fast enough from him. Now Simpson is alone and abandoned. He can't go back to his old life, and he can't even envision a new one. Locked behind the iron bars of his Rockingham estate, surrounded by bodyguards and lawyers, he's a prisoner in his own house.

Chapter 27

AFTERMATH

God bless you, and may you find peace in your life. Move on.
You've done your duty.

—FROM A LETTER TO MARK FUHRMAN

O.J. SIMPSON'S TRIAL CONTINUES as it will even after the civil trial is over. For some reason, we cannot put the case behind us, even those of us who would prefer it end. It has become an unending national soap opera.

But at least some things have changed. The media is no longer staked out in front of my house, and my family and I can begin to have some semblance of a normal life. Eventually, the media got tired of having the people of Sandpoint telling them to get off their street and out of their town.

I finished fixing up our house in town, and we put it on the market in January of last year. Although it was a time of year that few people buy houses, we were able to sell it and buy a new place. Our new home is on a twenty-acre farm outside Sandpoint. Once we moved, our lives improved immensely. People we did not want to see could not get to us; you can't drive two hundred yards down a driveway onto a farm and say it is not trespassing. The media couldn't plant themselves on the sidewalk and force us to sneak in and out of our own house.

But that doesn't mean that we were free of them entirely. One time a media car drove down my neighbor's driveway and parked. They started filming our house from inside their car. A friend of mine came by and saw them. He drove up right behind the media car, parked his truck and left it there. The media crew complained that they wouldn't be able to get out.

"Well, what the hell are you doing on this property?" my friend asked.

The media called the sheriff. When he arrived, they could not have been too happy when they saw the sheriff walk up laughing. He shook my friend's hand and joked about the media people, who were upset that they weren't getting the respect they are accustomed to.

The community here is filled with mature people who treat everybody equally. They have a laid-back, live-and-let-live attitude. There is no status system up here. I drive around in a 1970 Ford pickup truck. If I drove that truck around Los Angeles, everyone would laugh at me, including my friends.

What you are here in Sandpoint is not what someone says you are, but who you prove yourself to be. The people of Sandpoint do not have an agenda; they did not prejudge me. Instead, they gave me a chance to show who I really am, and many of them embraced me.

Sandpoint is a unique place. Situated fifty-five miles south of Canada at the base of the Selkirk and Cabinet mountain ranges, Sandpoint sits on a lake that is forty-three miles long and it offers spectacular natural beauty and a town with most of the amenities of a big city without any of the hassles. I am an outdoorsman, and the hunting and fishing opportunities afforded by the area are about the best you can find in the lower forty-eight states. Lake Pend Oreille holds the record for the largest trout (over thirty-seven pounds), and the game includes elk, mountain lion, bear, and deer.

But there is more in Sandpoint than just hunting and fishing. The town is filled with great restaurants, coffee shops, boutiques, and bookstores. There is a theater that attracts performing artists and musicians from all across the country. A local community theater group has shows all year long. Annual events include a winter festival, and art and music festivals. Several prominent artists live in the area.

When the media was hounding me about the Simpson trial, the only thing I would ever talk about was Sandpoint. I wanted them to know how great the people here were. But the media was not interested in hearing good news about good people, so they persisted in painting their distorted portrait of the town I now call home. While the media portrayed Sandpoint as a haven of hatred and anger, they would have done better looking into their own backyard. Then they might have found what they were looking for.

I liked Sandpoint from the first time I visited. In Los Angeles, you can live in a neighborhood for years and never even know your neighbors. In Sandpoint, already we have made friends I know I will have for the rest of my life.

While there are many Idaho natives, many others are newcomers like us. They have already made their bones and they do not come here with a chip on their shoulders or feeling they have something to prove. A lot of them escaped from big cities and came to Sandpoint to get away from the rat race while still being able to enjoy a civilized existence. They are retired, or semi-retired, or have professions that don't require

Eventually, I will have to explain all this to my kids.

them to go to an office every day. Out here they live a good life, enjoying the outdoors and taking an active part in their community. Sandpoint is a resort town, and in the summer there are a lot of tourists and season-long visitors. Many visitors fall in love with Sandpoint immediately and want to move here.

One of the main reasons we chose Sandpoint is that it is a great place to raise kids. My son and daughter go to good schools and enjoy other activities. They love living in Sandpoint.

My kids are growing up in a healthy environment without all the poisons of city life. We have lots of animals on the farm— horses, goats, and sheep. The kids raise their own rabbits and chickens and sell the eggs. At the last county fair, my daughter won a blue ribbon for her eggs and my son won a blue ribbon for his rabbit named Cookie. Winning blue ribbons at the ages of 5 1/2 and 3 1/2 might have spoiled them a little for future county fairs. They're going to have to learn you don't win every time.

For Christmas, I bought my wife a horse and trailer. She owned a horse before, but this had been her dream for years. Her horse is bigger and healthier than my old nag, but then, marriage is based on concessions. And I would rather hunt or fish than ride. Last summer I caught a twelve-pound rainbow trout that I had to throw back—it was too small.

We don't watch the news and hardly watch television at all, so we are a bit out of touch. When the Simpson story undergoes one of its periodic mini-crises, we don't usually notice, and our neighbors also ignore it. But friends keep us posted, usually by phone.

Now that the case is over, it is being chewed up and spit out by the media. Defense attorneys like to take rational facts and turn them into a bowl of Jello, especially when there is a camera or tape recorder pointed at them. The law should be a fairly accurate science. Laws are written, and once certain criteria are met, there is either a violation or not. The factual finding of evidence should be a lot simpler than the criminal justice system makes it. Either the fingerprint belongs to the suspect or it does not.

But defense attorneys never say die. They stumble over any admission of guilt or error the same way *Home Improvement*'s Tim Allen trips over the words "I am wrong." Criminal defense attorneys (redundant?), including many who had nothing to do with the Simpson case, decided that I planted the glove. Nothing, not even a video of Simpson committing the murders in slow-motion, would convince them otherwise. It would be comical if it were not so tragic. I try not to think about the trial, but it never goes away.

One day I was out hunting with a friend, Casey Foster, when he spotted a nice mature whitetail deer, a four- or five-point buck. Casey shot him in the shoulder, but the deer ran away. From my read of the blood trail, Casey had shot him in the left shoulder, but the blood was to the right side of the deer tracks, which meant the bullet went through the left shoulder and out the other side. There was only a little bit of blood to track with. The deer was not bleeding very badly, and we started tracking him down deep ravines and drainages; sometimes a small speck of blood was all we had to go on.

After a few hours we sat down to rest. Casey looked at me and said, "I know exactly how you found the evidence in the Simpson case, because I've never seen someone track a deer like that. I wouldn't want you on my trail."

Now Casey, Jeff, and my other friends say that the worst is behind us. I am on probation for the next three years, and unless I get a pardon, I will be a convicted felon for the rest of my life. Meanwhile, LAPD Internal Affairs, the U.S. Department of Justice, the LA County Public Defender's Office, and the State Attorney General's Office have all conducted exhaustive investigations of my police career. Not one of these investigations have uncovered a single incident of racial bias, evidence planting, or suspect complaints. If they had found a scintilla of evidence linking me to any illegal activities, you would have heard all about it on the evening news. But because they couldn't find anything, they're not saying anything. And they're never going to make a public announcement exonerating me.

One investigation by the LAPD came to the conclusion that I was "lying and exaggerating" on the screenplay tapes. That means I was telling the truth when I said they're fictional, but the department isn't about to admit that. Unfortunately, they're caught in a double-bind. Either I'm innocent, and they have ruined the career and reputation of a good cop (which they can't admit because they wanted so badly to prove I'm supposedly a racist and a rogue); or, I'm guilty of everything they say I'm (for which they still haven't found any evidence), and somehow this awful person was promoted three times. Whichever way they play it, the LAPD looks bad. They should just leave me alone, but they can't. Now the U.S. Department of Justice is investigating the LAPD, and I'll be interested to see how that turns out.

Johnnie Cochran made millions of dollars suing the LAPD for wrongful arrests and civil rights violations. As a result of the trial, I was portrayed as a racist cop who was supposed to have planted evidence, harassed and beat suspects, and used racial epithets. Over the years I made thousands of arrests and had contacts with tens of thousands of suspects. That should make me a good target for a Cochran-style lawsuit—if I am what my accusers say I am. Yet not one lawsuit has been brought against me since the trial.

My personal and professional reputation is damaged beyond repair. Few people seem to realize that I'm not the rogue cop they wanted me to be. I'll have to live with this my entire life. I think about it all the time. I spend hours asking myself, what if...?

Of course, I'm not alone. From the beginning of the trial, I've received letters, now totaling in the hundreds. The letters of support are incredibly touching, there are no words to describe the commitment these people have. I'm not sure I'm that good a person. It amazes me that these people can take the time, expense, and effort to write. I find it difficult just to write a check and pop it in a return envelope. These folks write me letters that are several pages long.

The writers want to do something. They can't do anything about the defense attorneys or the district attorney's office or the criminal justice system. And they want to do something positive, so they send photos of themselves and their family, of their husbands and sons who have died in service. They have sent T-shirts, hats, flowers, Marine Corps statues, a Cross pen with my name engraved on it, candy, fruit, and cookies. When I had a legal defense fund, some donated money that they probably couldn't afford to give.

The letters come from all over the world. They are written by people from all walks of life. I get letters from folks in big cities and small rural towns. Letters from blue-collar workers, white-collar professionals, owners of small businesses, corporate executives, retired people, mothers, widows, and attorneys who want to apologize for people in their own profession. I have received many letters from black people, from black church groups, from entire classrooms full of kids. But despite the broad range of backgrounds, these letter writers share at least one thing in common: a feeling of disgust that a working man like me was screwed for doing his job.

Some of the letters are angry. I get a lot of mail complaining about F. Lee Bailey. They cannot believe that someone would try to set a double murderer free on my back. If I showed Bailey the letters I got about him, maybe he'd change his style. Or maybe not.

Many of the people who write see themselves in me. They see a regular guy who got the shaft because he wasn't rich or famous or well-connected, because a bunch of people screwed up and someone had to take the fall. Cops in particular understand that it could have been any one of them. I just happened to answer the call and do my job the best I knew how.

Most of my correspondents are not Simpson case groupies, just people who believe that an injustice has been done. They realized that the trial was a national crime drama, a one-season television special. And they also understand that this media event involved real people, not actors. They knew that as absurd and unrealistic as it sometimes seemed, the script wasn't made up. They realized that those of us who were involved in the case, particularly those of us who did not have any choice in the matter, would have to live through all of it. They had sympathy and spoke from the heart.

I read every letter that is sent to me. Unfortunately, there is no possible way I could respond to them all. It would be a full-time job for two or three people to answer the countless letters I have received. But I enjoy reading them, and many of them make me smile. It is good to know that there is somebody out there who believes in Mark Fuhrman.

One letter said so much in so few words that I reprint it here in full:

> I watched your interview with Diane Sawyer of *ABC Primetime*. I just wanted to drop you a note to let you know that I was impressed with your forthrightness and integrity. It takes a man of strong character to admit his wrongs, ask for forgiveness, and to move on to a better place of beingness. I applaud this most manly of acts and do forgive you for your error. Hopefully, this will lead to your recovery.
>
> You see, I am a black man. The courage it took for you to face me, (all other black men and women), should not go unnoticed nor unacknowledged. It is also a form of courage on my part to pardon you, but what else can a man do. You lead the way, in this instance, I'll follow your lead.
>
> God bless you, and may you find peace in your life. Move on. You've done your duty. Peace.

The trial and its aftermath have completely turned my life upside down. But there is hope, and that is what keeps me going. I have been confronted with challenges my whole adult life, and I have learned to never give up, to always keep fighting. When I was a cop out on the street, I lived under stress that kicked the hell out of me, and I learned how to beat it. But the stress of this trial and all the sideshows is different. It gnaws at me every day, and I have had to learn to live with it. For the past two years, I have had a knot in my stomach. I am not sure my body would be able to function if the stress ever went away.

Three years ago I was just another detective. Now I am a public figure, which means that anyone can say whatever they want to about me. They have taken away my career, my life, and my privacy. But I cannot lose my faith in myself, in who I am, and what I have done with my life. I have always believed that I could make a difference. Despite all that happened, I still believe this.

The whole ordeal has taken an incredible toll on my wife. She is a private and reserved person, and living under the scrutiny of the national media for the past two years has been very difficult. She knows the real me—which only makes what she had to go through even worse. I wish there could be some closure for her, but I do not know if that will ever happen.

We could build a house so far up in the woods that nobody could ever get to us. We could move out of the country entirely. But I am not sure that would change things, and I do not know if there ever will be an end to this, wherever we go or whatever we do. I cannot stop thinking about it. I only hope my wife and kids can. That does not mean I cannot be happy, but it is never going to be the same.

I did nothing wrong. I was only doing my job. I made some mistakes in life and corrected them. Everyone makes mistakes. Everyone says things they wish they had not. But not everybody is forced to stand naked in judgment before the rest of the world.

Eventually, I will have to explain all this to my kids. Every few years there will be anniversary specials about the Simpson case, and we will have to relive it all over again. They will hear something in school from someone who is just repeating what they heard on television. They will read about me in the library. I hope they will read this book and it will make things clear for them. I hope they will have the strength to believe in the father they know, rather than the cartoon figure portrayed in the media. I hope they will realize that some people are too star-struck to believe that a popular celebrity can actually murder two people. I hope they will understand that while I am not perfect, the only thing I was guilty of was doing my job. And when my son grows up, I hope he does not want to become a policeman.

No matter what happened in the Simpson case and how I felt about it, no matter how my life has been irrevocably changed, knowing everything I know now and everything that happened to me, my family, and others, there is one thing I can say without question. I still would have answered the call on June 13. I still would have gone to the crime scene and done everything at Bundy and Rockingham the same way I did it then. I still would have tried my best to catch the murderer of Ron and Nicole. What else would I do? I'm a cop.

Appendix A

INTERROGATION TEXT

P.V. …my partner, Detective Lange, and we're in an interview room in Parker Center. The date is June 13th, 1994, and the time is 13:35 hours, and we're here with O.J. Simpson. Is that Orenthal James Simpson?

O.J. Orenthal James Simpson.

P.V. And what is your birthdate, Mr. Simpson?

O.J. July 9, 1947.

P.V. Okay, prior to us talking to you, as we agreed with your attorney, I'm going to give you your constitutional rights. And I would like you to listen carefully. If you don't understand anything, tell me, okay?

O.J. All right.

P.V. Okay, Mr. Simpson, you have the right to remain silent. If you give up the right to remain silent, anything you say can and will be used against you in a court of law. You have the right to speak to an attorney and to have an attorney present during the questioning. If you so desire and cannot afford one, an attorney will be appointed for you without charge before questioning. Do you understand your rights?

O.J. Yes, I do.

P.V. Are there any questions about that?

O.J. (Unintelligble)

P.V. Okay, you've got to speak up louder than that.

O.J. Okay, no.

P.V. Okay, do you wish to give up your right to remain silent and talk to us?

O.J. Ah, yes.

P.V. Okay, and you give up your right to have an attorney present while we talk?

O.J. Mmm hmm. Yes.

P.V. Okay. All right, what we're gonna do is, we want to . . . We're investigating, obviously, the death of your ex-wife and another man.

T.L. Someone told us that.

P.V. Yeah, and we're going to need to talk to you about that. Are you divorced from her now?

O.J. Yes.

P.V. How long have you been divorced?

O.J. Officially? Probably close to two years, but we've been apart for a little over two years.

P.V. Have you?

O.J. Yeah.

P.V. What was your relationship with her? What was the . . .

O.J. WELL, we tried to get back together, and it just didn't work. It wasn't working, and so we were going our separate ways.

P.V. Recently, you tried to get back together?

O.J. We tried to get back together for about a year, you know, where we started dating each other and seeing each other. She came back and wanted us to get back together, and . . .

P.V. Within the last year, you're talking about?

O.J. She came back about a year and four months ago about us trying to get back together, and we gave it a shot. We gave it a shot the better part of a year. And I think we both knew it wasn't working, and probably three weeks ago or so we said it just wasn't working and we went our separate ways.

P.V. Okay, the two children are yours?

O.J. Yes.

T.L. She have custody?

O.J. We have joint custody.

T.L. Through the courts?

O.J. We went through the courts and everything. Everything is done. We have no problems with the kids, we do everything together, you know, with the kids.

P.V. How was your separation? Was that a…?

O.J. The first separation?

P.V. Yeah, was there problems with that?

O.J. For me, it was big problems. I loved her, I didn't want us to separate.

P.V. Uh huh. I understand she had made a couple of crime…crime reports or something?

O.J. Ah, we had a big fight about six years ago on New Year's, you know, she made a report. I didn't make a report. And then we had an altercation about a year ago maybe. It wasn't a physical argument. I kicked her door or something.

P.V. And she made a police report on those two occasions?

O.J. Mmm hmm. And I stayed right there until the police came, talked to them.

T.L. Were you arrested at one time for something?

O.J. No. I mean, five years ago we had a big fight, six years ago. I don't know. I know I ended up doing community service.

P.V. So you weren't arrested?

O.J. No, I was never really arrested.

T.L. They never booked you or…?

O.J. No.

P.V. Can I ask you, when's the last time you've slept?

O.J. I got a couple of hours sleep last night. I mean, you know, I slept a little on the plane, not much, and when I got to the hotel I was asleep a few hours when the phone call came.

T.L. Did Nicole have a housemaid that lived there?

O.J. I believe so, yes.

T.L. Do you know her name at all?

O.J. Evia, Elvia, something like that.

P.V. We didn't see her there. Did she have the day off, perhaps?

O.J. I don't know. I don't know what schedule she's on.

T.L. Phil, what do you think? Maybe we can just recount last night …

P.V. Yeah. When was the last time you saw Nicole?

O.J. We were leaving a dance recital. She took off and I was talking to her parents.

P.V. Where was the dance recital?

O.J. Paul Revere High School.

P.V. And was that for one of your children?

O.J. Yeah, for my daughter Sydney.

P.V. And what time was that yesterday?

O.J. It ended about six-thirty, quarter to seven, something like that, you know, in the ballpark, right in that area. And they took off.

P.V. They?

O.J. Her and her family, her mother and father, sisters, my kids, you know.

P.V. And then you went your separate way?

O.J. Yeah, actually she left, and then they came back and her mother got in a car with her, and the kids all piled into her sister's car, and they …

P.V. Was Nicole driving?

O.J. Yeah.

P.V. What kind of car was she driving?

O.J. Her black car, a Cherokee, a Jeep Cherokee.

P.V. What were you driving?

O.J. My Rolls-Royce, my Bentley.

P.V. Do you own that Ford Bronco that sits outside?

O.J. Hertz owns it, and Hertz lets me use it.

P.V. So that's your vehicle, the one that was parked there on the street?

O.J. Mm hmm.

P.V. And it's actually owned by Hertz?

O.J. Hertz, yeah.

P.V. Who's the primary driver on that? You?

O.J. I drive it, the housekeeper drives it, you know, it's kind of a …

P.V. All-purpose type vehicle?

O.J. All purpose, yeah. It's the only one that my insurance will allow me to let anyone else drive.

P.V. Okay.

T.L. When you drive it, where do you park it at home? Where it is now, it was in the street or something?

O.J. I always park in the street.

T.L. You never take it in the … ?

O.J. Oh, rarely. I mean, I'll bring it in and switch the stuff, you know, and stuff like that. I did that yesterday, you know.

T.L. When did you last drive it?

O.J. Yesterday

P.V. What time yesterday?

O.J. In the morning, in the afternoon.

P.V. Okay, you left her, you're saying, about six-thirty or seven, or she left the recital?

O.J. Yeah.

P.V. And you spoke with her parents?

O.J. Yeah.

P.V. Okay, what time did you leave the recital?

O.J. Right about that time. We were all leaving. We were all leaving then. Her mother said something about me joining them for dinner, and I said no thanks.

P.V. Where did you go from there, O.J.?

O.J. Ah, home, home for a while, got my car for a while, tried to find my girlfriend for a while, came back to the house.

P.V. Who was home when you got home?

O.J. Kato.

P.V. Kato? Anybody else? Was your daughter there, Arnelle?

O.J. No.

P.V. Isn't that her name, Arnelle?

O.J. Arnelle, yeah.

P.V. So what time do you think you got back home, actually physically got home?

O.J. Seven-something.

P.V. Seven-something? And then you left, and …

O.J. Yeah, I'm trying to think, did I leave? You know I'm always…I had to run and get my daughter some flowers. I was actually doing the recital, so I rushed and got her some flowers, and I came home, and then I called Paula as I was going to her house, and Paula wasn't home.

P.V. Paula is your girlfriend?

O.J. Girlfriend, yeah.

P.V. Paula who?

O.J. Barbieri.

P.V. Could you spell that for me?

O.J. B-A-R-B-I-E-R-I.

P.V. Do you know an address on her?

O.J. No, she lives on Wilshire, but I think she's out of town.

P.V. You got a phone number?

O.J. Yeah, of course, [310] 470–3468.

P.V. So you didn't see her last night?

O.J. No, we'd been to a big affair the night before, and then I came back home. I was basically at home. I mean, anytime I was…Whatever time it took me to get to the recital and back, to get to the flower shop and back, I mean, that's the time I was out of the house.

P.V. Were you scheduled to play golf this morning, some place?

O.J. In Chicago.

P.V. What kind of a tournament was it?

O.J. Ah, it was Hertz, with special clients.

P.V. Oh, okay. What time did you leave last night, leave the house?

O.J. To go to the airport?

P.V. Mmm hmm.

O.J. About…The limo was supposed to be there at ten forty-five. Normally, they get there a little earlier. I was rushing around, somewhere between there and eleven.

P.V. So approximately ten forty-five to eleven.

O.J. Eleven o'clock, yeah, somewhere in that area.

P.V. And you went by limo?

O.J. Yeah.

P.V. Who's the limo service?

O.J. Ah, you have to ask my office.

P.V. Did you converse with the driver at all? Did you talk to him?

O.J. No, he was a new driver. Normally, I have a regular driver I drive with and converse. No, just about rushing to the airport, about how I live my life on airplanes, and hotels, that type of thing.

T.L. What time did the plane leave?

O.J. Ah, eleven forty-five the flight took off.

T.L. What airline was it?

O.J. American.

P.V. American? And it was eleven forty-five to Chicago?

O.J. Chicago.

T.L. So yesterday you did drive the white Bronco?

O.J. Mmm hmm.

T.L. And where did you park it when you brought it home?

O.J. Ah, the first time probably by the mailbox. I'm trying to think, or did I bring it in the driveway? Normally, I park it by the mailbox, sometimes …

T.L. On Ashford, or Ashland?

O.J. On Ashford, yeah.

T.L. Where did you park yesterday for the last time, do you remember?

O.J. Right where it is.

T.L. Where is it now?

O.J. Yeah.

T.L. Where, on … ?

O.J. Right on the street there.

T.L. On Ashford?

O.J. No, on Rockingham.

T.L. You parked it there?

O.J. Yes.

T.L. About what time was that?

O.J. Eight-something, seven … eight, nine o'clock, I don't know, right in that area.

T.L. Did you take it to the recital?

O.J. No.

T.L. What time was the recital?

O.J. Over at about six-thirty. Like I said, I came home, I got my car, I was going to see my girlfriend. I was calling her, and she wasn't around.

T.L. So you drove the…you came home in the Rolls, and then you got in the Bronco?

O.J. In the Bronco 'cause my phone was in the Bronco. And because it's a Bronco. It's a Bronco, it's what I drive, you know. I'd rather drive it than any other car. And, you know, as I was going over there, I called her a couple of times, and she wasn't there, and I left a message, and then I checked my messages, and there were no messages. She wasn't there, and she may have to leave town. Then I came back and ended up sitting with Kato.

T.L. Okay. What time was this again that you parked the Bronco?

O.J. Eight-something, maybe. He hadn't done a Jacuzzi, we had…went and got a burger, and I'd come home and kind of leisurely got ready to go. I mean, we'd done a few things …

T.L. You weren't in a hurry when you came back with the Bronco?

O.J. No.

T.L. The reason I ask you, the car was parked kind of at a funny angle, stuck out in the street.

O.J. Well, it's parked because…I don't know if it's a funny angle or what. It's parked because when I was hustling at the end of the day to get all my stuff, and I was getting my phone and everything off it, when I just pulled it out of the gate there, it's like, it's a tight turn.

T.L. So you had it inside the compound, then?

O.J. Yeah.

T.L. Oh, okay.

O.J. I brought it inside the compound to get my stuff out of it, and then I put it out, and I'd run back inside the gate before the gate closes.

T.L. O.J., what's your office phone number?

O.J. 820–5702.

P.V. And is that area code 310?

O.J. Yes.

P.V. How did you get the injury on your hand?

O.J. I don't know. The first time, when I was in Chicago and all, but at the house I was just running around.

P.V. How did you do it in Chicago?

O.J. I broke a glass. One of you guys had just called me, and I was in the bathroom, and I just went bonkers for a little bit.

T.L. Is that how you cut it?

O.J. Mmm, it was cut before, but I think I just opened it again, I'm not sure.

T.L. Do you recall bleeding at all in your truck, in the Bronco?

O.J. I recall bleeding at my house, and then I went to the Bronco. The last thing I did before I left, when I was rushing, was went and got my phone out of the Bronco.

T.L. Mmm hmm. Where's the phone now?

O.J. In my bag.

T.L. You have it?

O.J. In that black bag.

T.L. You brought a bag with you here?

O.J. Yeah, it's …

T.L. So do you recall bleeding at all?

O.J. Yeah, I mean, I knew I was bleeding, but it was no big deal. I bleed all the time. I play golf and stuff, so there's always something, nicks and stuff, here and there.

T.L. So did you do anything? When did you put the Band-Aid on it?

O.J. Actually, I asked the girl this morning for it.

T.L. And she got it?

O.J. Yeah, 'cause last night with Kato, when I was leaving, he was saying something to me, and I was rushing to get my phone, and I put a little thing on it, and it stopped.

P.V. Do you have the keys to the Bronco?

O.J. Yeah.

P.V. Okay. We've impounded the Bronco. I don't know if you know that or not.

O.J. No.

P.V. Take a look at it. Other than you, who's the last person to drive it?

O.J. Probably Gigi. When I'm out of town, I don't know who drives the car, maybe my daughter, maybe Kato.

P.V. The keys are available?

O.J. I leave the keys there, you know, when Gigi's there, because sometimes she needs it, or Gigi was off and wasn't coming back until today, and I was coming back tonight.

P.V. So you don't mind if she uses it, or … ?

O.J. This is the only one I can let her use. When she doesn't have her car, 'cause sometimes her husband takes her car, I let her use the car.

T.L. When was the last time you were at Nicole's house?

O.J. I don't go in. I won't go in her house. I haven't been in her house in a week, maybe five days. I go to her house a lot. I mean, I'm always dropping the kids off, picking the kids up, fooling around with the dog, you know.

P.V. How does that usually work? Do you drop them at the porch, or do you go in with them?

O.J. No, I don't go in the house.

P.V. Is there a kind of gate out front?

O.J. Yeah.

P.V. But you never go inside the house?

O.J. Up until five days, six days ago, I haven't been in the house. Once I started seeing Paula again, I kind of avoid Nicole.

P.V. Is Nicole seeing anybody else that you … ?

O.J. I have no idea. I really have absolutely no idea. I don't ask her, I don't know. Her and her girlfriends, they go out, you know, they've got some things going on right now with her girlfriends, so I'm assuming somethings happening because one of the girlfriends is having a big problem with her husband, because she's always saying she's with Nicole until three or four in the morning. She's not. You know, Nicole tells me she leaves her at one-thirty or two or two-thirty, and the girl doesn't go home until five, and she only lives a few blocks away.

P.V. Something's going on, huh?

T.L. Do you know where they went, the family, for dinner last night?

O.J. No. Well, no, I didn't ask.

T.L. I just thought maybe there's a regular place that they go.

O.J. No. If I was with them, we'd go to Toscano. I mean, not Toscano, Popino's.

P.V. You haven't had any problems with her lately, have you, O.J.?

O.J. I always have problems with her, you know? Our relationship has been a problem relationship. Probably lately for me, and I say this only because I said it to Ron yesterday at the—Ron Fischman, whose wife is Cora—at the dance recital, when he came up to me and went "Oooh, boy, what's going on?" And everybody was beefing with everybody. And I said, "Well, I'm just glad I'm out of the mix." You know, because I was like dealing with him and his problems with his wife and

Nicole and evidently some new problems that a guy named Christian was having with his girl, and he was staying at Nicole's house, and something was going on, but I don't think it's pertinent to this.

P.V. Did Nicole have words with you last night?

O.J. Pardon me?

P.V. Did Nicole have words with you last night?

O.J. No, not at all.

P.V. Did you talk to her last night?

O.J. To ask to speak to my daughter, to congratulate my daughter, and everything.

P.V. But you didn't have a conversation with her?

O.J. No, no.

P.V. What were you wearing last night, O.J.?

O.J. What did I wear on the golf course yesterday? Some of these kind of pants, some of these kind of pants, I mean I changed different for whatever it was. I just had on some …

P.V. Just these black pants?

O.J. Just these … They're called Bugle Boy.

P.V. These aren't the pants?

O.J. No.

P.V. Where are the pants that you wore?

O.J. They're hanging in my closet.

P.V. These are washable, right? You just throw them in the laundry?

O.J. Yeah, I got a hundred pair. They give them to me free, Bugle Boys, so I've got a bunch of them.

P.V. Do you recall coming home and hanging them up, or…?

O.J. I always hang up my clothes. I mean it's rare that I don't hang up my clothes unless I'm laying them in my bathroom for her to do something with them. But those are the only things I don't hang up. But when you play golf, you don't necessarily dirty pants.

T.L. What kind of shoes were you wearing?

O.J. Tennis shoes.

T.L. Tennis shoes? Do you know what kind?

O.J. Probably Reebok, that's all I wear.

T.L. Are they at home, too?

O.J. Yeah.

T.L. Was this supposed to be a short trip to Chicago, so you didn't take a whole lot?

O.J. Yeah, I was coming back today.

T.L. Just overnight?

O.J. Yeah.

P.V. That's a hectic schedule, drive back here to play golf and come back.

O.J. Yeah, but I do it all the time.

P.V. Do you?

O.J. Yeah. That's what I was complaining with the driver about, you know, about my whole life is on and off airplanes.

P.V. O.J., we've got sort of a problem.

O.J. Mmm hmm.

P.V. We've got some blood on and in your car, we've got some blood at your house, and sort of a problem.

O.J. WELL, take my blood test.

T.L. Well, we'd like to do that. We've got, of course, the cut on your finger that you aren't real clear on. Do recall having that cut on your finger the last time you were at Nicole's house?

O.J. A week ago?

T.L. Yeah.

O.J. No. It was last night.

T.L. Okay, so last night you cut it?

P.V. Somewhere after the recital?

O.J. Somewhere when I was rushing to get out of my house.

P.V. Okay, after the recital?

O.J. Yeah.

P.V. What do you think happened? Do you have any idea?

O.J. I have no idea, man. You guys haven't told me anything. I have no idea. When you said to my daughter, who said something to me today that somebody else might have been involved, I have absolutely no idea what happened. I don't know how, why, or what. But you guys haven't told me anything. Every time I ask you guys, you say you're going to tell me in a bit.

P.V. Well, we don't know a lot of the answers to these questions yet ourselves, O.J., okay?

O.J. I've got a bunch of guns, guns all over the place. You can take them, they're all there, I mean, you can see them. I keep them in my car for an incident that happened a month ago that my in-laws, my wife, and everybody knows about that.

P.V. What was that?

O.J. Going down to…And cops down there know about it because I've told two marshals about it. At a mall, I was going down for a christening, and I had just left and it was like three-thirty in the morning and I'm in a lane, and also the car in front of me is going real slow, and I'm slowing down 'cause I figure he sees a cop, 'cause we were all going pretty fast and I'm going to change lanes, but there's a car next to me, and I can't change lanes. Then that goes for a while, and I'm going to slow down and go around him, but the car butts up to me, and I'm like caught between three cars. They were Oriental guys, and they were not letting me go anywhere. And finally I went on the shoulder, and I sped up, and then I held my phone up so they could see the light part of it, you know, 'cause I have tinted windows, and they kind of scattered, and I chased one of them for a while to make him think I was chasing him before I took off.

T.L. Were you in the Bronco?

O.J. No.

T.L. What were you driving?

O.J. My Bentley. It has tinted windows and all, so I figured they thought they had a nice little touch.

T.L. Did you think they were trying to rip you off?

O.J. Definitely, they were. And then the next thing, you know, Nicole and I went home. At four in the morning I got there to Laguna, and when we woke up, I told her about it, and told her parents about it, told everybody about it, you know? And when I saw two marshals at a mall, I walked up and told them about it.

P.V. What did they do, make a report on it?

O.J. They didn't know nothing. I mean, they'll remember me and remember I told them.

P.V. Did Nicole mention that she'd been getting any threats lately to you? Anything she was concerned about or the kids' safety?

O.J. To her?

P.V. Yes.

O.J. From?

P.V. From anybody?

O.J. No, not at all.

P.V. Was she very security conscious? Did she keep that house locked up?

O.J. Very.

P.V. The intercom didn't work, apparently, right?

O.J. I thought it worked.

P.V. Oh, okay. Does the electronic buzzer work?

O.J. The electronic buzzer works to let people in.

P.V. Did you ever park in the rear when you go over there?

O.J. Most of the time.

P.V. You do park in the rear?

O.J. Most times when I'm taking the kids there, I come right into the driveway, blow the horn, and she, or a lot of times the housekeeper, either the housekeeper opens or they'll keep a garage door open up on the top of the thing, you know, but that's when I'm dropping the kids off, and I'm not going in, and sometimes I go to the front because the kids have to hit the buzzer and stuff.

P.V. Did you say before that up until about three weeks ago you guys were going out again and trying to…?

O.J. No, we'd been going out for about a year, and then the last six months we've had…it ain't been working, so we tried various things to see if we can make it work. We started trying to date and that wasn't working, and so, you know, we just said the hell with it, you know.

P.V. And that was about three weeks ago?

O.J. Yeah, about three weeks ago.

P.V. So you were seeing her up to that point?

O.J. It's, it's…seeing her, yeah, I mean yeah, yeah, it was a done deal, it just wasn't happening. I mean, I was gone. I was in San Juan doing a film, and I don't think we had sex since I've been back from San Juan, and that was like two months ago. So it's been like…for the kids we tried to do things together, you know. We didn't, we didn't really date each other. Then we decided let's try to date each other. We went out one night, and it just didn't work.

P.V. When you say it didn't work, what do you mean?

O.J. Ah, the night we went out it was fun. Then the next night we went out it was actually when I was down in Laguna, and she didn't want to go out. And I said, "well, let's go out 'cause I came all the way down here to go out," and we kind of had a beef. And it just didn't work after that, you know? We were only trying to date to see if we could bring some romance back into our relationship. We just said, let's treat each other like boyfriend and girlfriend instead of, you know, like seventeen-year-old married people. I mean, seventeen years together, whatever that is.

P.V. How long were you together?

O.J. Seventeen years.

P.V. Seventeen years. Did you ever hit her, O.J.?

O.J. Ah, one night we had a fight. We had a fight, and she hit me. And they never took my statement, they never wanted to hear my side, and they never wanted to hear the housekeeper's side. Nicole was drunk. She did her thing, she started tearing up my house, you know? And I didn't punch her or anything, but I …

P.V. Slapped her a couple times?

O.J. No, no, I wrestled her, is what I did. I didn't slap her at all. I mean, Nicole's a strong girl. She's a…one of the most conditioned women. Since that period of time, she's hit me a few times, but I've never touched her after that, and I'm telling you, it's five, six years ago.

P.V. What's her birthdate?

O.J. May 19th.

P.V. Did you get together with her on her birthday?

O.J. Yeah, her and I and the kids, I believe.

P.V. Did you give her a gift?

O.J. I gave her a gift.

P.V. What'd you give her?

O.J. I gave her either a bracelet or the earrings.

P.V. Did she keep them or…?

O.J. Oh, no, when we split she gave me both the earrings and the bracelet back. I bought her a very nice bracelet, I don't know if it was Mother's Day or her birthday, and I bought her the earrings for the other thing, and when we split, and it's a credit to her, she felt that it wasn't right that she had it, and I said good, because I want them back.

P.V. Was that the very day of her birthday, May 19, or was it a few days later?

O.J. What do you mean?

P.V. You gave it to her on the 19th of May, her birthday, right, this bracelet?

O.J. I may have given her the earrings. No, the bracelet. May 19th. When was Mother's Day?

P.V. Mother's Day was around that …

O.J. No, it was probably her birthday, yes.

P.V. And did she return it the same day?

O.J. Oh, now she…I'm in a funny place here on all this, right? She returned it—both of them—three weeks ago or so, because when I say I'm in a funny place on this it was because I gave it to my girlfriend and told her it was for her, and that was three weeks ago. I told her I bought it for her. You know? What am I going to do with it?

T.L. Did Mr. Weitzman, your attorney, talk to you anything about this polygraph we brought up before? What are your thoughts on that?

O.J. Should I talk about my thoughts on that? I'm sure eventually I'll do it, but it's like I've got some weird thoughts now. I've had weird thoughts…You know, when you've been with a person for seventeen years, you think everything. I've got to understand what this thing is. If it's true blue, I don't mind doing it.

T.L. Well, you're not compelled at all to take this, number one, and number two, I don't know if Mr. Weitzman explained it to you—this goes to the exclusion of someone as much as to the inclusion so we can eliminate people. And just to get things straight.

O.J. But does it work for elimination?

T.L. Oh, yes. We use it for elimination more than anything.

O.J. Well, I'll talk to him about it.

T.L. Understand, the reason we're talking to you is because you're the ex-husband.

O.J. I know I'm the number one target, and now you tell me I've got blood all over the place.

T.L. Well, there's blood in your house and in the driveway, and we've got a search warrant and we're going to go get the blood. We found some in your house. Is that your blood that's there?

O.J. If it's dripped, it's what I dripped running around trying to leave.

T.L. Last night?

O.J. Yeah, and I wasn't aware that it was…I was aware that I…You know, I was trying to get out of the house. I didn't even pay any attention to it. I saw it when I was in the kitchen, and I grabbed a napkin or something, and that was it. I didn't think about it after that.

P.V. That was last night after you got home from the recital, when you were rushing?

O.J. That was last night when I was...I don't know what I was, I was in the car getting my junk out of the car. I was in the house throwing hangers and stuff in my suitcase. I was doing my little crazy what I do, I mean, I do it everywhere. Anybody who has ever picked me up says that O.J.'s a whirlwind. He's running, he's grabbing things, and that's what I was doing.

P.V. Well, I'm going to step out and I'm going to get a photographer to come down and photograph your hand there. And then here pretty soon we're going to take you downstairs and get some blood from you. Okay? I'll be right back.

T.L. So it was about five days ago you last saw Nicole? Was it at the house?

O.J. Okay, the last time I saw Nicole, physically saw Nicole, I saw her obviously last night. The time before, I'm trying to think. I went to Washington, D.C., so I didn't see her, so I'm trying to think. I haven't seen her since I went to Washington. I went to Washington—what's the date today?

T.L. Today's Monday, the 13th of June.

O.J. Okay, I went to Washington on maybe Wednesday. Thursday I think I was in...Thursday I was in Connecticut, then Long Island Thursday afternoon and all of Friday. I got home Friday night, Friday afternoon, I played, you know...Paula picked me up at the airport. I played golf Saturday, and when I came home I think my son was there. So I did something with my son. I don't think I saw Nicole at all then. And then I went to a big affair with Paula Saturday night, and I got up and played golf Sunday, which pissed Paula off, and I saw Nicole at...It was about a week before, I saw her at the ...

T.L. Okay, the last time you saw Nicole, was that at her house?

O.J. I don't remember. I wasn't in her house, so it couldn't have been at her house, so it was, you know, I don't even physically remember the last time I saw her. I may have seen her even jogging one day.

T.L. Let me get this straight. You've never physically been inside the house?

O.J. Not in the last week.

T.L. Ever. I mean, how long has she lived there? About six months?

O.J. Oh, Christ, I've slept at the house many, many, many times, you know? I've done everything at the house, you know? I'm just saying...you're talking in the last week or so.

T.L. Well, whatever. Six months she's lived there?

O.J. I don't know. Roughly. I was at her house maybe two weeks ago, ten days ago. One night her and I had a long talk, you know, about how can we make it better for the kids, and I told her we'd do things better. And, okay, I can almost say when that was. That was when I, I don't know, it was about ten days ago. And then we...The next day I had her have her dog do a flea bath or something with me. Oh, I'll tell you, I did see her one day. One day I went...I don't know if this was the early part of last week, I went 'cause my son had to go and get something, and he ran in, and she came to the gate, and the dog ran out, and her friend Faye and I went looking for the dog. That may have been a week ago, I don't know.

T.L. (To Vannatter) Got a photographer coming?

P.V. No, we're going to take him up there.

T.L. We're ready to terminate this at 14:07.

Appendix B

SEARCH WARRANTS

STATE OF CALIFORNIA - COUNTY OF LOS ANGELES   SW No. 94-0093

SEARCH WARRANT AND AFFIDAVIT 00216
(AFFIDAVIT)

Philip L. Vannatter
(Name of Affiant)
, being sworn, says that on the basis of the information contained with this Search Warrant and Affidavit and the attached and incorporated Statement of Probable Cause, he/she has probable cause to believe and does believe that the property described below is lawfully seizable pursuant to Penal Code Section 1524 as indicated below, and is now located at the locations set forth below. Wherefore, affiant requests that this Search Warrant be issued.

(Signature of Affiant) Philip L. Vannatter , NIGHT SEARCH REQUESTED: YES [ ] NO [X

(SEARCH WARRANT)

THE PEOPLE OF THE STATE OF CALIFORNIA TO ANY SHERIFF, POLICEMAN OR PEACE OFFICER IN THE COUNTY OF LOS ANGELES: proof by affidavit having been made before me by ____Philip L. Vannatter____
(Name of Affiant)
that there is probable cause to believe that the property described herein may be found at the locations set forth herein and that it is lawfully seizable pursuant to Penal Code Section 1524 as indicated below by "x" (s) in that it
____X____ was stolen or embezzled
_____ was used as the means of committing a felony
_____ is possessed by a person with the intent to use it as means of committing a public offense or is possessed by another to whom he or she may have
____X____ delivered it for the purpose of concealing it or preventing its discovery,
_____ tends to show that a felony has been committed or that a particular person has committed a felony,
_____ tends to show that sexual exploitation of a child, in violation of P.C. Section 311.3, has occurred or is occurring;
YOU ARE THEREFORE COMMANDED TO SEARCH:

360 Rockingham, Avenue, West Los Angeles, California. A single family residence located on the southeast corner of Rockingham Avenue and Ashford Street. The residence is two stories constructed of light brown wood trim and beige stucco. The property is fence by a solid plant hedge with green wrought iron gates facing Rockingham Avenue and Ashford Street. The number 360 is clearly painted on the curb adjacent to the Rockingham Gate.

FOR THE FOLLOWING PROPERTY:
Presence of traces of human blood, clothing, surfaces, or any material that may contain blood, any object that may have been used to inflict the fatal injuries to the victims, including but not limited to objects capable of inflicting blunt force trauma, firearms or knives. Paperwork indicating the identity of the occupants of the residence to show dominion and control of the residence. Any and all garages or outbuildings associated to the residence to which the occupants have access, and the 1994 Ford Bronco, California license 3CWZ788.

AND TO SEIZE IT IF FOUND and bring it forthwith before me, or this court, at the courthouse of this court. This Search Warrant and incorporated Affidavit was sworn to and subscribed before me this _13_ day of _June_ , 19 _94_. at ____ A.M./P.M. Wherefore, I find probable cause for the issuance of this Search Warrant and do issue it.

Linda K. Bakcurt (Signature of Magistrate) , NIGHT SEARCH APPROVED: YES [ ] NO [ ]
Judge of the Superior/Municipal Court, _Los Angeles_ _____ Judicial District
0A-1508-A-768346W3—4 88

1   Your affiant Philip L. Vannatter #14877 is a Police Detective

2 for the Los Angeles Police Department, assigned to Robbery-Homicide

3 Division, Homicide Special Section. Your affiant has been a police

4 officer for the City of Los Angeles for over 25 years. Your

5 affiant has been assigned to Robbery-Homicide Division for the past

6 15 years working the Officer-Involved Shooting Section and Homicide

7 Special Section.

8   Your affiant worked homicide at West Los Angeles and Wilshire

9 Division prior to being assigned to Robbery-Homicide Division, and

10 has investigated in excess of 200 homicides. Your affiant has

11 attended numerous training sessions and seminars, and has qualified

12 in Los Angeles County Municipal and Superior Court as a homicide

13 expert.

14   On Monday June 13, 1994 at 0430 hours you affiant and his

15 partner F.D. Lange #13552 were assigned the investigation of the

16 double murder of Nicole Brown AKA Nicole Simpson and an

17 unidentified male, White at 875 South Bundy Drive, West Los Angeles

18 the residence of Nicole Brown. The facts contained herein are

19 summarized as follows:

20   During the course of the investigation it was determined that

21 Nicole Brown was the ex-wife of O.J. Simpson and had two children

22 by Simpson. The children were located and were removed from the

23 residence on Bundy Drive.

24   During the course of the investigation detectives followed up

25 to 360 Rockingham Avenue; West Los Angeles, the residence of O.J.

26 Simpson in an attempt to make a notification. Upon arriving at the

27 location detectives were unable to arouse anyone at the residence.

00218

1   Detectives observed a 1994 White Ford Bronco, California license
2   3CWZ788 registered to Hertz Corporation parked at the west side of
3   the residence headed north on Rockingham Avenue.   Detectives
4   observed what appeared to be human blood, later confirmed by
5   Scientific Investigation personnel to be human blood on the drivers
6   door handle of the vehicle.

7   Detectives subsequently aroused O.J. Simpson's daughter,
8   Arnell Simpson at the residence and determined Simpson was not at
9   home. During the interview of Simpson's daughter, she identified
10   the Ford Bronco as belonging to her father who was the primary
11   driver. Blood droplets were subsequently observed leading from the
12   vehicle on the street to the front door of the residence.

13   During the securing of the residence a man's leather glove
14   containing human blood was also observed on the south side of the
15   residence.   This glove closely resembled a brown leather glove
16   located at the crime scene at the feet of the unidentified male,.
17   White victim. *and by interviews of Simpson's daughter and a friend*
     Brian Kaelin
18   It was determined Simpson had left on an unexpected flight to
19   Chicago during the early morning hours of June 13, 1994, and was
20   last seen at the residence at approximately 2300 hours, June 12,
21   1994.

22   It is prayed that a search warrant be issued to search 360
23   Rockingham Avenue for the presence of traces of human blood,
24   clothing, surfaces, or any material that may contain blood, any
25   object that may have been used to inflict the fatal injuries to the
26   victims, including but not limited to objects capable of inflicting
27   blunt force trauma, firearms or knives. Paperwork indicating the

00213

1   identity of the occupants of the residence to show dominion and

2   control of the residence.   Any and all garages or outbuildings

3   associated to the residence to which the occupants have access, and

4   the 1994 Ford Bronco, California license 3CWZ788.

5

6

7

8

9

10

11

12

13

14

15

16

17

18

19

20

21

22

23

24

25

26

27

SW No. 94-009
00220

STATE OF CALIFORNIA - COUNTY OF LOS ANGELES

RETURN TO SEARCH WARRANT

__Philip L. Vannatter__ , being sworn, says that he/she conducted a search pursuant to
(Name of Affiant)
below described search warrant:

Issuing Magistrate: __Linda K. Lefkowitz__ ,

Magistrate's Court: Superior/Municipal Court, __Municipal__ , Judicial Dis

Date of Issuance: __6-13-94__ ,

Date of Service: __6-13-94__ ,

and searched the following location(s), vehicle(s), and person(s):

360 Rockingham Avenue
West Los Angeles, CA

R-1

94-009:
00251

and seized the items*

___X___ described in the attached and incorporated inventory.

_____ described below:

I further swear that this is a true and detailed account of all the property taken by me pursuant to the sear warrant, and that pursuant to Penal Code Sections 1528 and 1536 this property will be retained in r custody, subject to the order of this court or of any other court in which the offense in respect to which tl seized property is triable.

_____
(Signature of Affiant)

Sworn to and subscribed before me this _____ day of _____ , 19 _____.

_____
(Signature of Magistrate)

Judge of the Superior/Municipal Court, _____ , Judicial Distri

*List all items seized, including those not specifically listed on the warrant.

0 647 ·   SW No. 36824

STATE OF CALIFORNIA - COUNTY OF LOS ANGELES

SEARCH WARRANT AND AFFIDAVIT
(AFFIDAVIT)

Philip L. Vannatter

_____ , being sworn, says that on the basis of the information contained within
(Name of Affiant)

this Search Warrant and Affidavit and the attached and incorporated **Statement of Probable Cause**, he/she has probable
cause to believe and does believe that the property described below is lawfully seizable pursuant to Penal Code Section 1524,
as indicated below, and is now located at the locations set forth below. Wherefore, affiant requests that this Search Warrant be
issued.

_____ , NIGHT SEARCH REQUESTED: YES [   ] NO [   ]
(Signature of Affiant)

(SEARCH WARRANT)

THE PEOPLE OF THE STATE OF CALIFORNIA TO ANY SHERIFF, POLICEMAN OR PEACE OFFICER IN THE COUNTY
OF LOS ANGELES: proof by affidavit having been made before me by _____Philip L. Vannatter_____ ,
(Name of Affiant)

that there is probable cause to believe that the property described herein may be found at the locations set forth herein and that it
is lawfully seizable pursuant to Penal Code Section 1524 as indicated below by "x" (s) in that it:

_____ was stolen or embezzled

✓ _____ was used as the means of committing a felony

✓ _____ is possessed by a person with the intent to use it as means of committing a public offense or is possessed by another to whom he or she may have
delivered it for the purpose of concealing it or preventing its discovery,

✓ _____ tends to show that a felony has been committed or that a particular person has committed a felony,

_____ tends to show that sexual exploitation of a child, in violation of P.C. Section 311.3, has occurred or is occurring;

YOU ARE THEREFORE COMMANDED TO SEARCH:

SEE ATTACHED.

FOR THE FOLLOWING PROPERTY:

SEE ATTACHED.

AND TO SEIZE IT IF FOUND and bring it forthwith before me, or this court, at the courthouse of this court. This Search Warrant
and incorporated Affidavit was sworn to and subscribed before me this __15__ day of __June__ , 19 __94__ ,
at __ __ A.M./P.M. Wherefore, I find probable cause for the issuance of this Search Warrant and do issue it.

_____ , NIGHT SEARCH APPROVED: YES [   ] NO [✕]
(Signature of Magistrate)

Judge of the Superior/Municipal Court, _____ Judicial District

DA-1506-A—765346HO—8/86   SW & A1

0 648

LOCATION TO BE SEARCHED:

1.   360 ROCKINGHAM AVENUE, WEST LOS ANGELES, CA. A single-
family residence located on the southeast corner of
Rockingham Avenue and Ashford Street. The residence is two
stories constructed of light brown wood trim and beige
stucco. The property is fence by a solid plant hedge with
green wrought iron gates facing Rockingham Avenue and
Ashford Street. The number 360 is clearly painted on the
curb adjacent to the Rockingham gate, and all rooms, attics,
cellars, lofts, storage areas, and other parts therein, and
the surrounding grounds and any storage rooms or outbuilding
of any kind located thereon; any combination safes or locked
boxes therein.

        Included at the above-described location is any and all
rooms, attics, cellars, lofts, storage areas, and other
parts therein, and the surrounding grounds and any storage
rooms or outbuildings or garages of any kind located
thereon.

2.   1988 black Bently, CA license 2LVB161.

SW & A2

0 649

PROPERTY TO BE SEIZED:

A Stiletto brand knife, packaging material for said knife, brown leather men's gloves, black long sleeves cotton-type sweat-suit, a 1988 black Bently, CA license 2LVB161, any surfaces, objects or materials that contained blood or blood stains.

SW & A3

0 650

1   Your affiant, Philip L. Vannatter, #14877, is a police

2 detective for the Los Angeles Police Department, assigned to

3 Robbery-Homicide Division, Homicide Special Section. Your

4 affiant has been a police officer for the City of Los Angeles for

5 over 25 years. Your affiant has been assigned to Robbery-

6 Homicide Division, for the past 15 years, working the Officer-

7 Involved Shooting Section and Homicide Special Section.

8   Your affiant worked homicide at West Los Angeles and

9 Wilshire Division prior to being assigned to Robbery-Homicide

10 Division, and has investigated in excess of 200 homicides. Your

11 affiant has attended numerous training sessions and seminars, and

12 has qualified in Los Angeles County Municipal and Superior Court

13 as a homicide expert.

14   On Monday, June 13, 1994, at 0430 hours, your affiant and

15 his partner, F.D. Lange (13552), were assigned the investigation

16 of the double murder of Nicole Brown, aka, Nicole Simpson, and an

17 unidentified male, white, subsequently identified as Ronald

18 Goldman, at 875 South Bundy Drive, West Los Angeles, the

19 residence of Nicole Brown. The facts contained herein are

20 summarized as follows:

21   On 6/13/94, at approximately 0010 hours, Victim 1, Nicole

22 Brown (Simpson), age 35, and Victim 2, Ronald Goldman, age 25,

23 were found stabbed to death on the front walkway of the residence

24 of Victim 1 at 875 South Bundy Drive, West Los Angeles.

25

26

SW & A4

0 651

Upon arrival at the crime scene, detectives were met by Det. III Ron Phillips, West Los Angeles Division Homicide Coordinator. Phillips stated that Victim Brown was the ex-wife of O. J. SIMPSON, the well known athlete/actor. Additionally, Phillips stated that Mr. SIMPSON and Victim 1 had been embroiled in previous domestic violence situations, one of these resulting in the arrest of Mr. SIMPSON. Mr. SIMPSON resided at 360 North Rockingham Place, Brentwood, approximately two miles from the crime scene.

Detectives followed up to the SIMPSON residence for the purposes of death notification and to check on SIMPSON's welfare. Upon arrival at 360 Rockingham, detectives observed a 1994 white Ford Bronco (CA license 3CWZ788) parked facing northbound at the east curb near the entrance gate to the SIMPSON residence. The vehicle was parked at an angle to the curb with the rear end jutting out into the roadway.

Peering into the locked vehicle's rear window, detectives observed a package with a label indicating a return address to O. J. Simpson Enterprises. A registration check of the vehicle revealed it to belong to Hertz Rental. Upon closer observation of the vehicle, detectives observed what appeared to be blood near the handle on the driver's door. A subsequent test at the location did indeed confirm the presence of blood.

Due to the fact that detectives were unable to get a response from the residence after several attempts with the gate

SW & AS

0 652

phone, detectives entered the property by climbing over the wall.
Detectives were unable to contact anyone in the main house so
they entered the rear area of the property, finding a single-
story guest house. At this location, detectives were able to
arouse the daughter of O. J. SIMPSON, Arnell Simpson. Ms.
Simpson stated that the aforementioned Ford Bronco belonged to
her father, who was the primary driver.

Detectives were also informed by Ms. Simpson that her father
was in Chicago, Illinois, after leaving the Los Angeles area late
the night before. Ms. Simpson further stated she had returned
home at approximately 0100 hours after attending the movies in
Westwood.

While securing the Simpson residence, a leather glove,
right-handed, was observed on a walkway behind the guest house
near the south property line. There were what appeared to be
bloodstains on the glove. Additionally, this glove closely
resembled the left-handed brown leather glove located at the 875
South Bundy (crime scene) address on the ground adjacent to the
victims.

Another resident and acquaintance of Mr. SIMPSON, Brian
Kaelin, was contacted in the guest house and interviewed. Kaelin
stated that he had been in the company of Mr. SIMPSON until
approximately 2200 hours on Sunday, 6/13/94. At that time,
Kaelin had returned to his room in the guest house to eat after

SW & A6

APPENDIX B

0 053

1 he and SIMPSON had stopped at a fast food restaurant to pick up
2 food.

3   At approximately 2245 hours, Kaelin was in his room when he
4 felt what he thought to be an "earthquake". He described it as a
5 loud noise that disturbed the pictures on the wall. The noise
6 appeared to emanate from the south wall area behind his room.
7 (NOTE: It should be noted here that this location is the same
8 general area [walkway] where the aforementioned leather glove was
9 found.) At this point, Kaelin went outside with a flashlight to
10 investigate the noise. While outside, Kaelin observed a
11 limousine and driver at the Ashford Street gate of the residence.
12 The limo had arrived to transport O. J. SIMPSON to LAX for a pre-
13 arranged business flight to Chicago, Illinois. Kaelin spoke with
14 the limo driver (Allan Park), who stated that SIMPSON was late
15 for the pick up. Some time between 2300 hours and 2310 hours,
16 SIMPSON exited his residence, walking directly to the waiting
17 limo and drove off without comment to Kaelin.

18   Subsequent to daybreak on 6/13/94, detectives at the SIMPSON
19 residence discovered what appeared to be blood droplets in the
20 driveway trailing from the aforementioned Ford Bronco to the
21 front door of the residence. Three additional droplets were
22 observed inside the main entryway of the residence.

23   At this point in time, the SIMPSON residence was secured and
24 detectives proceeded to the West Los Angeles Station to complete
25 a search warrant for the premises.

26

SW & A7

0 654

1   Meanwhile, a crime scene investigation was in progress at
2   875 South Bundy Drive. A cursory examination of both victims
3   revealed that there was extensive cutting to the neck areas and
4   both had bled profusely. Additional cutting/stabbing wounds were
5   visible, as well as defense wounds evident on the hands of both
6   victims. Both victims were lying in pools of blood. It would
7   appear that both succumbed at the location where they were found.

8   The previously-mentioned brown leather glove was found on
9   the ground near the feet of Victim 2 (Goldman) and adjacent to a
10 dark blue knit watch cap. A ring of five keys was also located
11 near Victim 2, as was a white envelope containing a pair of
12 prescription glasses, Nicole Simpson printed on front of
13 envelope. Bloody shoe prints were evident leading up the steps
14 from the decedents going in a westerly direction along the north
15 side of the residence. Additionally, several blood droplets were
16 observed on the walkway between the decedents positions and the
17 rear of the residence. These droplets were found in conjunction
18 with and near the bloody shoe prints. (Note: On 6-15-94, a
19 serological examination/comparison was completed on five of these
20 crime scene blood droplets. It was determined that of the five
21 samples, one showed no results, one was inconclusive and three
22 matched a whole blood sample obtained from O.J. SIMPSON, to the
23 exclusion of some 93 percent of the population. (These results
24 were obtained utilizing DQ Alpha sub typing.) The droplets
25 appeared to be separate and apart from the immediate location of
26

SW & A8

G 655

1 the decedents. Additionally, both victims were eliminated

2 serologically from the droplets.

3   On 6-13-94, at approximately 1200 hours, O.J. SIMPSON

4 arrived at his residence. At this time, Simpson accompanied

5 detectives to Robbery-Homicide Division Parker Center. Mr.

6 Howard Weitzman, attorney-at-law representing SIMPSON,

7 accompanied him. SIMPSON was advised of his Constitutional

8 Rights, which he waived, and a taped conversation then took

9 place.

10   Simpson stated he attended a recital for his daughter on the

11 evening of 6-12-94 in West Los Angeles. His ex-wife (Victim

12 Brown) and her family were present. SIMPSON sat apart from them.

13 After the recital, Victim Brown's father, Louis Brown, invited

14 SIMPSON to have dinner with them. SIMPSON declined. SIMPSON

15 went on to state that after leaving the recital, he returned home

16 where he parked his Rolls Royce then left again, driving his

17 white Ford Bronco. SIMPSON stated he drove around for awhile

18 attempting to telephonically contact his girlfriend with his

19 mobile phone. This to no avail.

20   Later that evening (6-12-94), SIMPSON stated he returned

21 home in the white Ford Bronco. He parked the vehicle in the

22 driveway where he unloaded something from the vehicle. He then

23 drove the Bronco out through the gate and parked it at the curb

24 in front of the residence, where it was later observed by

25 detectives. SIMPSON states he was in a hurry to park in

26

SW & A9

0 656

1   anticipation of a limousine arrival that would take him to LAX
2   for a flight to Chicago.
3   When questioned as to an apparent fresh laceration on his
4   left middle finger, SIMPSON stated he did not recall how he was
5   injured. He went on to state that he was always getting cut or
6   scraped and thought little of it. SIMPSON could offer no
7   explanation for the apparent bloodstains on the Ford Bronco or
8   the apparent blood droplets at his residence. Additionally,
9   SIMPSON alluded to past altercations with victim Brown but felt
10 that these were either initiated by her or they were mutual. He
11 indicated he felt that their relationship was improving.
12   Subsequent to the interview, SIMPSON, gave detectives a
13 whole blood sample at the Parker Center Jail Dispensary.
14 Additionally, detectives photographed SIMPSON'S lacerated finger.
15 He was also finger-printed.
16   On 6-15-94, autopsies were conducted on both decedents by
17 Dr. Golden at the Los Angeles County Coroner's Office. Dr.
18 Golden attributed both deaths to multiple sharp instrument wounds
19 to the neck and body. The weapon involved was described as a
20 single edged bladed knife, blade at least 6" in length with a
21 thickness of approximately 1/32". The weapon would be sharp.
22   Victim Brown had a full stomach of undigested food.
23 Considering stomach contents, liver temperature and various
24 indicator markers, Dr. Golden affixed death "closer to 9:00 p.m.
25 than 12 o'clock" on 6-12-94.
26   T-7

SW & A10

0 657

1   On June 14, 1994, detectives were contacted by a private
2 citizen, David Prestholt, who related that O.J. SIMPSON, while
3 filming a motion picture in the downtown area, purchased a knife
4 at Ross Cutlery, 310 S. Broadway. A subsequent follow-up to Ross
5 Cutlery revealed that on 5-3-94, between 1400 hours and 1800
6 hours, SIMPSON entered the store and purchased a 15" overall, 6"
7 bladed folding knife for $74.98. He paid in cash. Detectives at
8 this time purchased a duplicate of the knife bought by SIMPSON.
9 (Note: On 6-15-94, the duplicate knife purchased was examined by
10 Dr. Golden. Dr. Golden was of the opinion that the knife
11 dimensions were consistent with the stab and cut wounds on both
12 victims.)
13   On 6-15-94, the limosine driver, Allan Park, was interviewed
14 by detectives. Park responded to the Simpson residence to pick
15 up O.J. SIMPSON. He arrived at 2225 hours on 6-12-94. Park had
16 been advised to pick up SIMPSON at 2245 hours, but arrived 20
17 minutes early. After his arrival, Park drove up to the
18 Rockingham gate of the Simpson residence. He observed no
19 vehicles parked at the curb. Park then backed the limo
20 northbound on Rockingham to the Ashford gate where he attempted
21 to contact anyone inside the residence with the gate phone. No
22 one responded. At approximately 2250 hours, Park observed a male
23 black, he later stated he believed to be O.J. SIMPSON, walk up
24 the driveway from the direction of the Rockingham gate "at a fast
25 pace" and enter the residence. Park then again attempted to
26

SW & A11

0 658

1   raise someone inside the house on the gate phone. A male, he
2   identifies as O.J. SIMPSON emerged from the residence carrying
3   two black nylon duffle bags. Additionally, there was a golf bag
4   on the walkway at the front of the house. Brian Kaelin was
5   standing in the front yard. As SIMPSON exited the residence,
6   Kaelin started towards an additional dark colored bag that was
7   lying in the driveway closest to the Rockingham gate. Kaelin
8   stated he would pick up the bag. He was stopped from doing this
9   by SIMPSON, who himself retrieved the bag. All three bags, plus
10 the golf bag, were loaded into the limosine.

11   Park went on to state that Simpson was sweating profusely
12 and complained of the heat several times while en route to the
13 airport. The air conditioner was on and SIMPSON had the rear
14 window down.

15   On 6-16-94, detectives were contacted by L.A.P.D., S.I.D.
16 Serology supervisor Greg Matheson regarding the right handed
17 leather glove found at the residence of O.J. SIMPSON.
18 Preliminary DNA typing of this item revealed that the glove
19 contains bloodstains that could include both victims' blood as
20 well as that of O.J. SIMPSON. All of the blood could not have
21 come from O.J. SIMPSON.

22   With regard to the five bloodstains located on the Ford
23 Bronco driven by O.J. SIMPSON, two were inconclusive and three
24 were sub-typed to O.J. SIMPSON.
25
26

SW & A12

0 059

With regard to two bloodstains lifted from the foyer area of
SIMPSON'S residence, both were sub-typed to SIMPSON.

Additionally, it was reported by Criminalist Wong that
caucasian hairs were removed from the exterior of both leather
gloves in question.

As noted above, a search warrant was issued and served on
June 13, 1994, for the residence located at 360 Rockingham Avenue
and for the Ford Bronco, 3CWZ788. (The first page of that
warrant is attached and incorporated as Exhibit I.) Since the
service of that warrant, your affiant has obtained additional
information which necessitates issuance of a new warrant for 360
Rockingham Avenue, a 1988 Bentley, black in color, registered to
Orenthal Productions, license plate 2LVB161, last seen in the
driveway of the SIMPSON residence.

The initial search warrant granted permission to search for
clothing or any material that may contain blood. When that
warrant was executed, your affiant found literally hundreds of
items of male clothing in both a large walk-in closet as well as
in the drawers of the bedroom itself. Because your affiant had
no description of any specific clothing worn by the suspect at
the time of the murders, a cursory examination was made of the
clothing found with the purpose of locating and seizing only
clothing bore obvious signs of blood stains. As noted above,
bloodstains were found within the residence in the foyer.

SW & A13

O 060

1 Evidence of blood was also found in the master bathroom of the
2 residence.
3 Since the service of the first warrant, witness Brian Kaelin
4 has told your affiant that when he last saw O. J. SIMPSON at
5 approximately 10:00 p.m. on the night of the killings, SIMPSON
6 was wearing a black cotton-type sweat-suit. In asmuch as this
7 information was not available at the service of the first
8 warrant, your affiant did not know which specific clothing to
9 look for and can no longer remember whether clothing of that
10 description was present at the location, as literally hundreds of
11 items of clothing were seen. Your affiant now wishes to examine
12 the clothing in the residence for the specific black cotton-type
13 sweat-suit described, and if found, to examine that clothing more
14 closely for traces of blood.
15 It is your affiant's training and experience that blood is
16 not always visible on dark clothing and can sometimes be detected
17 through closer examination.
18 Your affiant also requests permission to search the above
19 described premises for the specific knife described above, and a
20 cash register receipt in the amount approximately $74.95,
21 packaging in which it was sold, photographs depicting the suspect
22 in possession of that knife, knife sharpening or cleaning
23 equipment and receipts therefor dated on or after the purchase of
24 the knife. This request is based upon information acquired since
25 the execution of the first warrant which revealed that:
26

SW & A14

0 661

1.   The cause of death was determined to be severe knife
wounds inflicted upon both victims, one of such wounds penetrated
to a depth of more than five inches. This would indicate that a
knife with a blade of at least five inches in length had to have
been used to commit these murders.

2.   Mr. SIMPSON had purchased a Stiletto brand knife with a
locking blade, six inches in length, with an overall length of 15
inches, from a knife store in downtown Los Angeles, on or about
May 3, 1994, for approximately $75. The person who sold the
knife to SIMPSON had a specific memory of both the exact knife
purchased and the fact that the identity of the purchaser was Mr.
SIMPSON. Your affiant purchased an identical knife from that
store for evidentiary purposes. A copy of the photograph of the
knife purchased by your affiant is attached and incorporated
herein as Exhibit 2.

Your affiant has shown the knife to the Deputy Medical
Examiner who performed the autopsies on the victims in this case
to determine whether that knife or one identical to it could have
inflicted the wounds he observed on the victim's bodies. It was
the examiner's opinion that this knife could have inflicted the
fatal wounds.

When the first warrant was executed, your affiant had not
yet been informed as to cause of death, nor did your affiant know
the depth of the wounds inflicted upon the victims. This
information combined with the information concerning the purchase

SW & A15

0 662

1   of the Stiletto knife, makes another search of the premises

2   necessary. The knife is a folding knife which could be hidden in

3   smaller spaces or containers than were searched at the time of

4   the execution of the first warrant. In addition, it is your

5   affiant's training and experience that suspects often keep

6   receipts, pictures, and other indicia of ownership of knifes even

7   when they have disposed of the weapon.

8   Your affiant also believes that an additional search of the

9   SIMPSON residence, which reveals the absence of the above-

10   described knife and clothing, may provide evidence tending to

11   demonstrate Mr. SIMPSON's guilt. It is your affiant's opinion

12   that Mr. SIMPSON as the perpetrator of the two killings, would

13   have a strong motive to dispose of the items sought, which

14   according to witnesses he did possess. Therefore, if they are

15   not in the house, this would strongly suggest that he has hidden

16   or disposed of them and did, in fact, commit the murders.

17   Further, your affiant has learned from witness Brian Kaelin,

18   that Mr. SIMPSON and Mr. Kaelin went out together in the Bently

19   registered to Orenthal Productions, license 2LVB161, at

20   approximately 9:00 p.m. on the night of June 12, 1994. Mr.

21   SIMPSON drove to McDonald's at 26th and San Vicente, and returned

22   to the residence at approximately 9:45 p.m. During the service

23   of the first search warrant your affiant observed this vehicle

24   parked in the driveway of SIMPSON's residence. Your affiant has

25   also learned since the service of the first warrant, that blood

26

SW & A16

APPENDIX B

0 6E3

1 recovered in the interior of SIMPSON's rented Ford Bronco was
2 determined to be consistent with SIMPSON's blood type. Based on
3 the evidence above, your affiant believes that a search,
4 specifically for blood, in the Bentley, will tend to show that
5 SIMPSON was not cut or bleeding before 10:00 p.m. Additionally,
6 since the service of the first warrant, other officers present
7 during that service have told your affiant that they saw another
8 pair of gloves inside SIMPSON's residence. These officers had
9 also seen the glove found at the murder location and have told
10 your affiant that the gloves in the residence appeared to be of
11 the same type as the one from the crime scene. Your affiant
12 wishes to seize the gloves left in the SIMPSON residence because
13 they will tend to further establish that the bloody gloves
14 recovered belong to SIMPSON in that he favored this type, style
15 and size of glove. (These gloves were inadvertently left behind
16 at the SIMPSON residence.) Accordingly, your affiant also
17 requests permission to locate and seize said gloves and other
18 evidence from the SIMPSON residence, and or any outbuildings or
19 grounds in which they may be found at 360 Rockingham Avenue.

20
21 cme
22 ref: vannatter.sw<sw>
23 6/28/94
24
25
26

SW & A17

0 684

APPENDIX B

0888

SW No. 36824

STATE OF CALIFORNIA - COUNTY OF LOS ANGELES

RETURN TO SEARCH WARRANT

PHILIP L. VANNATTER #14877
(Name of Affiant) , being sworn, says that he/she conducted a search pursuant to the
below described search warrant:

Issuing Magistrate: Honorable Michael Tynan

Magistrate's Court: **Superior/Municipal** Court, Department 113 , Judicial District

Date of Issuance: June 28th, 1994

Date of Service: June 28th, 1994 ,

and searched the following location(s), vehicle(s), and person(s):

See attached.

FILED
MUNICIPAL COURT
LOS ANGELES

'94 JUL -6 P2:44

JUDICIAL DISTRICT
EDWARD KRITZMAN C...

R-1

0889

and seized the items*

    __X__ described in the attached and incorporated inventory.

    _____ described below:

I further swear that this is a true and detailed account of all the property taken by me pursuant to the search warrant, and that pursuant to Penal Code Sections 1528 and 1536 this property will be retained in my custody, subject to the order of this court or of any other court in which the offense in respect to which the seized property is triable.

_____
(Signature of Affiant)

Sworn to and subscribed before me this _____ day of _____, 19 94.

_____
(Signature of Magistrate)

Judge of the Superior/Municipal Court, _____, Judicial District

*List all items seized, including those not specifically listed on the warrant.

RON GOLDMAN STAB WOUNDS

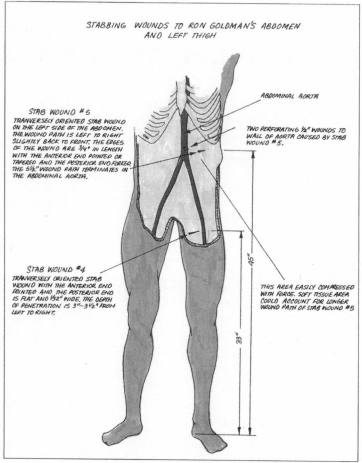

STABBING WOUNDS TO RON GOLDMAN'S ABDOMEN AND LEFT THIGH

ABDOMINAL AORTA

STAB WOUND #6
TRANVERSELY ORIENTED STAB WOUND ON THE LEFT SIDE OF THE ABDOMEN. THE WOUND PATH IS LEFT TO RIGHT SLIGHTLY BACK TO FRONT. THE EDGES OF THE WOUND ARE ¾" IN LENGTH WITH THE ANTERIOR END POINTED OR TAPERED AND THE POSTERIOR END FORKED. THE 5½" WOUND PATH TERMINATES IN THE ABDOMINAL AORTA.

TWO PERFORATING ½" WOUNDS TO WALL OF AORTA CAUSED BY STAB WOUND #5.

STAB WOUND #4
TRANVERSELY ORIENTED STAB WOUND WITH THE ANTERIOR END POINTED AND THE POSTERIOR END IS FLAT AND ½2" WIDE. THE DEPTH OF PENETRATION IS 3"–3½" FROM LEFT TO RIGHT.

THIS AREA EASILY COMPRESSED WITH FORCE. SOFT TISSUE AREA COULD ACCOUNT FOR LONGER WOUND PATH OF STAB WOUND #5.

45"

33"

DRAWING BY MARK FUHRMAN, NOT TO SCALE.

RON GOLDMAN
STAB WOUNDS TO RIGHT SIDE OF CHEST

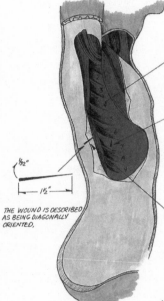

RIBS ARE NUMBERED AND
SHOWN COVERED BY
INTERCOSTAL MUSCLES.

STAB WOUND #1

22" BELOW THE TOP OF THE HEAD, 5"
FROM BACK OF BODY. 7th RIB AT MID
LINE IS TOTALLY INCISED. BRUISING
IN THE ADJACENT MUSCULATURE.
ESTIMATED LENGTH OF WOUND PATH
4". DIRECTION IS RIGHT TO LEFT, BACK
TO FRONT. PLEURAL WOUNDS ½-¾ INCH
     WOUND SEEMS TO BE INFLICTED WITH
GREAT FORCE, BUT ONLY A 4" WOUND?

THE WOUND IS DESCRIBED
AS BEING DIAGONALLY
ORIENTED.

STAB WOUND #2

21" BELOW THE TOP OF THE HEAD, 2"
FROM THE BACK OF THE BODY. PENETRATES
THROUGH 8th RIGHT INTERCOSTAL SPACE
WITHOUT STRIKING RIB. WOUND PATH
ENTERS PLEURAL CAVITY WITH AN
ESTIMATED MINIMUM TOTAL DEPTH OF
PENETRATION IS 2-3 INCHES. PLEURAL
WOUNDS ½-¾ INCH.

ALTHOUGH I AM NOT A PATHOLOGIST THESE
TWO WOUNDS SEEM TO BE THE MOST DIRECT
STABBING FROM THE RIGHT HANDED SUSPECT.
THE WOUNDS WERE INFLICTED WITH POWER,
BUT STILL THEY DID NOT PENETRATE
DEEPER THAN 4 INCHES. IT WOULD SEEM
THAT IF THE GERMAN STILETTO WAS THE MURDER
WEAPON ATLEAST ONE OF THESE WOUNDS
WOULD BE 6 INCHES IN LENGTH.

DRAWING BY MARK FUHRMAN, NOT TO SCALE.

INDEX

R

race card
  Cochran and, 75, 223
  first use, 74
  Judge Ito allows, 130
  prosecution's lack of strategy,
    193
  as racism, 227
  Shapiro reservations about,
    219–20
race and racism
  America's problems with, 94–95,
    97
  Bundy murders and, 97
  Darden and, 194–96, 264
  defense strategy. *See* race card
  Fuhrman testimony, 202
  motion to prevent cross-
    examination on, 96
  police and, 4, 263–65
  race card as racism, 227
racial epithet
  apology for unrest caused by, 4
  motion to prevent cross-
    examination on, 96
  prior allegations, 101–3
racial slurs
  Cordoba testimony, 211–12
  Fuhrman testimony on the "N"
    word, 213–15
  the "N" word, 199
  on tape, 232
racism. *See* race and racism
Rappe, Judge Curtis, 124, 127,
  129–30, 234
reasonable inference, 82
recital. *See* dance recital

Redondo Beach, 102, 112
Reid, Judge John, 235
religion, Cochran's use of, 226
reputation, damage to, 1, 273
retirement plans, 112
Riske, Robert, 8, 10–11, 17, 79,
  203–5, 208
Roberts, Brad
  Bundy crime scene, arrival at, 12
  Rockingham estate, arrival at,
    27
  Rockingham estate, during slow-
    speed pursuit, 66
  Simpson arrival, 32
  as trial witness, prosecution's
    intent not to call, 188–89,
    191–92, 245
The Rock, 262
Rockingham estate
  airline luggage tags, 31
  bandage package, 26
  blood evidence, 27–33
    list of, 137
  as crime scene, 27–28
  during slow-speed pursuit,
    66–67
  evidence map, 20
  Ford Bronco. *See* Bronco
  glove. *See* glove
  grounds investigation, 22,
    24–25, 27
  interior investigation, 29, 31, 33
  June 13, 1994, search warrant,
    29, 32–34, 36–38
  June 28, 1994, search warrant,
    168–69
    compared to June 13 warrant,
      37–38